# Four Corners

## Jack C. Richards · David Bohlke

**3**

# Student's Book

**CAMBRIDGE**
UNIVERSITY PRESS

CAMBRIDGE UNIVERSITY PRESS
Cambridge, New York, Melbourne, Madrid, Cape Town, Singapore,
São Paulo, Delhi, Dubai, Tokyo, Mexico City

Cambridge University Press
32 Avenue of the Americas, New York, NY 10013-2473, USA

www.cambridge.org
Information on this title: www.cambridge.org/9780521127363

First published 2012

Printed in Hong Kong, China, by Golden Cup Printing Company Limited

*A catalog record for this publication is available from the British Library.*

ISBN 978-0-521-12736-3 Full Contact 3 with Self-study CD-ROM
ISBN 978-0-521-12747-9 Teacher's Edition 3 with Assessment Audio CD / CD-ROM
ISBN 978-0-521-12743-1 Class Audio CDs 3
ISBN 978-0-521-12712-7 Classware 3
ISBN 978-0-521-12740-0 DVD 3

For a full list of components, visit www.cambridge.org/fourcorners

Cambridge University Press has no responsibility for the persistence or
accuracy of URLs for external or third-party Internet Web sites referred to in
this publication, and does not guarantee that any content on such Web sites is,
or will remain, accurate or appropriate. Information regarding prices, travel
timetables, and other factual information given in this work are correct at
the time of first printing, but Cambridge University Press does not guarantee
the accuracy of such information thereafter.

Art direction, book design, photo research, and layout services: Adventure House, NYC
Audio production: CityVox, NYC
Video production: Steadman Productions

# Authors' acknowledgments

Many people contributed to the development of *Four Corners*. The authors and publisher would like to particularly thank the following **reviewers**:

Nele Noe, **Academy for Educational Development, Qatar Independent Secondary School for Girls**, Doha, Qatar; Yuan-hsun Chuang, **Soo Chow University**, Taipei, Taiwan; Celso Frade and Sonia Maria Baccari de Godoy, **Associaçao Alumni**, São Paulo, Brazil; Pablo Stucchi, **Antonio Raimondi School** and **Instituto San Ignacio de Loyola**, Lima, Peru; Kari Miller, **Binational Center**, Quito, Ecuador; Alex K. Oliveira, **Boston University**, Boston, MA, USA; Elisabeth Blom, **Casa Thomas Jefferson**, Brasilia, Brazil; Henry Grant, **CCBEU – Campinas**, Campinas, Brazil; Maria do Rosário, **CCBEU – Franca**, Franca, Brazil; Ane Cibele Palma, **CCBEU Inter Americano**, Curitiba, Brazil; Elen Flavia Penques da Costa, **Centro de Cultura Idiomas – Taubate**, Taubate, Brazil; Inara Lúcia Castillo Couto, **CEL LEP – São Paulo**, São Paulo, Brazil; Geysa de Azevedo Moreira, **Centro Cultural Brasil Estados Unidos (CCBEU Belém)**, Belém, Brazil; Sonia Patricia Cardoso, **Centro de Idiomas Universidad Manuela Beltrán**, Barrio Cedritos, Colombia; Geraldine Itiago Losada, **Centro Universitario Grupo Sol (Musali)**, Mexico City, Mexico; Nick Hilmers, **DePaul University**, Chicago, IL, USA; Monica L. Montemayor Menchaca, **EDIMSA**, Metepec, Mexico; Angela Whitby, **Edu-Idiomas Language School**, Cholula, Puebla, Mexico; Mary Segovia, **El Monte Rosemead Adult School**, Rosemead, CA, USA; Dr. Deborah Aldred, **ELS Language Centers, Middle East Region**, Abu Dhabi, United Arab Emirates; Leslie Lott, **Embassy CES**, Ft. Lauderdale, FL, USA; M. Martha Lengeling, **Escuela de Idiomas**, Guanajuato, Mexico; Pablo Frias, **Escuela de Idiomas UNAPEC**, Santo Domingo, Dominican Republic; Tracy Vanderhoek, **ESL Language Center**, Toronto, Canada; Kris Vicca and Michael McCollister, **Feng Chia University**, Taichung, Taiwan; Flávia Patricia do Nascimento Martins, **First Idiomas**, Sorocaba, Brazil; Andrea Taylor, **Florida State University in Panama**, Panamá, Panama; Carlos Lizárraga González, **Groupo Educativo Angloamericano**, Mexico City, Mexico; Dr. Martin Endley, **Hanyang University**, Seoul, Korea; Mauro Luiz Pinheiro, **IBEU Ceará**, Ceará, Brazil; Ana Lúcia da Costa Maia de Almeida, **IBEU Copacabana**, Copacabana, Brazil; Ana Lucia Almeida, Elisa Borges, **IBEU Rio**, Rio de Janeiro, Brazil; Maristela Silva, **ICBEU Manaus**, Manaus, Brazil; Magaly Mendes Lemos, **ICBEU São José dos Campos**, São José dos Campos, Brazil; Augusto Pelligrini Filho, **ICBEU São Luis**, São Luis, Brazil; Leonardo Mercado, **ICPNA**, Lima, Peru; Lucia Rangel Lugo, **Instituto Tecnológico de San Luis Potosí**, San Luis Potosí, Mexico; Maria Guadalupe Hernández Lozada, **Instituto Tecnológico de Tlalnepantla**, Tlalnepantla de Baz, Mexico; Greg Jankunis, **International Education Service**, Tokyo, Japan; Karen Stewart, **International House Veracruz**, Veracruz, Mexico; George Truscott, **Kinki University**, Osaka, Japan; Bo-Kyung Lee, **Hankuk University of Foreign Studies**, Seoul, Korea; Andy Burki, **Korea University, International Foreign Language School**, Seoul, Korea; Jinseo Noh, **Kwangwoon University**, Seoul, Korea; Nadezhda Nazarenko, **Lone Star College**, Houston, TX, USA; Carolyn Ho, **Lone Star College-Cy-Fair**, Cypress, TX, USA; Alice Ya-fen Chou, **National Taiwan University of Science and Technology**, Taipei, Taiwan; Gregory Hadley, **Niigata University of International and Information Studies, Department of Information Culture**, Niigata-shi, Japan; Raymond Dreyer, **Northern Essex Community College**, Lawrence, MA, USA; Mary Keter Terzian Megale, **One Way Línguas-Suzano**, São Paulo, Brazil; Jason Moser, **Osaka Shoin Joshi University**, Kashiba-shi, Japan; Bonnie Cheeseman, **Pasadena Community College** and **UCLA American Language Center**, Los Angeles, CA, USA; Simon Banha, **Phil Young's English School**, Curitiba, Brazil; Oh Jun Il, **Pukyong National University**, Busan, Korea; Carmen Gehrke, **Quatrum English Schools**, Porto Alegre, Brazil; Atsuko K. Yamazaki, **Shibaura Institute of Technology**, Saitama, Japan; Wen hsiang Su, **Shi Chien University, Kaohsiung Campus**, Kaohsiung, Taiwan; Richmond Stroupe, **Soka University, World Language Center**, Hachioji, Tokyo, Japan; Lynne Kim, **Sun Moon University (Institute for Language Education)**, Cheon An City, Chung Nam, Korea; Hiroko Nishikage, **Taisho University**, Tokyo, Japan; Diaña Peña Munoz and Zaira Kuri, **The Anglo**, Mexico City, Mexico; Alistair Campbell, **Tokyo University of Technology**, Tokyo, Japan; Song-won Kim, **TTI (Teacher's Training Institute)**, Seoul, Korea; Nancy Alarcón, **UNAM FES Zaragoza Language Center**, Mexico City, Mexico; Laura Emilia Fierro López, **Universidad Autónoma de Baja California**, Mexicali, Mexico; María del Rocío Domíngeuz Gaona, **Universidad Autónoma de Baja California**, Tijuana, Mexico; Saul Santos Garcia, **Universidad Autónoma de Nayarit**, Nayarit, Mexico; Christian Meléndez, **Universidad Católica de El Salvador**, San Salvador, El Salvador; Irasema Mora Pablo, **Universidad de Guanajuato**, Guanajuato, Mexico; Alberto Peto, **Universidad de Oxaca**, Tehuantepec, Mexico; Carolina Rodriguez Beltan, **Universidad Manuela Beltrán, Centro Colombo Americano**, and **Universidad Jorge Tadeo Lozano**, Bogotá, Colombia; Nidia Milena Molina Rodriguez, **Universidad Manuela Beltrán** and **Universidad Militar Nueva Granada**, Bogotá, Colombia; Yolima Perez Arias, **Universidad Nacional de Colombia**, Bogota, Colombia; Héctor Vázquez García, **Universidad Nacional Autónoma de Mexico**, Mexico City, Mexico; Pilar Barrera, **Universidad Técnica de Ambato**, Ambato, Ecuador; Deborah Hulston, **University of Regina**, Regina, Canada; Rebecca J. Shelton, **Valparaiso University, Interlink Language Center**, Valparaiso, IN, USA; Tae Lee, **Yonsei University**, Seodaemun-gu, Seoul, Korea; Claudia Thereza Nascimento Mendes, **York Language Institute**, Rio de Janeiro, Brazil; Jamila Jenny Hakam, **ELT Consultant**, Muscat, Oman; Stephanie Smith, **ELT Consultant**, Austin, TX, USA.

The authors would also like to thank the Four Corners editorial, production, and new media teams, as well as the Cambridge University Press staff and advisors around the world for their contributions and tireless commitment to quality.

# Scope and sequence

| Functional language | Listening and Pronunciation | Reading and Writing | Speaking |
|---|---|---|---|
| **Interactions:**<br>Expressing prohibition<br>Expressing obligation | **Listening:**<br>Office rules<br>An interview about homeschooling<br>**Pronunciation:**<br>Stress and rhythm | **Reading:**<br>"Homeschooling"<br>A magazine article<br>**Writing:**<br>Advantages and disadvantages of distance education | • Information exchange about school and work<br>• *Keep talking:* "Find someone who" activity about everyday activities<br>• List of class rules<br>• Information exchange about personal behavior<br>• *Keep talking:* Comparison of behaviors<br>• Discussion about distance education |
| **Interactions:**<br>Announcing news<br>Closing a conversation | **Listening:**<br>News about other people<br>A camping trip<br>**Pronunciation:**<br>Intonation in complex sentences | **Reading**<br>"Embarrassing Experiences"<br>An article<br>**Writing:**<br>An embarrassing moment | • Group story about a past event<br>• *Keep talking:* Description of simultaneous past actions<br>• Celebrity news<br>• Personal stories and anecdotes<br>• *Keep talking:* Picture stories<br>• Descriptions of embarrassing moments |
| **Interactions:**<br>Asking where things are<br>Asking for an alternative | **Listening:**<br>Clothing purchases<br>An interview with a fashion designer<br>**Pronunciation:**<br>*Used to* and *use to* | **Reading:**<br>"Favorite Fashions"<br>A survey<br>**Writing:**<br>Class survey | • Interview about style and fashion<br>• *Keep talking:* Comparison of two people's past and present styles<br>• Role play of a shopping situation<br>• Opinions on fashion and style<br>• *Keep talking:* Interview about what's hot<br>• Class survey about style and fashion |
| **Interactions:**<br>Checking meaning<br>Clarifying meaning | **Listening:**<br>Unusual habits<br>An interview with a grandmother<br>**Pronunciation:**<br>Contrastive stress in responses | **Reading:**<br>"The Life of an Astronaut"<br>An interview<br>**Writing:**<br>Interesting people, places, or things | • Interviews about experiences<br>• *Keep talking:* Information exchange about experiences never had<br>• Information exchange about unusual habits<br>• True and false information about life experiences<br>• *Keep talking:* "Find someone who" activity about everyday experiences<br>• Description of an interesting person or place |
| **Interactions:**<br>Expressing disbelief<br>Saying you don't know | **Listening:**<br>An interesting city<br>The Great Barrier Reef<br>**Pronunciation:**<br>Intonation in tag questions | **Reading:**<br>"Seven Wonders of the Natural World"<br>An article<br>**Writing:**<br>A natural wonder | • Comparison of different places<br>• *Keep talking:* Information gap activity about impressive places<br>• Information exchange about human-made structures<br>• Discussion about experiences in different places<br>• *Keep talking:* Advice for foreign visitors<br>• List of the most wonderful places in the country |
| **Interactions:**<br>Offering to take a message<br>Leaving a message | **Listening:**<br>Weekend plans<br>Phone messages<br>**Pronunciation:**<br>Reduction of *could you* and *would you* | **Reading:**<br>"How to Manage Your Time"<br>An article<br>**Writing:**<br>Tips for success | • "Find someone who" activity about weekend plans<br>• *Keep talking:* Information exchange about upcoming plans<br>• Role play with phone messages<br>• Class favors, offers, and promises<br>• *Keep talking:* Role play with requests<br>• Quiz about overdoing things |

| LEVEL 3 | Learning outcomes | Grammar | Vocabulary |
|---|---|---|---|
| **Unit 7**     Pages 63–72 | | | |
| **Personalities**<br>A *You're extremely curious.*<br>B *In my opinion, . . .*<br><br>C *We've been friends for six years.*<br>D *What is your personality?* | Students can . . .<br>☑ talk about personality traits<br>☑ give an opinion<br>☑ ask for agreement<br>☑ describe people's personalities<br>☑ talk about their personality | Adverbs modifying<br>  adjectives and verbs<br>Present perfect with<br>  *for* and *since* | Personality traits<br>More personality traits |
| **Unit 8**     Pages 73–82 | | | |
| **The environment**<br>A *Going green*<br>B *I'd rather not say.*<br><br>C *What will happen?*<br>D *Finding solutions* | Students can . . .<br>☑ discuss environmental problems<br>☑ give an approximate answer<br>☑ avoid answering<br>☑ talk about future possibilities<br>☑ discuss solutions to problems | Quantifiers<br>First conditional | Environmental impacts<br>Tips to help the<br>  environment |
| **Unit 9**     Pages 83–92 | | | |
| **Relationships**<br>A *Healthy relationships*<br>B *I'm really sorry.*<br><br>C *That can't be the problem.*<br>D *Getting advice* | Students can . . .<br>☑ discuss what's important in relationships<br>☑ apologize and give excuses<br>☑ accept an apology<br>☑ speculate about people<br>☑ give advice about relationships | *It's* . . . expressions<br>Expressions with<br>  infinitives<br>Modals for speculating | Relationship behaviors<br>Inseparable phrasal<br>  verbs |
| **Unit 10**     Pages 93–102 | | | |
| **Living your life**<br>A *He taught himself.*<br>B *I'll give it some thought.*<br><br>C *What would you do?*<br>D *What an accomplishment!* | Students can . . .<br>☑ talk about themselves and their experiences<br>☑ advise against something<br>☑ consider advice<br>☑ talk about imaginary situations<br>☑ ask and talk about accomplishments | Reflexive pronouns<br>Second conditional | Qualities for success<br>Separable phrasal verbs |
| **Unit 11**     Pages 103–112 | | | |
| **Music**<br>A *Music trivia*<br>B *The first thing you do is* . . .<br>C *Music and me*<br>D *Thoughts on music* | Students can . . .<br>☑ talk about music<br>☑ give instructions<br>☑ talk about things they've done recently<br>☑ talk about memorable songs | Past passive<br>Present perfect with *yet*<br>  and *already* | Compound adjectives<br>Verb and noun formation |
| **Unit 12**     Pages 113–122 | | | |
| **On vacation**<br>A *Travel preferences*<br>B *Don't forget to* . . .<br><br>C *Rules and recommendations*<br>D *Seeing the sights* | Students can . . .<br>☑ discuss travel preferences<br>☑ ask about preferences<br>☑ remind someone of something<br>☑ talk about rules and recommendations<br>☑ describe their dream trip | Gerunds<br>Modals for necessity and<br>  recommendations | Vacation activities<br>Extreme sports |

| Functional language | Listening and Pronunciation | Reading and Writing | Speaking |
|---|---|---|---|
| **Interactions:**<br>Giving an opinion<br>Asking for agreement | **Listening:**<br>Common proverbs<br>A personality quiz<br>**Pronunciation:**<br>Reduction of *don't you* | **Reading:**<br>"The Signs of the Zodiac"<br>Descriptions<br>**Writing:**<br>My personality | • Interview about personality traits<br>• *Keep talking:* Left-brain versus right-brain quiz<br>• Discussion about personality assumptions<br>• Information exchange about friends and their personalities<br>• *Keep talking:* Interviews about special people and things<br>• Guessing game to match people and their personality descriptions |
| **Interactions:**<br>Giving an approximate answer<br>Avoiding answering | **Listening:**<br>A survey on grocery shopping habits<br>Award winners for environmental work<br>**Pronunciation:**<br>Stress in compound nouns | **Reading:**<br>"One-of-a-Kind Homes"<br>An article<br>**Writing:**<br>A letter about an environmental issue | • Discussion about community environmental problems<br>• *Keep talking:* "Green" quiz<br>• Survey about water usage<br>• Cause and effect<br>• *Keep talking:* Possible outcomes in different situations<br>• Solutions to environmental issues |
| **Interactions:**<br>Apologizing<br>Accepting an apology | **Listening:**<br>Apologetic phone calls<br>A radio call-in show<br>**Pronunciation:**<br>Sentence stress | **Reading:**<br>"Addy's Advice"<br>Emails<br>**Writing:**<br>A piece of advice | • Tips for healthy relationships<br>• *Keep talking:* Advice for relationship problems<br>• Role play to apologize and make excuses<br>• Speculations about classmates<br>• *Keep talking:* Speculations about people<br>• Discussion about relationship problems |
| **Interactions:**<br>Advising against something<br>Considering advice | **Listening:**<br>Three problems<br>Interviews about accomplishments<br>**Pronunciation:**<br>Stress shifts | **Reading:**<br>"A Walk Across Japan"<br>An interview<br>**Writing:**<br>An accomplishment | • Interview about personal experiences<br>• *Keep talking:* "Find someone who" activity about personal experiences<br>• Role play to give and consider advice<br>• Discussion about hypothetical situations<br>• *Keep talking:* Interview about hypothetical situations<br>• "Find someone who" activity about accomplishments |
| **Interactions:**<br>Beginning instructions<br>Continuing instructions<br>Ending instructions | **Listening:**<br>How things work<br>Song dedications<br>**Pronunciation:**<br>Syllable stress | **Reading:**<br>"Richie Starr"<br>A fan site<br>**Writing:**<br>A music review | • Guessing game about music<br>• *Keep talking:* Discussion about music<br>• Information exchange with instructions<br>• "Find someone who" activity about recent actions<br>• *Keep talking:* "Find the differences" activity about two friends<br>• Information exchange about songs and memories |
| **Interactions:**<br>Asking about preferences<br>Reminding someone of something | **Listening:**<br>Hostel check-in<br>A white-water rafting trip<br>**Pronunciation:**<br>Reduction of verbs | **Reading:**<br>"A Taste of Cairo"<br>A food blog<br>**Writing:**<br>A walking tour | • Interview about vacation activities<br>• *Keep talking:* Comparison of travel preferences<br>• Role play about checking into a hotel<br>• Discussion about extreme sports<br>• *Keep talking:* Plan for a backpacking trip<br>• Information exchange about dream trips |

# Classroom language

**A** 🔊 Complete the conversations with the correct sentences. Then listen and check your answers.

| |
|---|
| ✓ What page are we on?     ✓ Excuse me. I'm very sorry I'm late. |
| Can you repeat that, please?    May I go to the restroom, please? |
| What's our homework?      Which role do you want to play? |

**A:** *Excuse me. I'm very sorry I'm late.*

**B:** That's OK. Next time try to arrive on time.

**A:** What page are we on?

**B:** Thirteen. We're doing the Warm-up for Unit 2.

**A:** _____

**B:** Yes. I said, "Please work with a partner."

**A:** _____

**B:** I'll be Student A. You can be Student B.

**A:** _____

**B:** No problem. Please try to be quick.

Homework
Workbook
Unit 2

**A:** _____

**B:** Please complete the activities for Unit 2 in your workbook.

**B** **Pair work** Practice the conversations.

2

# Education

## Warm-up

**A** Describe the pictures. What do you see? What are the students doing?

**B** How are the classrooms similar or different from your own classroom experiences?

# A I'm taking six classes.

## 1 Vocabulary School subjects

**A** 🔊 Match the words and the pictures. Then listen and check your answers.

✓ a. algebra กลัว
✓ b. art
✓ c. biology
✓ d. chemistry เคมี
✓ e. geometry
✓ f. history
✓ g. music
✓ h. physics
✓ i. world geography

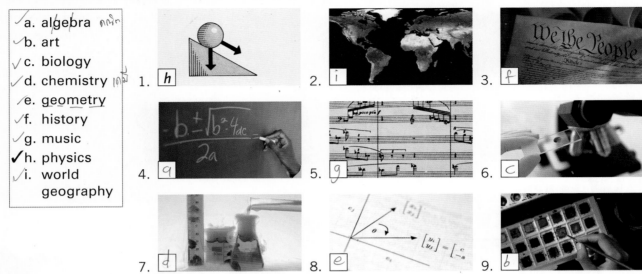

1. h
2. i
3. f
4. g
5. g
6. c
7. d
8. e
9. b

**B** 🔊 Complete the chart with the correct school subjects. Then listen and check your answers.

| Arts | Math | Science | Social studies |
|------|------|---------|----------------|
| _art_ | | | |
| | | | |
| | | | |

**C Pair work** Which school subjects are or were easy for you? Which are or were difficult? Tell your partner.

*"History and music were easy subjects for me, but algebra was difficult!"*

## 2 Language in context Busy schedules

**A** 🔊 Listen to three people talk about their schedules. Who doesn't have a job?

I'm a high school student. I love history and world geography. I have a part-time job, too. My parents own a restaurant, so I work there on Saturdays. I guess I'm pretty busy.      – *Kenji*

I'm a full-time student. I want to be a doctor. I'm taking six classes and preparing for my medical school entrance exams. I study biology and chemistry every night.    K    – *Jan*

I'm really busy! I work full-time at a bank. I'm also taking an English class at night with my friend Ricardo. Actually, I'm going to class now. I think I'm late!      – *Amelia*

**B** What about you? Do you have a busy schedule? What do you do in a typical week?

กว่า
เป็นตัวอย่าง

# 3 Grammar ◄))  Simple present vs. present continuous

*Use the simple present to describe routines and permanent situations.*

Kenji **works** on Saturdays.
Jan **studies** every night.
Kenji's parents **own** a restaurant.

*Use the present continuous to describe actions in progress or temporary situations.*
Amelia **is going** to class right now.
Jan **is preparing** for her medical school entrance exams.
Amelia and Ricardo **are taking** an English class together.

**Verbs not usually used in continuous tenses**

| | |
|---|---|
| believe | mean |
| have | own |
| hope | remember |
| know | seem |
| like | understand |
| love | want |

**A** Complete the conversations with the simple present or present continuous forms of the verbs. Then practice with a partner.

1. **A:** _____*Are*_____ you _____*taking*_____ (take) a lot of classes these days?
   **B:** I'm _____taking_____ (take) just two: world geography and physics. I _____have_____ (have) a full-time job, so I _____don't have_____ (not / have) a lot of free time.

2. **A:** How often _____do_____ you _____go_____ (go) to the library?
   **B:** I _____go_____ (go) every Saturday. But I _____study_____ (study) at home a lot, too. I'm _____preparing_____ (prepare) for an important exam.

3. **A:** How _____is_____ (be) your English class?
   **B:** It's _____ (be) fine. I _____like_____ (like) English and _____want_____ (want) to improve my speaking. But we _____are_____ (be) only in the first lesson!

4. **A:** What _____is_____ the teacher _____doing_____ (do) now?
   **B:** She's _____helping_____ (help) some students. They _____are asking_____ (ask) her questions. They _____seem_____ (seem) confused about something.

**B Pair work** Ask and answer the questions in Part A. Answer with your own information.

# 4 Speaking  School and work

**A Pair work** Read the list. Add one set of questions about school or work. Then ask and answer the questions with a partner.

- What's your favorite class? Are you learning anything interesting?
- Do you have a job? If so, what do you do?
- Are you studying for any exams? Do you study alone or with others?
- What job do you want someday? Are you doing anything to prepare for it?
- Why are you studying English? What do you hope to do in this class?
- _____ ? _____ ?  *Do you like this class*

**B Group work** Share any interesting information from Part A.

# 5 Keep talking!

Go to page **123** for more practice.

I can *ask and talk about routines.* ☑

## 1 Interactions | Prohibition and obligation

**A** Do you always follow rules? Do you ever break rules? If so, when?

**B** 🔊 Listen to the conversation. What *can* students do in the class? Then practice the conversation.

**Justin:** Excuse me. Do you mind if I sit here?

**Fei:** Not at all. Go ahead.

**Justin:** Thanks. I'm Justin, by the way.

**Fei:** Hi. I'm Fei. Are you new in this class?

**Justin:** Yeah. Today is my first day. Hey, can we drink coffee in class?

**Fei:** No. You can't eat or drink in class. It's one of the rules.

**Justin:** Really? Good to know.

**Fei:** Oh, and there's another rule. You have to turn off your cell phone.

**Justin:** OK. Thanks for letting me know.

**Fei:** Sure. Do you want to be my language partner today? We can choose our speaking partners in this class.

**Justin:** OK. Thanks.

**C** 🔊 Read the expressions below. Complete each box with a similar expression from the conversation. Then listen and check your answers.

| *Expressing prohibition* | *Expressing obligation* |
|---|---|
| You can't . . . | _____ |
| You're not allowed to . . . | You need to . . . |
| You're not permitted to . . . | You must . . . |

**D** **Pair work** Look at the common signs. Say the rules. Take turns.

*"You're not permitted to use cell phones."*

6

# 2 Listening First day at work

**A** 🔊 Listen to Joel's co-workers explain the office rules on his first day at work. Number the pictures from 1 to 6.

**B** 🔊 Listen again. Write the office rules.

1. You can't wear blue jeness in the office
2. You have to ture off your cell phone
3. You cant listen to music
4. You need to wash your cup
5. You are not pernitted to eat at your desh
6. You have to put more paper in the copy machine

# 3 Speaking Class rules

**A Pair work** Make a list of five important rules for your class like the one below.

_Class rules_

1. You must raise your hand to speak.
2. You can't send or read text messages.
3. You have to turn off your cell phone.
4. You're not permitted to chew gum.
5. You're allowed to sit anywhere you want.

- You have to bring the books come to class every day
- You can't use your cell phone in class

**B Group work** Compare your list with another pair. Choose the five most important rules.

**C Class activity** Share your lists. Can you and your teacher agree on a list of class rules?

I can express prohibition and obligation. ☑

# C My behavior

## 1 Vocabulary Feelings and emotions

**A** 🔊 Match the words and the pictures. Then listen and check your answers.

| | | | | |
|---|---|---|---|---|
| a. angry | c. hungry | e. lonely | g. scared | i. thirsty |
| b. busy | d. jealous | f. nervous | h. sleepy | j. upset |

1. h
2. d
3. j
4. a
5. f
6. b
7. c
8. g
9. i
10. e

**B Pair work** Why do you think the people in the pictures feel the way they do? Discuss your ideas.

## 2 Conversation Feeling nervous

**A** 🔊 Listen to the conversation. Why is Nate eating so late?

**Nate:** Hello?

**Laura:** Hi, Nate. It's Laura. Are you busy?

**Nate:** Not really. I'm just eating some ice cream.

**Laura:** Really? Why are you eating so late?

**Nate:** Oh, I have an exam tomorrow, and I'm kind of nervous about it. I eat when I'm nervous. I'm not even hungry! It's not good, I know.

**Laura:** Well, a lot of people eat when they're nervous. If I'm nervous about something, I just try not to think about it.

**Nate:** That's easier said than done! But what do you do if you have a really important exam?

**Laura:** I study a lot, of course!

**B** 🔊 Listen to the rest of the conversation. Why did Laura call Nate?

*few*

# 3 Grammar 🔊 Zero conditional

*Zero conditional sentences describe things that are generally true.* (usually) *Use the simple present for both the* if *clause (the condition) and the main clause.*

What **do** you **do** if you **have** a really important exam?

  If I **have** a really important exam, I **study** a lot.

  I **study** a lot if I **have** a really important exam.

*You can usually substitute* when *for* if *in zero conditional sentences.*

**If** I'm nervous about something, I just try not to think about it.

**When** I'm nervous about something, I just try not to think about it.

**A** Match the conditions and the main clauses. Then compare with a partner.

1. If I'm nervous before an exam, __f__
2. When I'm busy with chores at home, __a__
3. If I wake up and feel hungry, __c__
4. When I get angry at someone, __d__
5. If my friends don't call me for a few days, __b__
6. When I feel sleepy on Sunday mornings, __e__

 a. I ask a family member to do some.
 b. I start to get lonely.
 c. I have something healthy, like an apple.
 d. I usually don't say anything to him or her.
 e. I like to stay in bed.
 f. I take a deep breath and try to relax.

**B Pair work** Make true sentences about your behavior with the conditions in Part A. Tell your partner.

*"If I'm nervous before an exam, I study with a friend."*

angry → person = angry with ___.
  → thing = angry at ___.

# 4 Pronunciation Stress and rhythm

**A** 🔊 Listen and repeat. Notice how stressed words occur with a regular rhythm.

When I'm **lonely**, I **like** to **chat** or **talk** on the **phone** with my **friends**.

**B Pair work** Practice the sentences from Exercise 3A. Pay attention to your stress and rhythm.

# 5 Speaking Different behaviors

**Group work** Read the list. Add two more questions with *if* or *when*. Then ask and answer them.

bullets

cheat

Sm.

- How do you feel when you're home alone at night?
- What do you do when you get jealous?
- What do you do if you feel sleepy in class?
- How do you feel when you speak English in class?
- What do you do if someone mad at you?
- What do you do when someone do something you don't like.

# 6 Keep talking!

Go to page 124 for more practice.

Go to page 124 for more practice.

*I can ask and talk about feelings and reactions.* ☑

**Alternative education**

## 1 Reading

**A** What is homeschooling? Do you know any homeschooled students?

**B** Read the article. What is a "curriculum," and who chooses it for homeschooled students?

# Homeschooling

Homeschooling is a choice made by some parents to provide education to their children in their own homes. It's popular in the United States, and it is becoming more popular in the United Kingdom, Australia, South Africa, and Japan.

There are several advantages to homeschooling. For example, parents choose what their children learn. Because parents can teach their children one on one, they often understand the curriculum better and more quickly, too. On the other hand, if their children need more time to learn something, parents can work with them at a slower pace. Parents also like to spend more time together as a family, and children feel safe at home. A safe environment often leads to better learning.

There are disadvantages as well. Homeschooled students often feel lonely because they don't spend as much time with other kids their age. They don't get to talk with classmates about things like parents and homework. Parents also feel lonely because they must spend time teaching children and don't get to talk with other adults at work. In addition, homeschooled students sometimes cannot play school sports or participate in other activities and programs available to people in a school.

Only you can decide if homeschooling is right for you and your family. Take the time to do the research and consider the pros and cons.

*Source:* www.wisegeek.com/what-is-home-schooling.htm

**American Parents' Reasons for Homeschooling**

| | | | |
|---|---|---|---|
| Better education at home | 48.9% | Disagree with school's curriculum | 12.1% |
| Religious reasons | 38.4% | School is too easy | 11.6% |
| Poor learning environment at school | 25.6% | No schools nearby | 11.5% |
| Family reasons | 16.8% | Child's behavior problems | 9.0% |
| To develop child's character | 15.1% | Child's special needs | 8.2% |

*Source:* nces.ed.gov/pubs2001/Homeschool/reasons.asp

**C** Read the article again. Complete the chart with at least three advantages and three disadvantages of homeschooling.

| Advantages of homeschooling (+) | Disadvantages of homeschooling (−) |
|---|---|
| *parents choose the curriculum* | *kids can feel lonely* |
| | |
| | |

**D Pair work** Do you think you and your family would like homeschooling? Why or why not? Tell your partner.

## 2 Listening Is homeschooling for you?

**A** 🔊 Listen to Julie and her parents discuss homeschooling. What do they like about it, and what are their challenges? Check (✓) the correct answers.

| | Likes | Challenges | Advice |
|---|---|---|---|
| Julie | ☐ the classroom<br>☐ the hours<br>☐ the teachers | ☐ texting friends<br>☐ not seeing friends in class<br>☐ being in a real school | |
| Julie's parents | ☐ teaching together<br>☐ choosing the curriculum<br>☐ working at home | ☐ scheduling<br>☐ giving grades<br>☐ knowing every subject | |

**B** 🔊 Listen again. What advice do Julie and her parents give to people considering homeschooling? Complete the chart with their advice.

## 3 Writing Distance education

**A Pair work** Read the definition of distance education. Then make a list of its advantages and disadvantages.

Distance education is a type of education where students work on their own at home and communicate with teachers and other students using email, message boards, instant messaging, chat rooms, and other forms of computer-based communication.

**B** Do you think learning English by distance education is a good idea or a bad idea? Write a paragraph to explain your opinion. Use the model and your list from Part A.

> *Advantages of Distance Education*
> *I think learning English by distance education is a very good idea. There are many advantages. For example, students can work at their own speed. This is good for people with full-time jobs or people who can't go to regular classes . . .*

**C Pair work** Compare your ideas.

## 4 Speaking Advantages and disadvantages

**A Group work** What are the advantages and disadvantages of these types of learning? Discuss your ideas.

| | | |
|---|---|---|
| large classes | private lessons with a tutor | studying abroad |
| small classes | online learning | watching movies in English |

**B Class activity** How do you prefer to learn? What type of learning is the most popular?

*I can discuss advantages and disadvantages.* ☑

# Wrap-up

## 1 Quick pair review

**Lesson A** **Do you remember?** Cross out the word that doesn't belong. Then write the category. You have two minutes.

1. _____math_____    algebra    ~~history~~    geometry
2. _____music_____    art    history    world geography
3. _____history_____    music    art    algebra
4. _____algebra_____    biology    geometry    chemistry

**Lesson B** **Guess!** Think of a place that has rules. Tell your partner things you can and can't do there, but don't say the name of the place. Can your partner guess it? You have two minutes.

**A:** *You're not permitted to talk. You must turn off your cell phone.*
**B:** *Is it a library?*

**Lesson C** **Find out!** What is one thing both you and your partner do in each situation? You have three minutes.

- What do you do if you feel scared?
- What do you do if you get a phone call in class?
- What do you do if you have a lot of homework?

**A:** *If I'm scared, I turn on the lights. Do you?*
**B:** *No. I lock the doors if I'm scared. Do you?*
**A:** *Yes.*

**Lesson D** **Give your opinion!** What are two advantages and two disadvantages of taking a class online? You have three minutes.

## 2 In the real world

What is a multi-age classroom? Go online and find information in English about one. Then write about it.

- What ages or grades are in the classroom?
- What are some advantages?
- What are some disadvantages?

> *A Multi-Age Classroom*
> *At Ambuehl Elementary School, first-, second-, and third-graders are in the same classroom. One advantage is that younger students learn from older students. Another advantage is that . . .*

# Personal stories

| **LESSON A** | **LESSON B** | **LESSON C** | **LESSON D** |
|---|---|---|---|
| • Sentence adverbs<br>• Past continuous vs. simple past | • Announcing news<br>• Closing a conversation | • Verbs to describe reactions<br>• Participial adjectives | • Reading: "Embarrassing Experiences"<br>• Writing: An embarrassing moment |

## Warm-up

**A** Look at the pictures. Which story would you like to hear? Rank them from 1 (very much) to 6 (not much).

**B** Do you prefer to tell stories about yourself or hear stories about other people? Why?

# A *What were you doing?*

## 1 Vocabulary Sentence adverbs

**A** 🔊 Match the pictures and the sentences. Then listen and check your answers.

1.     2.     3.     4.

<u>2</u> **Amazingly,** she came home last night.

<u>4</u> **Fortunately,** she was very healthy.
ติดโรคอ

<u>1</u> **Sadly,** my cat disappeared last year.

<u>3</u> **Strangely,** she had on a little sweater.
น่าแปลกใจ

5.     6.     7.     8.

<u>7</u> **Luckily,** someone found it.

<u>6</u> **Suddenly,** I realized I didn't have it.
ฉุกกระหันคิดขึ้น

<u>8</u> **Surprisingly,** she brought it to my home.

<u>5</u> **Unfortunately,** I lost my wallet yesterday.
ฝาเงิน ตง

**B Pair work** Use sentence adverbs to describe incidents that happened to you or people you know. Tell your partner.

*"Amazingly, my brother passed his physics exam last week. He didn't study at all!"*

## 2 Language in context Lights out!

**A** 🔊 Listen to two people describe what they were doing when the power went out last night. What did they do after the power went out?

I was cooking pasta when suddenly everything went dark. Luckily, I had some candles. I couldn't finish making my meal, so I just ate cereal for dinner.

*– Angela*

While my friends and I were watching a movie at home, the lights went out. Unfortunately, no one knew how the movie ended. So, we took turns telling our own endings.

*– Tetsu*

**B** What about you? Have you ever been in a blackout? What did you do?

# **3 Grammar** 🔊 | Past continuous vs. simple past

*Use the past continuous to describe an action in progress in the past.*

Angela **was cooking** pasta last night.     Tetsu and his friends **were watching** a movie.

*Use the simple past for an event that interrupts that action in progress.*

Angela **was cooking** pasta when everything **went** dark.
While Tetsu and his friends **were watching** a movie, the lights **went** out.

**A** Complete the conversations with the past continuous or simple past forms of the verbs. Then practice with a partner.

1. **A:** What _____*were*_____ you ____*doing*____
   (do) last night when the storm
   _____*began*_____ (begin)?
   **B:** I ___*was using*___ (use) my computer.
   While I ____*wroet*____ (write) my report,
   the electricity suddenly ____*went*____
   (go) off.
   **A:** ____*Were*____ you ____*losed.*____
   (lose) your work?
   **B:** Yeah. Unfortunately, I ___*needded*___
   (need) to do it again.

2. **A:** How ____*did*____ you
   ____*break*____ (break) your foot?
   **B:** Oh, I ___*was skiing*___ (ski).
   **A:** Really? ____*did*____ it
   ____*hurt*____ (hurt)?
   **B:** Of course! But fortunately, someone
   ____*called*____ (call) an ambulance.
   **A:** That's good.
   **B:** Yeah, and while I ___*was waiting*___ (wait),
   my friends ____*brought*____ (bring) me
   hot chocolate.

**B Pair work** Ask and answer questions about what you were doing at the times below.

7:00 this morning     10:00 last night     4:30 yesterday afternoon     this time yesterday

# **4 Pronunciation** Intonation in complex sentences

🔊 Listen and repeat. Notice how each clause has its own intonation pattern.

Angela was cooking pasta when everything went dark.

When everything went dark, Angela was cooking pasta.

# **5 Speaking** Story time

**Group work** Complete a sentence below with your own idea. Your group adds
sentences with adverbs to create a story. Take turns.

- I was talking to my best friend when . . .
- I was sleeping one night when . . .
- I was walking down the street when . . .
- I was checking my messages when . . .

**A:** *I was talking to my best friend when my phone rang.*
**B:** *Strangely, it was a phone number I didn't know.*
**C:** *Luckily, I answered the phone, because it was . . .*

# **6 Keep talking!**

Go to page **125** for more practice.

*I can describe what was happening in the past.* ☑

# B Guess what!

## 1 Interactions    Sharing news

**A** Think about different people you know. Do you have any news about them?

**B** 🔊 Listen to the conversation. What news is Diana sharing?
Then practice the conversation.

**Ruben:** Hi, Diana. How are you?
**Diana:** I'm fine. Guess what!
**Ruben:** What?
**Diana:** Do you remember Joe from our photography class?
**Ruben:** Joe? Oh, yeah. Is he OK?
**Diana:** Oh, he's fine. It's just that he got into film school in Los Angeles. He's wants to be a director.
**Ruben:** Really? Good for him.
**Diana:** Yeah. I hear he really likes it.
**Ruben:** That's fantastic!
**Diana:** Yeah. Hey, I need to get going. I'm late for work.
**Ruben:** Oh, OK. I'll call you later.

**C** 🔊 Read the expressions below. Complete each box with a similar expression from the conversation. Then listen and check your answers.

### Announcing news

_____
Did you hear what happened?
You'll never guess what happened!

### Closing a conversation

_____
Listen, I've got to run.
Sorry, I have to go.

**D** **Pair work** Have conversations like the one in Part B. Use these ideas.

Your classmate Lucy Kim moved away. She moved to Spain to study art.

Your teacher Bill Jones got married. He married his girlfriend from high school.

Your friend Pedro Garcia was on TV. He was on a game show and won!

## 2 **Listening** You'll never guess!

**A** 🔊 Listen to Michael and Wendy talk about four different people they know. Number the people from 1 to 4 in the order they talk about them. There is one extra person.

4 a classmate    5 a co-worker    1 a family member เพื่อนบ้าน    2 a neighbor    3 a teacher

**B** 🔊 Listen again. Check (✓) the true sentences. Correct the false ones.

1. ☑ Greg is graduating from middle school.
2. ☐ Eva bought a brand-new red car. *won*
3. ☐ Mr. Landers is going to teach a new class.
4. ☑ Cathy is going to be in the school play.

## 3 **Speaking** Celebrity news

**A Pair work** Think of four famous people. What is some interesting news about them? Complete the chart.

| | Famous person | News |
|---|---|---|
| 1. | Silindero | News consend |
| 2. | Maroon 5 | New singer |
| 3. | Rehunna | Her song is number 1 |
| 4. | Beyongse | New consend |

**B Class activity** Announce your news about the famous people to a classmate. Then close the conversation and talk to another classmate.

**C Class activity** Who heard the most interesting news?

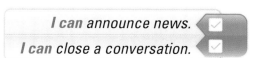

I can announce news. ✓
I can close a conversation. ✓

# C *I was really frightened!*

## 1 **Vocabulary** Verbs to describe reactions

**A** 🔊 Match the words and the pictures. Then listen and check your answers.

| | | | |
|---|---|---|---|
| a. amuse | c. confuse | e. embarrass | g. frighten |
| b. challenge | d. disgust | f. excite | h. interest |

 1. c

 2. b

 3. h

 4. d

 5. e

 6. f

 7. a

 8. g

**B Pair work** What amuses you? challenges you? confuses you? etc.
Tell your partner.

## 2 **Conversation** Around the campfire

**A** 🔊 Listen to the conversation. What frightened Paul?

**David:** . . . and that's what was on the floor!

  **Jim:** Yuck! That story was disgusting!

  **Paul:** Well, listen to this. I was watching a movie at home one night when I heard a strange noise outside the window.

**David:** What did you do?

  **Paul:** I was really frightened! I was watching a horror movie, *and* I was sitting in the dark. Anyway, I walked to the window, opened the curtains, and saw a face!

  **Jim:** No way! That's frightening!

  **Paul:** Not really. It was just my roommate.

**David:** Your roommate?

  **Paul:** Yeah. Unfortunately, he lost his key and couldn't get in the house. He was really embarrassed!

**B** 🔊 Listen to the rest of the conversation.
How did Paul's roommate react?

## 3 Grammar 🔊   **Participial adjectives**

| | |
|---|---|
| *Use present participles (-ing) to describe someone or something that causes a reaction.* | *Use past participles (-ed) to describe a person's reaction to someone or something.* |
| That story was **disgusting**. | I was **disgusted** by that story. |
| The noise was really **frightening**. | I was really **frightened** by the noise. |
| His actions were really **embarrassing**. | He was really **embarrassed**. |

Circle the correct words. Then compare with a partner.

1. This short story is very (challenging)/ challenged. There's a lot of difficult vocabulary.
2. I'm really **exciting** / **excited** to hear about your trip. Tell me all about it!
3. I liked your story, but I'm **confusing** / **confused** by the ending. Can you explain it?
4. I think my neighbor's stories about her life are very **amusing** / **amused**.
5. I never feel **frightening** / **frightened** when people tell me ghost stories.
6. That joke wasn't funny at all. It was **disgusting** / **disgusted**.
7. That movie was **boring** / **bored**. It wasn't **interesting** / **interested** at all.
8. I'm **surprising** / **surprised** you were **embarrassing** / **embarrassed** by my story.

## 4 Listening   Is that really true?

**A** 🔊 Listen to Mark's story. Check (✓) the two adjectives that best describe it.

☐ challenging    ☑ frightening    ☐ disgusting    ☑ amusing

**B** 🔊 Listen again. Answer the questions.

1. What were Mark and his friend doing in the tent? They were reading Mark's book and talking
2. What did they first hear outside the tent? There heard a big animal
3. What did Mark's friend want to do? Mark's friend wanted to read it
4. What did the voice outside the tent say? "I'm hungry at a bear"

## 5 Speaking   My own experience

**A** Think about your own experiences. Choose one of the topics from the list below. Then take notes to prepare to talk about it.

| | |
|---|---|
| an exciting day | a frightening experience |
| a confusing moment | an amusing situation |
| a challenging situation | an interesting conversation |

**B Pair work** Tell your partner about your experience. Ask and answer questions for more information.

## 6 Keep talking!

Go to page 126 for more practice.

*I can tell personal stories.* ☑

## 1 Reading 🔊

**A** How do you react when you feel embarrassed? Do you turn red? Do you get angry if people laugh at you?

**B** Read the article. Where did each person's embarrassing moment happen?

# STUDENT TIMES

| Home | Metro | Sports | Opinions | Arts | Photos | Videos | Search |

### Embarrassing Experiences
*By Jack Preston*

Last week, *Student Times* reporter Jack Preston asked students, "What's the most embarrassing experience you've ever had?" Here are five of his favorite responses.

This happened at work a few years ago. I was on an elevator, and a man got on that I didn't know. He asked, "How are you?" I answered, "Pretty good." Then he asked, "What's new?" and I said, "Nothing much." Finally, he turned and said, "Do you mind?" He was on his cell phone! I was so embarrassed! [2] – *Susan*

I sing all the time. One time, a few years ago, I was singing in the shower when my sister came into the bathroom and recorded me! Later, we were driving, and my sister put on some music. [4] It was me! I was really embarrassed and turned bright red. – *Becky*

I fell asleep in math class once. I closed my eyes for a second, and the next thing I remember is my teacher's voice. He was asking me a question. When I didn't answer, he walked over to my desk. He asked the question again. [1] – *Alex*

My friend's parents had a birthday party for her at their new house last year. They had these glass doors that went out to the backyard. We were all outside, and I had to use the restroom. So I was running to the house and then – BAM! I hit the glass doors. I was really confused for a minute. I thought they were open, but they were closed! [5] – *Anita*

When I was in middle school, I bought this cool new sweater. I wore it to a school dance the next evening, and everyone laughed at me when I came in. The sweater was inside out! So I went into the restroom to change and came back out. [3] Everyone laughed at me again. – *Evan*

**C** Read the article again. Write the numbers of the missing sentences in the correct paragraphs.

1. Luckily, I knew the answer.
2. Fortunately, the doors opened, and I got off.
3. Unfortunately, it was now on backwards!
4. Suddenly, she started to laugh.
5. Amazingly, I wasn't hurt at all.

**D Pair work** Whose story do you think is the most embarrassing? Discuss your ideas.

## 2 Writing An embarrassing moment

**A** Think of an embarrassing moment that happened to you or someone you know. Answer the questions.

- When did it happen? _____
- Where did it happen? _____
- Who was there? _____
- Why was it embarrassing? _____

**B** Write a description of an embarrassing moment that happened to you or someone you know. Use the model and your answers in Part A to help you.

*Embarrassed at the Supermarket*
*When I was about six years old, I was at the supermarket with my mom. She was shopping for groceries. I wanted some candy, but my mom didn't want to buy me any. So, when my mother wasn't looking, I took some candy and put it into the cart. The problem was that I put the candy into the wrong cart. . . .*

**C Class activity** Post your papers around the classroom. Then read the stories and rate them from 1 (very embarrassing) to 4 (not embarrassing). Which stories are the most embarrassing?

## 3 Speaking It happened to me!

**A** Imagine you are the person in one of these pictures. Take notes to prepare to tell the story. Spill (หก)

**B Group work** Tell your stories. Ask and answer questions for more information.

A: *I was having dinner with a friend. We were eating pizza and drinking soda. Suddenly, I spilled my soda on my clothes.*
B: *Oh, no! What did you do?*

*I can describe embarrassing moments.* ☑

# Wrap-up

## 1 Quick pair review

**Lesson A** **Brainstorm!** Make a list of sentence adverbs. How many do you know? You have one minute.

**Lesson B** **Do you remember?** Complete the expressions with the correct words to announce news and close a conversation. You have one minute.

1. Did you hear ___what happened___ ?
2. You'll ___never guess___ what happened!
3. Guess ___what___ !
4. Listen, I've ___got to run___ run.
5. Hey, I need to ___get going___ .
6. Sorry, I ___have___ to go.

**Lesson C** **Test your partner!** Say four present or past participles. Can your partner use them correctly in a sentence? Take turns. You have two minutes.

**A:** *Disgusting.*
**B:** *In my opinion, hamburgers are disgusting!*

**Lesson D** **Find out!** What are two things both you and your partner do when you are embarrassed? You have one minute.

**A:** *When I'm embarrassed, I laugh a lot. Do you?*
**B:** *No, I don't. I turn red, though. Do you?*
**A:** *Yes, my cheeks turn red, too!*

## 2 In the real world

Go online and find an embarrassing, interesting, or amusing story in English about a famous person. Then write about it.

> *Beyoncé's Embarrassing Moment*
> *Beyoncé had an embarrassing experience at a concert. She was walking down the stairs on stage when she tripped and fell. Luckily, she didn't get hurt. Actually she got up and continued to sing! . . .*

# Style and fashion

## Warm-up

**A** Describe the picture. What are the people doing?

**B** Which styles do you like? Which don't you like? Why?

## 1 **Vocabulary** Fashion statements

**A** 🔊 Complete the chart with the correct words. Then listen and check your answers.

a bracelet

contact lenses

dyed hair

earrings

glasses

high heels

a leather jacket

a ponytail

sandals

a uniform

| Shoes | Clothing | Eyewear | Hairstyles | Jewelry |
|---|---|---|---|---|
| high heels | a leather jacket | contact lenses | dyed hair | a bracelet |
| sandals | a uniform | glasses | a ponytail | earrings |

**B Pair work** Which things in Part A do you wear or have? Tell your partner.

## 2 **Language in context** Fashion history

**A** 🔊 Read about three fashions from the past. Who wore each fashion?

**Togas** Two thousand years ago, Roman men used to wear sandals and a long piece of clothing called a toga.

**Wigs** In the seventeenth and eighteenth centuries, rich men and women in England and France used to wear long wigs. Some of the wigs had ponytails.

**Leather jackets** In the 1950s, many American men used to wear leather jackets with jeans. Before that time, most teenagers didn't use to wear jeans.

**B** Do people still wear the fashions from Part A today? If so, how are they similar or different?

# 3 Grammar 🔊 ~~Used to~~

> Used to *refers to something that was true in the past but isn't anymore or something that happened regularly in the past but doesn't anymore.*
>
> I **used to** have a black leather jacket.
>
> Men and women in England and France **used to** wear long wigs.
>
> **Did** you **use to** dye your hair?
>
>     Yes, I **used to** dye my hair all the time, but I don't dye it anymore.
>
>     No, I **didn't use to** dye my hair, but I do now.

**A** Write sentences with *used to* (✓) or *didn't use to* (✗). Then compare with a partner.

1. Max / (✓) dye his hair black      *Max used to dye his hair black.*
2. Carly / (✗) wear a uniform to school      _____
3. Tina and I / (✓) have ponytails      _____
4. Britney / (✓) wear the same bracelet every day      _____
5. Roberto and Ana / (✗) wear glasses      _____
6. Kendra / (✗) like leather skirts      _____

**B Pair work** Complete the sentences with true information. Tell your partner.

1. I used to _____ as a kid, but I don't now.
2. I didn't use to _____ , but some of my friends did.
3. Lots of people used to _____ , but they don't now.

# 4 Pronunciation *Used to* and *use to*

🔊 Listen and repeat. Notice how *used to* and *use to* sound the same.

/yustə/                             /yustə/

I **used to** wear a uniform.     I didn't **use to** dye my hair, but I do now.

# 5 Speaking Past and present

**A Pair work** Read the list. Add two more questions about style and fashion. Then interview your partner. Take notes.

- What kind of clothing did you use to wear?
- What kind of hairstyles did you use to have?
- What's something you didn't use to wear but do now?
- _____
- _____

**B Pair work** Tell another classmate any interesting information about your partner's style and fashion.

# 6 Keep talking!

Student A go to page **127** and
Student B go to page **128** for more practice.

> *I can ask about and describe past fashions.* ☑

## 1 Interactions — Shopping questions

**A** Where do you like to shop for clothes? What kinds of clothes do you like?

**B** 🔊 Listen to the conversations. What size does Jenny want?
Then practice the conversations.

> **Jenny:** Excuse me.
> **Salesclerk 1:** Yes?
> **Jenny:** Where are the raincoats?
> **Salesclerk 1:** They're on the second floor, in Outerwear.
> **Jenny:** Thank you.

> **Jenny:** Excuse me.
> **Salesclerk 2:** Can I help you?
> **Jenny:** Yes. Does this come in a medium?
> **Salesclerk 2:** I believe so. Let's see. . . . Yes, here you go.
> **Jenny:** Thank you.
> **Salesclerk 2:** If you want to try it on, the fitting rooms are over there.

**C** 🔊 Read the expressions below. Complete each box with a similar expression from the conversations. Then listen and check your answers.

| *Asking where things are* |
| --- |
| _____ |
| Where can I find the . . . ? |
| Could you tell me where the . . . are? |

| *Asking for an alternative* |
| --- |
| _____ |
| Do you have this in . . . ? |
| Can I get this in . . . ? |

**D Pair work** Have conversations like the ones in Part B. Use these items.

## 2 Listening Shopping for clothes

**A** 🔊 Listen to four customers shopping in a clothing store. Number the items they discuss from 1 to 4. There are two extra items.

**B** 🔊 Listen again. Does each customer ask the salesclerk for the location or an alternative of the item? Write L (location) or A (alternative).

1. ____    2. ____    3. ____    4. ____

## 3 Speaking In a department store

**Group work** Role-play the situation. Then change roles.

**Student A:** You are a salesclerk in a department store. Student B is shopping for a particular item. Direct Student B to the correct section of the store. Use the picture to help you.

**Student B:** You are shopping in a department store. Students A and C are salesclerks. Ask Student A where a particular clothing item is. Then ask Student C for a different item.

**Student C:** You are a salesclerk in a department store. Student B is shopping for a particular item in your section of the store. Help Student B get a different item.

**A:** *Good afternoon. Can I help you?*
**B:** *Yes. Where can I find women's shoes?*
**A:** *On the second floor, in Footwear.*

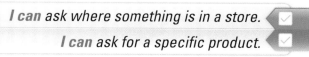

*I can ask where something is in a store.* ☑
*I can ask for a specific product.* ☑

## 1 Vocabulary Clothing styles

**A** 🔊 Write the correct adjectives to describe the clothing. Then listen and check your answers.

| fashionable |
| ✓flashy |
| glamorous |
| old-fashioned |

1. _flashy_
2. _____
3. _____
4. _____

| retro |
| tacky |
| trendy |
| ✓weird |

5. _weird_
6. _____
7. _____
8. _____

**B Pair work** Which styles do you like? Which don't you like? Why? Tell your partner.

## 2 Conversation People-watching

**A** 🔊 Listen to the conversation. What does Ryan think of the man's tie?

**Ryan:** Look at that woman's jacket!

**Jill:** Wow! It's pretty flashy. I definitely think she's someone who likes to stand out in a crowd.

**Ryan:** I know what you mean. I like clothes which don't attract a lot of attention.

**Jill:** Really?

**Ryan:** Yeah. I usually shop for clothes that are simple and inexpensive. Hey, check out that guy's tie. Talk about old-fashioned!

**Jill:** Do you think so? Actually, I think it's pretty fashionable. It's kind of retro.

**Ryan:** Well, I'd never wear anything like that.

**B** 🔊 Listen to the rest of the conversation. How does Jill describe her style?

# 3 Grammar 🔊 Defining relative clauses

*Defining relative clauses specify which or what kind of people or things you are describing.*

| | |
|---|---|
| *Use* that *or* who *for people.* | *Use* that *or* which *for things.* |
| I'm a person **that** loves flashy clothes. | I shop for clothes **that** are simple and inexpensive. |
| She's someone **who** likes to stand out in a crowd. | He likes clothes **which** don't attract a lot of attention. |

**A** Complete each sentence with *that, who,* or *which*. Then compare with a partner.

1. I prefer salesclerks _____ are honest with me.
2. I'm the kind of person _____ rarely follows fashion.
3. I hardly ever wear clothes _____ are trendy.
4. I know someone _____ loves expensive clothes.
5. Some of my friends wear stuff _____ is a little too weird.
6. I usually buy clothes _____ are on sale.
7. I'm someone _____ likes reading fashion magazines.
8. I buy shoes _____ go with lots of different clothing.

**B** **Pair work** Make the sentences in Part A true for you. Tell your partner.

**A:** *I prefer salesclerks who don't say anything. I know what looks good on me.*
**B:** *Not me. I need all the help I can get!*

# 4 Speaking Thoughts on fashion

**A** Complete the sentences with your own ideas.

1. I really don't like clothes that are _____ .
2. _____ is a word which describes my personal style.
3. When shopping, I like friends who _____ .
4. _____ is a person who always looks fashionable.
5. I think _____ is a color that looks good on me.
6. A _____ is something that I never wear.
7. _____ is a designer who's very popular now.

**B** **Group work** Compare your ideas. Ask and answer questions for more information.

**A:** *I really don't like clothes that are expensive.*
**B:** *Really? I only like expensive clothes!*
**C:** *I like clothes that are comfortable.*

# 5 Keep talking!

Go to page 129 for more practice.

*I can express opinions about style and fashion.* ☑

# D Views on fashion

## 1 Reading 🔊

**A** What's in style these days? Do you like the current fashions for men and women?

**B** Read the article. What is the survey about? Who took it, and where are they from?

## FAVORITE FASHIONS

Image is important to many people, but what do men and women really think of each other's fashion choices? What do people actually think looks good on the opposite sex? An equal number of male and female university students in southern California recently answered some questions about fashion. Here are the results.

### WHAT THE **GIRLS** SAID

*What's the best color on a guy?*
- **50%** Black
- **25%** White
- **25%** Whatever matches his eyes

*What footwear looks the best on a guy?*
- **60%** Flip-flops
- **25%** Dress shoes
- **15%** Skater shoes

*What should a guy wear on a first date?*
- **80%** Jeans, a nice shirt, and a jacket
- **15%** Shorts, a T-shirt, and flip-flops
- **5%** A shirt, a tie, and nice pants

### WHAT THE **GUYS** SAID

*What's the best color on a girl?*
- **40%** Red
- **35%** White
- **25%** Black

*What footwear looks the best on a girl?*
- **45%** High heels
- **30%** High-top sneakers
- **25%** Flip-flops

*What should a girl wear on a first date?*
- **60%** Jeans and a classy top
- **25%** A black dress
- **15%** A short shirt and skirt

*Source:* Adapted from San Diego State University's student newspaper, *The Daily Aztec.*

**C** Read the article again. Are the sentences true or false? Write T (true) or F (false).

1. Fifty percent of the girls think a bright color looks best on a guy. _____
2. Girls like nice dress shoes on guys more than skater shoes. _____
3. Most girls think a guy should wear flip-flops on a first date. _____
4. Guys think white is the best color on a girl. _____
5. Guys like sneakers more than flip-flops on girls. _____
6. Most guys think girls should wear a black dress on a first date. _____

**D** **Pair work** Do you agree with the survey results? Why or why not? Discuss your ideas.

## 2 Listening An interview with Eduardo

**A** 🔊 Listen to an interview with Eduardo, a fashion designer. Number the questions from 1 to 5 in the order you hear them.

☐ Are high heels old-fashioned? _____

☐ Should belts and shoes be the same color? _____

☐ Does black go with everything? _____

☐ Is it OK for men to wear earrings? _____

☐ Can guys wear pink? _____

**B** 🔊 Listen again. How does Eduardo answer each question? Write Y (yes) or N (no).

**C** Do you agree with Eduardo's opinions? Why or why not?

## 3 Writing and speaking Class survey

**A Group work** Create a survey with four questions about fashion and style. Use the topics below or your own ideas.

| | |
|---|---|
| cool places to shop | popular colors |
| current clothing styles | the latest gadgets |
| current hairstyles | trendy accessories |
| popular brands | unpopular colors |

*Fashion Survey*
1. *What color is popular right now?*
2. *What's the most popular brand of jeans?*
3. *Where is a cool place to buy jewelry?*
4. *What gadget does everyone want now?*

**B Class activity** Ask and answer the questions in your surveys. Take notes.

**C Group work** Share and summarize the results.

*Our Class Survey Results*

*Most people think blue is popular right now. Red was second and green was third. Only a few people think black, orange, or purple are popular. Only one person thinks yellow is popular.*

*The most popular brand of jeans is Sacco. A lot of people have these. Next was a brand called Durango. These were the only two brands that people mentioned.*

*Over half of the people in class think Glitter is a cool place to buy jewelry. Some people think the best place to buy jewelry is from people who sell it on the street. Two people . . .*

**D Class activity** Share your most interesting results. Do you agree with the answers you heard? Give your own opinions.

*I can ask and talk about current fashions.* ☑

# Wrap-up

## 1 Quick pair review

**Lesson A** **Do you remember?** Cross out the word that doesn't belong. Then write the category. You have two minutes.

1. _Shoes_        high heels        sandals        glasses
2. _Jewelry_      a bracelet        contact lenses   earrings
3. _Hairstyles_   dyed hair         a uniform       a ponytail
4. _Clothing_     a uniform         high heels      a leather jacket
5. _eyewear_      glasses           contact lenses   earrings

**Lesson B** **Brainstorm!** Make a list of three ways to ask where something is and three ways to ask for an alternative. You have two minutes.

**Lesson C** **Test your partner!** Say each pair of sentences. Can your partner make them into one sentence with *which* or *who*? You have two minutes.

**Student A**

1. I'm a trendy person. I don't like old-fashioned clothes.
2. I usually wear glasses. They aren't glamorous.
3. Julie shops for stuff. It is affordable.

**Student B**

1. I usually wear hats. They are weird.
2. I know someone. She likes flashy bracelets.
3. Kyle is a guy. He wears tacky clothes.

**A:** *I'm a trendy person. I don't like old-fashioned clothes.*
**B:** *I'm a trendy person who doesn't like old-fashioned clothes.*

**Lesson D** **Find out!** What are two colors that both you and your partner think are good for girls to wear? What are two colors you both think are good for guys to wear? You have two minutes.

**A:** *I think pink is a good color for girls to wear. Do you?*
**B:** *No, but I think purple is a good color. Do you?*
**A:** *Yes.*

## 2 In the real world

What clothes used to be trendy? Go online and find examples of trendy clothes from one decade in the past. Then write about them.

| 1950s | 1960s | 1970s | 1980s | 1990s |
| --- | --- | --- | --- | --- |

> *Trends in the 1980s*
> *Leg warmers used to be trendy in the 1980s. Tight jeans used to be popular, too. Women used to . . .*

# Interesting lives

## Warm-up

**A** Describe the pictures. What are the people doing?

**B** Check (✓) the two most interesting activities. Have you ever done them? If not, would you like to try them?

# Have you ever been on TV?

## 1 Vocabulary Experiences

**A** 🔊 Complete the phrases with the correct words. Then listen and check your answers.

| an award | a famous person | on TV | to a new city |
|---|---|---|---|
| a bone | ✓in a play | seasick | your phone |

1. act *in a play*
2. be *on TV*
3. break *a bone*
4. get *seasick*

5. lose *your phone*
6. meet *famous person*
7. move *to a new city*
8. win *an award*

**B Pair work** Which experiences in Part A are good to have? Which are not good to have? Discuss your ideas.

*"It's good to win an award. It's not good to get seasick."*

## 2 Language in context A local hero

**A** 🔊 Read Brian's online chat with some friends. Why is Brian excited?

○ ○ ○

**Brian:** You'll never believe what happened! I'm going to be on the TV news tonight! My first time!

**Jill:** You're kidding! Why?

**Brian:** It's a surprise. You have to watch. Have you ever been on TV?

**Jill:** No, I haven't. One of my friends is an actress, though, and I've seen her on TV a couple of times.

**Hideo:** I've never been on TV, but my sister Kumiko has been on TV lots of times. She's a TV reporter!

**B** What about you? Would you like to be on TV? Why or why not?

34

# 3 Grammar ◀)) Present perfect

*Use the present perfect to describe events or experiences that happened at an unspecified time in the past. Use* have / has *and the past participle of the verb.*

**Have** you ever **seen** a friend on TV?     **Has** your sister ever **been** on TV?
   Yes, I **have**.                              Yes, she **has**.
   No, I **haven't**.                            No, she **hasn't**.

*Use frequency expressions with the present perfect to give more information.*

I've **never** been on TV.              My sister has been on TV **lots of times**.

**A** Complete the conversations with the present perfect forms of the verbs. Then practice with a partner.

1. **A:** ___Have___ you ever ___been___ (be) to another country?
   **B:** Yes, I ___have___ . I ___went___ (be) to Canada.
2. **A:** ___Have___ you ever ___eaten___ (eat) sushi?
   **B:** Yes, I ___have___ . I ___had___ (have) it many times.
3. **A:** ___Have___ you ever ___lost___ (lose) your wallet?
   **B:** No, I ___haven't___ . Luckily, I ___have___ never ___lost___ (lose) it.
4. **A:** ___Have___ your best friend ever ___call___ (call) you in the middle of the night?
   **B:** No, she ___hadn't___ . But I ___did___ (do) that to her once or twice!

◀)) **Regular past participles**

| act | ➤ | act**ed** |
| chat | ➤ | chat**ted** |
| try | ➤ | tr**ied** |

**Irregular past participles**

| be | ➤ | **been** |
| break | ➤ | **broken** |
| do | ➤ | **done** |
| eat | ➤ | **eaten** |
| go | ➤ | **gone** |
| have | ➤ | **had** |
| lose | ➤ | **lost** |
| meet | ➤ | **met** |
| see | ➤ | **seen** |
| win | ➤ | **won** |

Turn to page 151 for a list of more past participles.

**B** **Pair work** Ask and answer the questions in Part A. Answer with your own information.

# 4 Speaking Yes, I have!

**A** Complete the questions with your own ideas. Then check (✓) the things you've done, and write how often you've done them.

| Have you ever . . . ? | Me | Name: _____ | Name: _____ |
|---|---|---|---|
| eaten _____ | ☐ | ☐ | ☐ |
| been _____ | ☐ | ☐ | ☐ |
| seen _____ | ☐ | ☐ | ☐ |
| had _____ | ☐ | ☐ | ☐ |
| won _____ | ☐ | ☐ | ☐ |
| met _____ | ☐ | ☐ | ☐ |

**B** **Group work** Interview two classmates. Complete the chart with their answers. Who has had similar experiences?

# 5 Keep talking!

Go to page **130** for more practice.

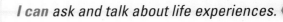

*I can ask and talk about life experiences.* ☑

## 1 Interactions · Checking and clarifying meaning

**A** How often do you eat out? Do you ever cook at home? Do you ever order takeout?

**B** 🔊 Listen to the conversation. How often does Sam eat out? Then practice the conversation.

**Elena:** I'm getting hungry.
**Sam:** Me, too.
**Elena:** Hey, Sam, there's a great Mexican restaurant near the school. Have you ever tried it?
**Sam:** No, I haven't. Actually, I don't eat in restaurants.
**Elena:** Really? Are you saying you never go to restaurants?
**Sam:** Well, no, not *never*. I mean I just don't eat out very often.
**Elena:** Why not?
**Sam:** I'm allergic to certain foods, like peanuts. If I eat them, my skin gets red and itchy.
**Elena:** That sounds awful!
**Sam:** It is!

**C** 🔊 Read the expressions below. Complete each box with a similar expression from the conversation. Then listen and check your answers.

| *Checking meaning* | *Clarifying meaning* |
|---|---|
| _____ | _____ |
| Do you mean . . . ? | What I mean is, . . . |
| Does that mean . . . ? | What I'm saying is, . . . |

**D** Number the sentences in the conversation from 1 to 7. Then practice with a partner.

____5____  **A:** What? Do you mean you never eat pizza?

____7____  **A:** I see. So, when can I come over for homemade pizza?

____1____  **A:** I feel a little hungry.

____3____  **A:** Have you ever been to Pizza Palace? We can go there.

____2____  **B:** So do I.

____6____  **B:** No, not *never*. What I mean is, I usually make it myself.

____4____  **B:** Actually, I never go to fast-food places.

## 2 Pronunciation Contrastive stress in responses

**A** 🔊 Listen and repeat. Notice how the stressed words emphasize contrast.

Are you saying you never go to restaurants?

Well, not **never**. I mean I just don't eat out **very often**.

**B Pair work** Practice the conversation in Exercise 1D again. Stress words to emphasize contrast.

## 3 Listening Why not?

**A** 🔊 Listen to four conversations about habits and preferences. Correct the false information.

*never*
1. Danielle ~~often~~ goes to hair salons.

2. Todd ~~loves~~ *hates* going to the beach.

3. Jessica always walks to school. *work*

4. Mitch ~~never~~ *always* rents DVDs.

**B** 🔊 Listen again. How do the people explain their habits and preferences? Check (✓) the correct answers.

1. Danielle's explanation:
   - ☐ She finds it too expensive.
   - ☑ Her sister cuts her hair.
   - ☐ She cuts her own hair.

2. Todd's explanation:
   - ☑ It's not easy to get there.
   - ☐ He doesn't know how to swim.
   - ☐ He doesn't like to be in the sun.

3. Jessica's explanation:
   - ☐ The school is only five minutes away.
   - ☐ She doesn't have a driver's license.
   - ☑ She prefers to walk for the exercise.

4. Mitch's explanation:
   - ☐ The movie theater is too far away.
   - ☐ He thinks tickets are too expensive.
   - ☑ He prefers to watch DVDs at home.

## 4 Speaking Unusual habits

**A** Write four statements about any unusual or interesting habits and behaviors you have. Use the questions to help you, or think of your own ideas.

- Is there a food you eat all the time?
- Is there a place you never go?
- Is there someone you talk to every day?
- Is there something you never do?
- Is there an expression you say all the time?

1. Is there the gym you go to every day?
2. Is there the school you go to every day
3. Is there a snak you eat all the time?
4. Is there the rasturant you never go

**B Pair work** Tell your partner about each habit or behavior. Your partner checks the meaning, and you clarify it. Take turns.

A: *I eat chocolate all the time.*
B: *Does that mean you eat it every day?*
A: *Well, no, not every day. I mean I have chocolate several times a week.*

*I can check and clarify meaning.*

# C Life experiences

## 1 Vocabulary Fun things to do

**A** 🔊 Match the phrases and the pictures. Then listen and check your answers.

| | | | |
|---|---|---|---|
| a. climb a mountain | c. go camping | e. go whale-watching | g. try an exotic food |
| b. eat in a fancy restaurant | d. go to a spa | f. ride a roller coaster | h. try an extreme sport |

1. ☐

2. ☐

3. ☐

4. a

5. ☐

6. c

7. h

8. f

**B Pair work** Have you ever done the fun things in Part A? Tell your partner.

## 2 Conversation A fancy restaurant

**A** 🔊 Listen to the conversation. Do you think Alice will order frog legs?

**Alice:** Wow! This place is nice!

**Emma:** Have you ever eaten in a fancy restaurant before?

**Alice:** Yes, I have. I've eaten in a few expensive restaurants, but this place is amazing.

**Emma:** You can try a lot of exotic food here, and all of their dishes are excellent. Oh, look. Tonight's special is frog legs.

**Alice:** Frog legs? Umm, I don't know. . . .

**Emma:** Have you ever tried them?

**Alice:** No, I haven't. But my brother tried them once a few years ago.

**Emma:** Did he like them?

**Alice:** I don't think so. He got sick later that night.

**B** 🔊 Listen to the rest of the conversation. What do Alice and Emma order?

## 3 Grammar 🔊 ━ Present perfect vs. simple past

*Use the present perfect to describe events or experiences at an unspecified time in the past.*

**Have** you ever **eaten** in a fancy restaurant?   X━━━━→

  Yes, I **have**. I**'ve eaten** in a few expensive restaurants.

*Use the simple past to describe events or experiences that happened at a specific time in the past.*

Have you ever tried frog legs?

  No, I haven't. But my brother **tried** them once **a few years ago**.
**Did** he **like** them?

  I don't think so. He **got** sick later **that night**.

**A** Complete the conversations with the present perfect or simple past forms of the verbs. Then practice with a partner.

1. **A:** _____have_____ you ever _____seen_____ (see) a whale?
   **B:** No, I _____have not_____ . But I _____have_____ always _____wanted_____ (want) to.
2. **A:** _____Did_____ you _____have_____ (do) anything fun last weekend?
   **B:** Yes, I _____did_____ . I _____went_____ (go) camping with my sister.
3. **A:** _____have_____ you ever _____eaten_____ (eat) in a fancy restaurant?
   **B:** Yes, I _____have_____ . I _____went_____ (go) to Lucia's last year.
4. **A:** What extreme sports _____have_____ you _____tried_____ (try)?
   **B:** I _____haven't try_____ (not / try) any. But my sister
   _____went_____ (go) skydiving once!
5. **A:** What _____did_____ you _____do_____ (do) on your last vacation?
   **B:** My friend and I _____went_____ (go) to a spa.

**B Pair work** Ask and answer the questions in Part A. Answer with your own information.

## 4 Speaking  Is that true?

**A** Write two true sentences and one false sentence about interesting life experiences you've had.

1. _I went to ohio for work at the park_
2. _I finished schcool of law_
3. _I like my majer school of law_

**B Group work** Share your sentences. Your group asks you questions and guesses the false sentence. Take turns.

  **A:** *I've been to a wrestling match.*
  **B:** *Really? Who did you go with?*

## 5 Keep talking!

Go to page 131 for more practice.

I can describe details of my experiences. ☑

## D What a life!

## 1 Reading 🔊

**A** What do you think an astronaut's life is like? What do people need to do or know to become astronauts?

**B** Read the interview. According to Dr. Pettit, what's the most exciting thing he's experienced?

# THE LIFE OF AN ASTRONAUT

*Dr. Donald Pettit is a NASA astronaut.*

**Interviewer:** I'm sure people ask you this question all of the time, Dr. Pettit, but I have to ask it: Have you ever been to space?

**Dr. Pettit:** Yes, I have. I was a crew member of *Expedition 6*, and I spent five and a half months at the International Space Station. We call it the ISS.

**Interviewer:** How many times have you gone up on the space shuttle?

**Dr. Pettit:** I've ridden the space shuttle to the ISS twice.

**Interviewer:** And what was the best part about being in space?

**Dr. Pettit:** Being able to float. It was the worst part, too.

**Interviewer:** Have you visited any other interesting places while working for NASA?

**Dr. Pettit:** Well, I lived in Russia for about two years while I was training to fly to the ISS. I've also been to Antarctica.

**Interviewer:** Not many people can say that! I understand that you like to work with tools. Have you ever invented anything?

**Dr. Pettit:** Yes. During my second trip into space, I made a special coffee cup so we could drink in space, much like we do here on earth. I just couldn't get used to drinking coffee out of a small bag through a straw!

**Interviewer:** I don't think I could get used to that, either. But why did you have to drink coffee that way before?

**Dr. Pettit:** Without the bag or my special cup, the coffee floats in space, too.

**Interviewer:** Of course! Well, you've accomplished so much, Dr. Pettit. Considering all of it, what's the most exciting thing that you've experienced?

**Dr. Pettit:** Seeing the birth of my twin boys.

**Interviewer:** Wow, what a life! Thanks so much for sharing, Dr. Pettit.

**C** Read the interview again. What things has Dr. Pettit done? Check (✓) the correct answers.

☐ walked on the moon     ☐ been to the ISS     ☐ ridden the space shuttle
☐ traveled to Antarctica     ☐ had twin daughters     ☐ invented something

**D Pair work** Would you like to travel to space? Why or why not? What would be the most interesting thing about it? Discuss your ideas.

# 2 Listening A memorable life

**A** 🔊 Listen to Leo ask his grandmother about her life. Number the questions from 1 to 5 in the order that you hear them.

4 When did you meet Grandpa? _22 olds_

5 What's something interesting you've done? _met Pablo Picasso_

3 Where else have you lived? _USA and Macico_

1 Where were you born? _in Gamany_

2 Have you been back? _Yes, She has 2 time_

**B** 🔊 Listen again. Write the grandmother's answers to the questions in Part A.

# 3 Writing and speaking Interesting people, places, or things

**A** Choose one of the topics. Answer the questions.

| Topics | Questions |
|---|---|
| A close friend I've had | Who is your friend?<br>How exactly did you meet?<br>Is this person your friend now? Why or why not? |
| A special place I've been | Where is this place?<br>What made this place so special?<br>Have you ever been back? Why or why not? |
| An interesting thing I've done | What did you do?<br>How did you feel after doing it?<br>Would you like to do it again? Why or why not? |

**B** Write a paragraph about your topic. Use the model and your answers in Part A to help you.

### My Friend Lucas

I've had several good friends, but one that was very special to me was my friend Lucas. He moved into the house next door when I was eight. We became good friends. We walked to school together and always played together at his house. He had a great bike, and I used to ride it. He moved to another city after a year. I've tried to find him online, but haven't had any luck. I . . .

**C Pair work** Read your partner's paragraph. Write five questions to get more information.

**D Pair work** Ask and answer your questions.

"So, tell me, why did you become friends?"

*I can ask and talk about a memorable experience.* ✓

# Wrap-up

## 1 Quick pair review

**Lesson A  Find out!**  What is one place both you and your partner have been? one food you both have tried? one movie you both have seen? You have two minutes.

A: *I've been to the art museum downtown. Have you?*
B: *No, I haven't. I've been to our university library. Have you?*
A: *Yes, I have.*

**Lesson B  Do you remember?**  What can you say to clarify meaning? Check (✓) the correct answers. You have one minute.

☐ What I mean is, . . .          ☐ I didn't use to . . .
☐ What time is . . . ?           ☐ I mean . . .
☐ What I'm saying is, . . .      ☐ I used to go . . .

**Lesson C  Brainstorm!**  Imagine you and your partner are going on vacation together. Make a list of eight fun things to do on your trip. You have two minutes.

**Lesson D  Guess!**  Describe a memorable experience you've had, but don't say where it was. Can your partner guess where you were? You have two minutes.

## 2 In the real world

What do you think would be a memorable vacation? Find information in English online or in a travel magazine about one place. Then write about it.

*A Vacation in Hawaii*
*Hawaii is a good place for a vacation. I've always wanted to go whale-watching, and I read that you can see whales in the Pacific Ocean from December to early May. The best places to see them are Maui, Molokai, and Lanai.*

*I've also read about Haleakala National Park in Hawaii. A lot of people climb Mount Haleakala. I've seen pictures of it. It looks really beautiful. The weather is usually . . .*

# Our world

# Warm-up

Shanghai World Financial Center – China

Tikal's Temple 4 – Guatemala

Poseidon Underwater Hotel – Fiji

The Parthenon – Greece

Grand Canyon Skywalk – U.S.

Palm Island – the U.A.E.

**A** Look at the pictures. Rank the places you would like to visit from 1 (the most) to 6 (the least).

**B** Why do you want to visit your top three places?

# A *Older, taller, and more famous*

## 1 Vocabulary Human-made wonders

**A** 🔊 Label the pictures with the correct words. Then listen and check your answers.

| | | | |
|---|---|---|---|
| bridge | plaza | stadium | tower |
| canal | skyscraper | subway system | tunnel |

1. ___canal___   2. ___tower___   3. ___tunnel___   4. ___skyscraper___

5. ___subway system___   6. ___stadium___   7. ___bridge___   8. ___plaza___

**B Pair work** Can you name a famous example for each word? Tell your partner.

*"The Panama Canal is very famous."*

## 2 Language in context Two amazing views

**A** 🔊 Read the question posted on a website for visitors to New York City. Which view does the site recommend?

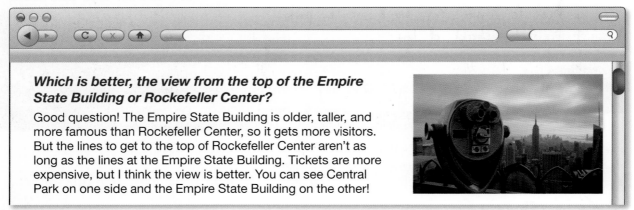

> **Which is better, the view from the top of the Empire State Building or Rockefeller Center?**
>
> Good question! The Empire State Building is older, taller, and more famous than Rockefeller Center, so it gets more visitors. But the lines to get to the top of Rockefeller Center aren't as long as the lines at the Empire State Building. Tickets are more expensive, but I think the view is better. You can see Central Park on one side and the Empire State Building on the other!

**B** What about you? Where can you go in your town or city for a great view? Have you ever been there?

44

## 3 Grammar ◀)) **Comparisons with adjectives and nouns**

*Use the* -er *ending or* more . . . than *with adjectives to make comparisons.*
The Empire State Building is **older, taller**, and **more famous than** Rockefeller Center.

*You can also use* not as . . . as *to make comparisons with adjectives.*
The lines at Rockefeller Center are**n't as long as** the lines at the Empire State Building.
Tickets to the Empire State Building are**n't as expensive as** tickets to Rockefeller Center.

*Use* more . . . than *to make comparisons with nouns.*
The Empire State Building gets **more visitors than** Rockefeller Center.
Rockefeller Center has **more observation space than** the Empire State Building.

**A** Read the information about the Lincoln and Holland tunnels. Make comparisons with
the adjectives and nouns below. Then compare with a partner.

### LINCOLN TUNNEL
Year opened: 1937
Cars each day: 120,000
Length: 2.4 kilometers
Width: 6.5 meters
Number of traffic lanes: 6
Cost to build: $75 million

### HOLLAND TUNNEL
Year opened: 1927
Cars each day: 100,000
Length: 2.6 kilometers
Width: 6 meters
Number of traffic lanes: 4
Cost to build: $48 million

1. (old)  The Lincoln Tunnel *isn't as old as the Holland Tunnel* .
2. (cars)  The Lincoln Tunnel isn't as cars as the Holland Tunel .
3. (long)  The Holland Tunnel is longer than Holland Tunnel
4. (wide)  The Holland Tunnel isn't as wide as Holland Tunnel .
5. (lanes)  The Lincoln Tunnel has more lanes than Holland Tunel
6. (expensive)  The Lincoln Tunnel is more expensive than Holland Tunel

**B** **Pair work** Which tunnel do you think is more crowded? Why? Discuss your ideas.

## 4 Speaking Comparisons

**Pair work** Complete the chart with two examples of each place. Then make
comparisons with the adjectives and nouns in the chart.

| Places | Example 1 | Example 2 | Comparisons |
|---|---|---|---|
| cities | | | people? / exciting? |
| stadiums | | | old? / big? |
| skyscrapers | | | tall? / modern? |
| universities | | | expensive? / students? |

**A:** *I'm sure . . . has more people than . . .*
**B:** *That's right. But I think . . . is more exciting than . . .*

## 5 Keep talking!

Student A go to page **132** and
Student B go to page **134** for more practice.

*I can compare human-made structures.* ☑

## B | I don't believe it!

**A** What are the oldest human-made structures in your country? How old are they?

**B** 🔊 Listen to the conversation. What question can't Rachel answer?
Then practice the conversation.

> **Rachel:** This is pretty interesting. Look at this.
> **Keith:** What's that?
> **Rachel:** I'm looking at this website about the statues on Easter Island. It says they've found almost 900 statues.
> **Keith:** No way!
> **Rachel:** Yes. Most of the statues face inland. Only a few of them face the sea.
> **Keith:** When did the Easter Islanders make them?
> **Rachel:** Let's see. . . . About 500 to 750 years ago.
> **Keith:** They look so heavy, don't they?
> **Rachel:** Yes, they do.
> **Keith:** How did they move them?
> **Rachel:** I really don't know. But let's see if we can find out.

**C** 🔊 Read the expressions below. Complete each box with a similar expression from the conversation. Then listen and check your answers.

| Expressing disbelief |
| --- |
| _____ <br> Seriously? <br> I don't believe it! |

| Saying you don't know |
| --- |
| _____ <br> I have no idea. <br> I don't have a clue. |

**D Pair work** Continue the conversation in Part B with these questions and answers. Use the expressions in Part C.

| | |
| --- | --- |
| How tall is the tallest statue? | more than 20 meters tall! |
| Why did they stop building them? | (say you don't know) |
| How far is Easter Island from Chile? | more than 3,200 kilometers! |
| Do you think you'll ever go there? | (say you don't know) |

## 2 Pronunciation Intonation in tag questions

**A** 🔊 Listen and repeat. Notice the falling intonation in tag questions when the speaker expects the listener to agree or expects something to be true.

The statues look so heavy, don't they?     The island is beautiful, isn't it?

**B Pair work** Practice the tag questions. Pay attention to your intonation.

1. Easter Island is part of Chile, isn't it?
2. You read that online, didn't you?
3. She wasn't sure, was she?
4. You've never been there, have you?
5. We should go there, shouldn't we?
6. They'll probably go there, won't they?

## 3 Listening "Manhattan of the Desert"

**A** 🔊 Listen to two people talk about the city of Shibam, in Yemen. Number the questions from 1 to 5 in the order you hear them.

[5] Is it easy to get to? _____ I don't have clue _____
[4] How many people live there? about 7,000 _____
[1] What's it famous for? _____ skyscraper _____
[3] How high are the tallest buildings? _____
[2] How old is the city? _____ more than 2000 years old _____

**B** 🔊 Listen again. Answer the questions in Part A.

## 4 Speaking Did you know . . . ?

**A** Make a list of three interesting facts about human-made structures. ก่อสร้าง

1. *There used to be soccer games and bullfights in the Plaza Mayor in Madrid, Spain.*

2. *More people ride the Tokyo Metro in Japan each year than any other subway system in the world.*

3. *The TV screen in Cowboys Stadium in Dallas, Texas, is almost 50 meters long!*

**B Group work** Share your interesting facts. Your group expresses disbelief and asks questions for more information. If you don't know the answers to their questions, say you don't know.

A: *Did you know that there used to be soccer games and bullfights in the Plaza Mayor in Madrid, Spain?*
B: *Bullfights? Seriously? Why is it famous?*
A: *I don't have a clue.*

**C** How many questions could you answer correctly about the structures on your list? Which classmate could answer the most questions?

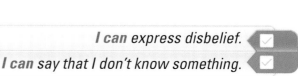

*I can express disbelief.* ☑
*I can say that I don't know something.* ☑

# C World geography

## 1 Vocabulary Geographical features

**A** 🔊 Match the descriptions and the pictures. Then listen and check your answers.

a. The largest **desert** in Asia is the Gobi Desert.
b. There are about 17,000 **island**s in Indonesia.
c. Siberia's Lake Baikal is the world's deepest **lake**.
d. The Indian **Ocean** covers 20% of the earth's surface.
e. **Rain forest**s cover almost 75% of Brunei.
f. China's Yangtze River is the longest **river** in Asia.
g. Langtang Valley is one of the prettiest **valley**s in Nepal.
h. The highest **waterfall** in India is Jog Falls.

1. c    2. d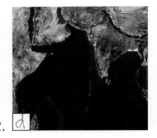

3. a    4. g

5. b    6. f    7. h    8. e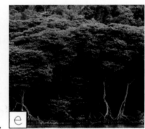

**B Pair work** What's another example of each geographical feature? Tell your partner.

## 2 Conversation Welcome to Bali.

**A** 🔊 Listen to the conversation. When does Bali get a lot of rain?

**Guide:** Welcome to Bali, one of the most beautiful islands in the world.

**Sam:** It's definitely the most beautiful island I've ever visited. Is Bali the biggest island in Indonesia?

**Guide:** No. Actually, it's one of the smallest, but it has a lot of people. The island of Java has the most people.

**Sam:** Is that right? The weather seems pretty nice right now. Is this the best time of year to visit?

**Guide:** Oh, yes. It's the dry season. We get the most sunshine this time of year. The wettest time is from November to April.

**Sam:** Well, that's good. Um, what's that?

**Guide:** Oh. It looks like rain.

**B** 🔊 Listen to the rest of the conversation.
Why is Sam visiting Bali?

## 3 Grammar 🔊   **Superlatives with adjectives and nouns**

*Use the -est ending or* the most *to express the superlative with adjectives.*

**The wettest** time is from November to April.

Bali is **the most beautiful** island I've ever visited.

The dry season is **the best** time to visit.

*Use* the most *to express the superlative with nouns.*

Java has **the most people** of all the islands in Indonesia.

Bali gets **the most sunshine** in the dry season.

**A** Complete the conversation with the superlative forms of the adjectives.
Then practice with a partner.

A: I'm thinking of visiting Chile next year.

B: Great! You should try to visit my hometown, Viña del Mar.
One of _the most popular_ (popular) beaches in the
country is there. It's north of Santiago.

A: OK. Should I try to go to the Atacama Desert?

B: Definitely. I think it's _the most beautiful_ (beautiful)
part of the country. It's one of _____ driest _____ (dry)
places in the world, too.

A: Cool. And how about Patagonia?

B: Well, that's in the south. Remember, Chile is
_____ longest _____ (long) country in the world. It takes
time to see it all.

A: When's _____ best _____ (good) time to visit?

B: Anytime is fine. But I think _____ nicest _____ (nice)
time is between November and May.

The Atacama Desert, Chile

**B Pair work** Make true sentences about your country with the phrases below.

the most cars     the most fun     the most rain     the most tourists

## 4 Speaking Tell me about it.

**A Group work** Discuss your experiences in different geographical locations.

- What's the most beautiful island you've ever seen?
- What's the coldest lake, river, or ocean you've ever swum in?
- What's the highest mountain you've ever climbed?
- What's the prettiest geographical location you've ever taken a picture of?
- What's the most amazing place you've ever walked through?

**B** Share your information. Who has had the most interesting experience?

## 5 Keep talking!

Go to page **133** for more practice.

*I can ask and talk about geographical features.* ✓

# D Natural wonders

## 1 Reading 🔊

**A** What do you think is the most amazing natural wonder in the world? Why?

**B** Read the article. What are the seven wonders, and where are they?

# Seven Wonders of the Natural World

Here is a list of some of the most fascinating places in the world.
*interesting*

The Rio de Janeiro Harbor in Brazil is one of the biggest and most amazing harbors in the world. It has beautiful beaches and the famous Sugar Loaf Mountain.

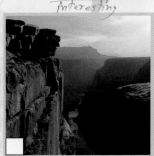

Over five million people visit the Grand Canyon in the U.S. state of Arizona every year. The breathtaking landscape is 445 kilometers long, 24 kilometers wide, and more than a kilometer deep!

The Great Barrier Reef is not just one colorful coral reef. It's actually almost 3,000 of them! Many plants and gorgeous tropical fish live among these reefs off the coast of Australia.
*beautiful*

Located in the Himalayas on the border of Nepal and Tibet, Mount Everest is the highest mountain in the world – and one of the most dangerous to climb. But that doesn't stop people from trying to get to the top of it every year!

Have you ever heard the crashing sound of millions of liters of water? The Zambezi River between Zambia and Zimbabwe falls 120 meters, making Victoria Falls one of the largest and loudest waterfalls on the planet.

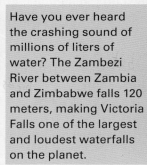

Paricutín Volcano in Mexico is more than 300 meters high, but it used to be a flat cornfield. In 1943, people saw the earth steam and crack. It grew into a new volcano in just two years!

The Northern Lights are exactly what their name suggests: bright, flashing lights of amazing shapes and colors in the northern sky. The North Pole has the best view of them.

**C** Read the article again. Complete the sentences with the correct natural wonders.

1. The Rio de Janeiro has beautiful beaches.
2. Victoria Falls is a very loud waterfall.
3. Gran Canyon is over a kilometer deep.
4. Volcano formed in two years.
5. Northern Lights change in shape and color.
6. Great Barrier Reef is off a country's coast.

**D Pair work** Rank the natural wonders from 1 (most amazing) to 7 (least amazing). Then compare answers.

## 2 Listening The Great Barrier Reef

**A** 🔊 Listen to a guide talk to two tourists at the Great Barrier Reef.
Which statements surprise the tourists? Check (✓) the correct answers.

☐ The Great Barrier Reef is made up of many smaller reefs.
☑ You can see the reef from space.
☑ You can see turtles near the reef.
☑ Global warming can make the coral appear white.

**B** 🔊 Listen again. Answer the questions.

1. How many kinds of coral are there? _____ 400 h _____
2. How does the coral look on TV? _____ V. colourful _____
3. What's the weather like today? _____ Sunny. _____
4. What does the guide say to do? _____ Plis stay together _____

## 3 Writing A natural wonder

**A** Think of a natural wonder in your country. Answer the questions.

- Where is it? _____
- What does it look like? _____
- What can you do there? _____
- When's a good time to go there? _____

**B** Write a paragraph about the natural wonder. Use the model and your answers in
Part A to help you.

*A Wonderful Mountain*
*Mount Toubkal is the highest mountain in*
*Morocco, and one of the prettiest. The most*
*popular time to visit is the summer. Many*
*people climb the mountain, and you can hike*
*it in two days. To me, the most interesting*
*time to visit is the winter because you can*
*ski. This is surprising to many people. . . .*

**C Group work** Share your paragraphs. Can anyone add more information?

## 4 Speaking Seven wonders of my country

**A Pair work** Make a list of the top seven natural or human-made wonders in your
country. Why are they wonderful? Take notes.

**B Class activity** Share your lists and reasons. Then vote on the top seven
wonders to create one list.

*I can describe natural wonders in my country.* ☑

# Wrap-up

## 1 Quick pair review

**Lesson A** **Brainstorm!** Make a list of human-made wonders. How many do you know? You have one minute.

**Lesson B** **Do you remember?** Is the sentence expressing disbelief, or is it saying you don't know? Write D (disbelief) or DK (don't know). You have one minute.

1. I have no idea. _____
2. Seriously? _____
3. No way! _____
4. I don't believe it! _____
5. I don't have a clue. _____
6. I really don't know. _____

**Lesson C** **Test your partner!** Say three comparative adjectives. Can your partner use the superlative forms in a sentence? Take turns. You have three minutes.

**A:** *More famous.*
**B:** *The most famous. The most famous person I've ever met is George Clooney.*

**Lesson D** **Guess!** Describe a natural wonder in your country, but don't say its name. Can your partner guess what it is? You have two minutes.

## 2 In the real world

What are the seven wonders of the modern world? Go online or to a library, and find information in English about the seven wonders of the modern world. Choose one and write about it.

> *A Wonder of the Modern World*
>    The Itaipu Dam is one of the seven wonders of the modern world. It's on the Paraná River between Brazil and Paraguay. Many people in South America depend on the dam for power and electricity. About 40,000 workers helped construct the dam, and it's one of the most expensive objects ever built. It's also huge. In fact, it's so big that . . .

# Organizing your time

## Warm-up

**A** Look at the pictures. What's happening? Do you think the man organizes his time well?

**B** Do you think you organize your time well? Why or why not?

# A | A busy week

## 1 Vocabulary Commitments

**A** 🔊 Match the words in columns A and B. Then listen and check your answers.

| A | B |
|---|---|
| 1. a birthday | appointment 5 |
| 2. a blind | call 4 |
| 3. a business | date 2 |
| 4. a conference | interview 6 |
| 5. a doctor's | lesson 8 |
| 6. a job | meeting 3 |
| 7. soccer | party 1 |
| 8. a violin | practice 7 |

**B** **Pair work** When was the last time you had each commitment? Tell your partner.

## 2 Language in context Weekend plans

**A** 🔊 Read George's plans for the weekend. Number the pictures from 1 to 8.

My parents are arriving from out of town this weekend. I'm picking them up at the airport on Friday night. Their flight doesn't get in until midnight. They're staying at my place for a couple of weeks. On Saturday, I'm preparing breakfast for them. Then I have a doctor's appointment. In the afternoon, I'm taking them for a drive around town. In the evening, I'm starting a new part-time job. There's a new movie I want to see on Sunday. I'm going with a friend of mine from school. It starts at 9:00 p.m., so we're having dinner first.

**B** Which things in Part A do you think George will enjoy? Do you have any of the same plans?

# 3 Grammar 🔊 **Present tenses used for future**

*Use the present continuous to describe plans or intentions.*
My parents **are arriving** from out of town this weekend.
They**'re staying** at my place for the weekend.

*Use the simple present to describe events that are on a schedule or a timetable.*
I **have** an appointment in the morning.
The movie **starts** at 9:00 p.m.

**A** Complete the conversation with the present continuous or the simple present forms of the verbs. Then practice with a partner.

A: What _____are_____ you _____doing_____ (do) tonight?
B: Oh, I _____am taking_____ (take) my sister to the airport. She _____going_____ (go) to Manila. Her flight _____leaving_____ (leave) at 9:00.
A: _____Are_____ you _____doing_____ (do) anything tomorrow?
B: I _____have_____ (have) soccer practice at 2:00.

**B Pair work** What are your plans after class? Tell your partner.

# 4 Listening A weekend away

**A** 🔊 Listen to Peter talk with his neighbor Nancy. Check (✓) the true sentences.

1. ☐ Nancy has a date this weekend. _____
2. ☑ Peter's train leaves Friday night at 8:30. _____
3. ☐ Peter's grandfather is turning 70. _____
4. ☐ Peter and Kevin are going to museums on Sunday. _They going to the museums_
5. ☑ Peter and Kevin arrive home on Sunday evening. _____
6. ☐ Peter has a job interview on Monday. _He had docter app_

**B** 🔊 Listen again. Correct the false sentences.

# 5 Speaking What are you doing this weekend?

**A Class activity** Find classmates who are going to do each thing. Write their names and ask questions for more information.

| Find someone who . . . this weekend. | Name | Extra information |
|---|---|---|
| is going out | | |
| is planning to stay home | | |
| has a lesson or an appointment | | |
| plans to meet friends | | |
| is spending time with relatives | | |

**B** Who has the most interesting plans? What are they?

# 6 Keep talking!

Go to page **135** for more practice.

*I can ask and talk about weekend plans.* ☑

# B Can I take a message?

## 1 Interactions | Phone messages

**A** How many phone calls do you make in a week? Do you leave many messages?

**B** 🔊 Listen to the conversation. What message does Rex leave for Jake? Then practice the conversation.

**Ben:** Hello?
**Rex:** Hi. Can I please speak to Jake?
**Ben:** Um, sorry. Jake's not here right now. I think he might be at the gym. Can I take a message?
**Rex:** Uh, sure. This is Rex Hanson. I'm calling about our class trip. Please tell him that we're leaving tomorrow at 8:00, not 9:00.
**Ben:** OK, got it. I'll give him the message.
**Rex:** Great. Thanks a lot. Bye.
**Ben:** Good-bye.

**C** 🔊 Read the expressions below. Complete each box with a similar expression from the conversation. Then listen and check your answers.

| *Offering to take a message* | *Leaving a message* |
| --- | --- |
| _____ | _____ |
| Do you want to leave a message? | Can you tell . . . that . . . ? |
| Would you like to leave a message? | Could you let . . . know that . . . ? |

**D Pair work** Have conversations like the one in Part B. Use these ideas.

| | |
| --- | --- |
| You're calling your friend Carrie at home, but she's at soccer practice. | You're calling your friend Gary at work, but he's in a meeting. |
| She needs to bring her laptop to class. | The birthday party starts at 7:00, not 8:00. |

## 2 Listening Taking messages

**A** 🔊 Listen to four people leave phone messages. Number the messages from 1 to 4.

---

**Manhattan Designs** [4]
**TO:** Mr. Philips
**FROM:** Julie Kim
**TIME:** 2:45
**MESSAGE:**
She needs the _____ for her office by
_____ .

---

Silvia – [3]
_____ Miller's office called. You
should come in for your _____ at
4:30, not 3:00.
– Beth

---

Paul, [1]
Your _____ Kurt called. Your parents'
anniversary party is at his place, not your
_____ .

---

**MESSAGE** [2]
**To:** Roberto
**From:** Hank
**Message:**
___class___ is canceled
___cancle___ .

---

**B** 🔊 Listen again. Complete the messages.

**C** 🔊 Listen to the people return the calls. What happens to whom?
Write M (Mr. Philips), P (Paul), R (Roberto), or S (Silvia).

1. __M__ gets a busy signal.   3. __S__ leaves a voicemail.
2. __P__ gets disconnected.   4. __R__ calls the wrong number.

## 3 Speaking Role play

**A** Complete the chart with your own ideas.

| | Who's the message for? | What's the message about? | What's the message? |
|---|---|---|---|
| 1. | Rosario | soccer practice | She needs to come 15 minutes early. |
| 2. | | the meeting | It's on Thursday, not Tuesday. It's still at 4:00. |
| 3. | Jennifer | docter app | It starts at 10:00 p.m. Bring dancing shoes. |
| 4. | | the job interview | |
| 5. | | | |

**B Pair work** Role-play the phone conversations. Then change roles.

**Student A:** Call the people in the chart. They can't talk, so leave messages for them.

**Student B:** Answer the phone. Explain why the people can't talk, and offer to take messages for them.

I can offer to take a message. ✓
I can leave a message. ✓

57

# C Can you do me a favor?

## 1 Vocabulary Favors ยื่นขอ/สับเปลี่ยนๆ

**A** 🔊 Match the phrases and the pictures. Then listen and check your answers.

| | | | |
|---|---|---|---|
| a. check my homework | c. get my mail | e. help me with my résumé | g. pick me up |
| b. feed my cat | d. give me a ride | f. lend me some money | h. water my plants |

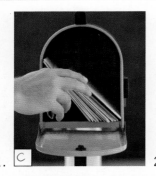 1. c     2. h     3. e     4. d

 5. b     6. f     7. a     8. g

**B Pair work** Who might you ask to do each thing in Part A? Discuss your ideas.

| | | | | | |
|---|---|---|---|---|---|
| a child | a classmate | a friend | a neighbor | a parent | a teacher |

## 2 Conversation Is that all?

**A** 🔊 Listen to the conversation. What things does Kate ask Ruth to do for her?

**Ruth:** Oh, hi, Kate. What's up?
**Kate:** Hi, Ruth. Listen, I'm going away this weekend.
Can you do me a favor?
**Ruth:** Sure. What do you need?
**Kate:** Can you feed my cat, please?
**Ruth:** No problem. I'll feed her. Is that all?
**Kate:** Well, could you please get my mail, too?
**Ruth:** Sure. I could do that for you. I'll put it on your kitchen table. Anything else?
**Kate:** If you don't mind, there's one more thing.
**Ruth:** What's that?
**Kate:** I'm getting back at 11:00 on Sunday night. Would you mind picking me up at the airport?

**B** 🔊 Listen to the rest of the conversation. Why can't Ruth pick Kate up?

## 3 Grammar 🔊 Requests; promises and offers with *will*

**Requests**
**Can** you **feed** my cat, please?
**Could** you please **get** my mail?
**Would** you **pick** me up at the airport?
**Would** you **mind picking** me up at the airport?

**Promises and offers**
No problem. I**'ll feed** her.
Sure. I**'ll put** it on your kitchen table.
All right. I **won't be** late. I promise.
No, I don't mind. I**'ll be** there.

**A** Match the requests and the responses. Then practice with a partner.

1. Can you lend me your car tonight? _____
2. Ms. Smith, would you check my homework, please? _____
3. Can you give me a ride to class? _____
4. Would you mind feeding my fish? _____
5. Could you water my plants this weekend? _____
6. Would you mind picking me up at the mall? _____

a. Sure. I'll look at it after I help Michael.
b. No problem. I'll do it on Saturday.
c. Not at all. What time?
d. I guess so. I'll give you the keys after I pick up Rachel from school.
e. Yeah, sure. I'll be at your house at 10:00.
f. No, I don't mind. I'll feed them after work.

**B Pair work** Ask and answer the questions in Part A. Answer with your own offer or promise.

## 4 Pronunciation Reduction of *could you* and *would you*

**A** 🔊 Listen and repeat. Notice how *could you* and *would you* are sometimes pronounced /kʊdʒə/ and /wʊdʒə/.

**Could you** please get my mail?    **Would you** pick me up at the airport?

**B Pair work** Practice requests with *could you*, *would you*, and the phrases from Exercise 1. Reduce *could you* and *would you*.

## 5 Speaking Unfavorable favors

**A** Think of three favors to ask your classmates. Use the ideas below or your own ideas. Be creative!

| | |
|---|---|
| feed my pet snake | lend me some money |
| check my homework | lend me your cell phone |
| help me clean my room | make my lunch |

**B Class activity** Find three different classmates to do the favors for you. If you decline a request, make an excuse. If you accept a request, make an offer or a promise.

## 6 Keep talking!

Go to page 136 for more practice.

*I can make requests, promises, and offers.*

# D Time management

## 1 Reading 🔊

**A** Do you have a busy schedule? What's the busiest day of your week?

**B** Read the headings in the article. Which things do you do to manage your time?

# HOW TO MANAGE YOUR TIME

These simple ideas can help you manage your time and work more effectively. Share these tips with your friends, family, or co-workers.

**1. Write things down.**
Don't try to remember every detail. This can cause information overload. Make a list so you don't forget what you have to do.

**2. Put your list in order.**
Put the most important things in your list at the top. This helps you spend time on the things that matter most.

**3. Plan your week.**
Spend some time at the beginning of each week to plan your schedule. All you need is 15 to 30 minutes each week.

**4. Carry a notebook.**
You never know when you'll have a great idea. Carry a small notebook with you so you can write down your thoughts.

**5. Learn to say no.**
Many people say yes when they should say no. Say no when you need to. Then you'll have time to spend on more important things.

**6. Think before you act.**
Don't always agree to do something right away. Think about it before you answer. You don't want to commit to too much.

**7. Continuously improve yourself.**
Make time to learn new things and develop your natural talents. Try to improve your knowledge and skills.

**8. Identify bad habits.**
Make a list of bad habits that are wasting your time and slowing your success. Then work on them one at a time.

**9. Don't do other people's work.**
Are you in the habit of doing other people's work? This can take up a lot of time. Think about your own goals. Leave some things for other people to do.

**10. Don't try to be perfect.**
Some things don't need your best effort. Learn the difference between more important and less important jobs.

**C** Read the article and the statements below. What's the best time-management tip for each person to follow? Write the number of the tip.

1. "I often make decisions quickly. Then, of course, I'm sorry I made them." _____

2. "I'm always forgetting things. My memory is terrible. It's embarrassing!" _____

3. "I spend too much time on tasks that don't matter." _____

4. "I find excuses to avoid doing my own work. I shouldn't do that, but I do." _____

5. "I always agree to things when I know I shouldn't. I feel like I need to say yes!" _____

6. "I want everything I do to be the best it can be." _____

**D Pair work** Which tips do you think are very useful? not very useful? Why? Discuss your ideas.

# 2 Writing Tips for success

**A Group work** Choose one of the topics below or your own idea. What tips for success can you think of? Discuss your ideas and make a list of your tips.

| | |
|---|---|
| how to find more time for family | how to remember important things |
| how to make and keep friends | how to study better |

**B Group work** Create a poster with the most useful tips. Write a short paragraph for each tip.

**C Class activity** Present your tips for success. Ask and answer questions for more information.

### HOW TO DEVELOP BETTER STUDY HABITS

1. **Take regular breaks.**
   It's important to take breaks. Get up and stretch, go for a walk, or call a friend for a chat. You'll feel ready for more!

2. **Listen to music.**
   Listen to relaxing music. This helps you . . .

# 3 Speaking Time management interview

**A Pair work** Interview your partner. Check (✓) his or her answers.

**Are you overdoing things?**

| Do you . . . ? | Often | Sometimes | Never |
|---|:---:|:---:|:---:|
| get nervous when you have to wait | ☐ | ☐ | ☐ |
| feel like you do things too quickly | ☐ | ☐ | ☐ |
| often do two or more things at once | ☐ | ☐ | ☐ |
| feel bad when you're not working or studying | ☐ | ☐ | ☐ |
| feel like things don't move fast enough for you | ☐ | ☐ | ☐ |
| forget important events, like birthdays | ☐ | ☐ | ☐ |
| get angry in situations you can't control | ☐ | ☐ | ☐ |
| get bored easily when you're not working or studying | ☐ | ☐ | ☐ |
| get angry when you make small mistakes | ☐ | ☐ | ☐ |
| make big decisions before you get all the facts | ☐ | ☐ | ☐ |

**B Pair work** Score your partner's answers. Add 2 for *often*, 1 for *sometimes*, and 0 for *never*. Tell your partner the results.

**13–20 You're overdoing it.**
You probably already know you're too busy. Take a deep breath and slow down.

**7–12 You're overdoing it a little.**
You're doing well, but try not to do too much. Make sure you make time for yourself.

**0–6 You're not overdoing it.**
Congratulations! You are managing your time well. Keep it up!

**C Pair work** Are you overdoing it? If so, what time-management tips can help? Discuss your ideas.

*I can discuss ways to manage time effectively.* ☑

# Wrap-up

## 1 Quick pair review

**Lesson A** **Find out!** What are two commitments both you and your partner have next month? You have two minutes.

**A:** *I'm going to a conference for work next month. Are you?*
**B:** *No, I'm not, but I have a dentist's appointment next month. Do you?*
**A:** *. . .*

**Lesson B** **Brainstorm!** Make a list of three ways to offer to take a message and three ways to leave one. You have two minutes.

**Lesson C** **Do you remember?** Match the requests and the responses. You have two minutes.

1. Could you water my plants for me? _____
2. Would you mind giving me a ride to work? _____
3. Can you feed my dog, please? _____
4. Could you please call me back at 4:00? _____
5. Can you meet me in the library tomorrow? _____

a. OK. I'll call your cell phone.
b. Sure. I'll water them.
c. Yes. I'll bring my books so we can study.
d. Yeah, I'll do that. What does he eat?
e. No problem. I'll pick you up at 8:00.

**Lesson D** **Give your opinion!** What three tips can you give someone who is always late for class? Decide together. You have two minutes.

## 2 In the real world

What are some tips for success? Go online and find tips in English about one of these topics or your own idea. Then write about them.

| | |
|---|---|
| how to get rich | how to make a good first impression |
| how to improve your pronunciation | how to write a good résumé |

*How to Save Money*
*It's important to save money every month. One way to save money is to turn off the lights when you aren't using them, because electricity is expensive. Another way to save money is to cook at home more often. Food can be very expensive, especially if you eat out a lot. You should look for coupons in newspapers. Also, . . .*

# Personalities

## Warm-up

**A** Describe the people in the picture. Where are they? What are they doing?

**B** What do you think each person is like? Why?

# A You're extremely curious.

## 1 Vocabulary  Personality traits

**A** 🔊 Match the adjectives and the sentences. Then listen and check your answers.

1. adventurous _C_       a. I'm interested in learning about people and things around me.
2. ambitious _____       b. I'm friendly, and I like people.
3. careful _____         c. I set high goals for myself.
4. curious _____         d. I look on the bright side of things.
5. easygoing _____       e. I do things slowly and with attention to detail.
6. optimistic _d_        f. I don't like to change my mind.
7. outgoing _b_          g. I am relaxed, and I don't worry about little things.
8. stubborn _____        h. I love trying new, exciting activities.

**B Pair work** Describe people you know with each personality trait.
Tell your partner.

*"My baby brother is very curious about the world. He wants to touch everything."*

## 2 Language in context  Are you a believer?

**A** 🔊 Read the personality descriptions. Underline the positive personality traits, and circle the negative ones.

## Are you adventurous?

Answer ten questions in this quick personality test to find out just how adventurous you are!

**Click here to begin.**

**Year of the Monkey**
*Born in years 1968, 1980, 1992, and 2004*
You're extremely curious and outgoing. You solve problems well, but you can be stubborn about some things.

**Personality Test Results**
Your score: **13**
You're very adventurous, but you're not a very careful person. Try not to make decisions quickly. Take time to consider your options seriously.

**Your Birth Order**
As the first-born child in your family, you are a natural leader. You're pretty ambitious and like to work hard. However, you don't work well without direction.

**B** What about you? Do you believe the things in Part A can tell you about your personality? Why or why not?

# 3 Grammar 🔊 — Adverbs modifying adjectives and verbs

Adverbs that modify adjectives come before the adjectives.

You're **pretty** ambitious.

You're **extremely** curious and outgoing.

Adverbs that modify verbs go after the verb or the verb and its object.

You don't work **well** without direction.

Try not to make decisions **quickly**.

Turn to page 152 for a list of adjective and adverb formations.

**A** Add the adverbs to the sentences. Then compare with a partner.

1. I move ˄slowly in the morning. (slowly)
2. I'm ˄really serious about my studies. (really)
3. I choose ˄carefully my words. (carefully)
4. I arrive ˄early at important meetings. (early)
5. My friends are ˄extremely important to me. (extremely) (กลัวว่า)
6. I work ˄well in large groups. (well)
7. I'm ˄very optimistic about the future. (very)
8. It's easy for me to share my feelings. (fairly)

**B** **Pair work** Which sentences in Part A are true for you? Tell your partner.

# 4 Speaking My true self

**A** **Pair work** Interview your partner and ask questions for more information. Take notes.

| | Name: _____ | Yes | No | Extra information |
|---|---|---|---|---|
| 1. | Are you very adventurous? | ☐ | ☐ | |
| 2. | Do you make new friends easily? | ☐ | ☐ | |
| 3. | Do you make decisions quickly? | ☐ | ☐ | |
| 4. | Are you really stubborn about anything? | ☐ | ☐ | |
| 5. | Do you work and study hard? | ☐ | ☐ | |
| 6. | Do you get to class early? | ☐ | ☐ | |
| 7. | Are you completely honest all the time? | ☐ | ☐ | |

A: *Are you very adventurous?*
B: *Yes, I think so.*
A: *What's the most adventurous thing you've ever done?*

**B** **Pair work** Share the most interesting information with another partner.

# 5 Keep talking!

Go to page 137 for more practice.

*I can talk about personality traits.* ☑

# B In my opinion, . . .

## 1 Interactions  Opinions

**A** Do you always tell people exactly what you think? Do you sometimes keep your opinions to yourself?

**B** 🔊 Listen to the conversation. Whose opinion do you agree with more? Then practice the conversation.

**Fei:** Have you seen Adam's new painting?

**Ralph:** Yes. I saw it last weekend.

**Fei:** It's not very good.

**Ralph:** No, it's not. He asked me what I thought of it. I said I didn't think it was his best painting.

**Fei:** You're kidding! How did he react?

**Ralph:** He didn't seem very happy to hear that. But he did ask.

**Fei:** In my opinion, it's better to say something positive, even if you don't really mean it. Don't you agree?

**Ralph:** I don't know. Why do you say that?

**Fei:** Well, it's not always easy to hear the truth.

**Ralph:** I'm not so sure. I find that honesty is always the best policy.

**C** 🔊 Read the expressions below. Complete each box with a similar expression from the conversation. Then listen and check your answers.

<table>
<tr><td>Giving an opinion</td><td>Asking for agreement</td></tr>
<tr><td>_____<br><br>If you ask me, . . .<br>Maybe it's just me, but I think . . .</td><td>_____<br><br>Don't you think so?<br>Don't you think that's true?</td></tr>
</table>

**D Pair work** Check (✓) the opinions you agree with. Then ask your partner for agreement.

1. ☐ Women are more stubborn than men.
   ☐ Men are more stubborn than women.

2. ☐ It's never OK to lie.
   ☐ It's sometimes OK to lie.

3. ☐ A small group of friends is better than a large group of friends.
   ☐ A large group of friends is better than a small group of friends.

## 2 **Pronunciation** Reduction of *don't you*

**A** 🔊 Listen and repeat. Notice how *don't you* is pronounced /dʌʊntʃə/.

Don't you agree?     Don't you think so?     Don't you think that's true?

**B Pair work** Say the opinions in Exercise 1D again. Ask your partner for agreement.
Reduce *don't you* to /dʌʊntʃə/.

## 3 **Listening** A book of proverbs

**A** 🔊 Listen to Tina and Cal talk about proverbs. Number the proverbs from 1 to 4 in
the order you hear them.

| Proverbs | Does Tina agree? | Does Cal agree? |
|---|---|---|
| ☐ Practice makes perfect. | yes / no | yes / no |
| ☐ Better late than never. | yes / no | yes / no |
| ☐ Beauty is only skin deep. | yes / no | yes / no |
| ☐ Two heads are better than one. | yes / no | yes / no |

**B** 🔊 Listen again. Do Tina and Cal agree with the proverbs in Part A?
Circle *yes* or *no*.

**C Pair work** Do you agree with each proverb? Why or why not?
Do you know any similar proverbs in your own language? Tell your partner.

## 4 **Speaking** Don't you think so?

**A** What's your opinion? Circle the words.

1. People are **more** / **less** ambitious these days.
2. Young people are **more** / **less** optimistic than older people.
3. **First-born** / **Last-born** children are usually very easygoing.
4. It's **possible** / **impossible** to change your personality.

**B Group work** Discuss your opinions from Part A.

A: *If you ask me, people are less ambitious these days. Don't you think so?*
B: *I'm not so sure. Why do you say that?*
C: *Well, maybe it's just me, but I feel no one wants to work hard these days.*
D: *I'm not sure I really agree. In my opinion, . . .*

**C Group work** Think of three other topics. Share your opinions about them.
Does anyone agree with you?

*"In my opinion, people worry about their appearance too much. Don't you agree?"*

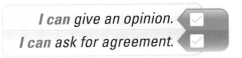

*I can give an opinion.* ✓
*I can ask for agreement.* ✓

# C  We've been friends for six years.

## 1 Vocabulary More personality traits

**A** 🔊 Match the adjectives and the definitions. Then listen and check your answers.

1. agreeable __a__       a. thinking of the needs of others
2. considerate __c__     b. treating people equally or right
3. decisive __d__        c. friendly and pleasing
4. fair __b__            d. making decisions quickly

5. honest __g__          e. waiting without getting annoyed
6. mature __f__          f. doing what is expected or promised
7. patient __e__         g. truthful
8. reliable __h__        h. behaving in a responsible way

**B** 🔊 Complete the chart with the opposites of the words in Part A. Then listen and check your answers.

| dis- | im- | in- | un- |
|------|-----|-----|-----|
| disagreeable | | | |
| | | | |

**C Pair work** What are the three best personality traits to have in a friend? What are the three worst? Discuss your ideas.

## 2 Conversation Time to say you're sorry

**A** 🔊 Listen to the conversation. How does Lance describe Jill's reaction?

**Lance:** I don't know what to do about my friend Jill. I haven't spoken to her since last weekend, and she won't answer my text messages.
**Emily:** Did something happen?
**Lance:** Yeah. I said something about her to another friend. She found out, and now I feel terrible. To be honest, it wasn't anything serious, though. I think she's being unfair and a little immature.
**Emily:** Well, put yourself in her shoes. Imagine a friend saying something about you behind your back.
**Lance:** You're probably right.
**Emily:** Have you been friends for a long time?
**Lance:** Yes. We've been friends for six years, and we used to talk all the time.
**Emily:** Then I think you should do the considerate thing and call to say you're sorry.

**B** 🔊 Listen to Lance and Jill's phone conversation. What word does Lance use to describe himself?

68

## 3 Grammar ◀)) Present perfect with *for* and *since*

*Use the present perfect to describe an action that began in the past and continues to now. Use* for *to specify the amount of time. Use* since *to specify the starting point.*

How long have you been friends?
   We've been friends **for six years**.
   We've been friends **since middle school**.
She's been upset **for several days**.
I haven't spoken to her **since last weekend**.

| for | since |
|---|---|
| ten minutes | 3:00 |
| two hours | last night |
| several days | Monday |
| a month | October |
| six years | 2009 |
| a long time | high school |
| quite a while | I was a kid |

**A** Complete the sentences with *for* or *since*. Then compare with a partner.

1. Rod has become more considerate _____ he got married.
2. Mr. and Mrs. Kim haven't had an argument _____ 1981.
3. Pete and Lisa have been on the phone _____ six hours.
4. Tim hasn't spoken with his brother _____ a long time.
5. Jay's been totally unreliable _____ he started his new job.
6. Inez has been in her new job _____ three months.
7. Annie has become less immature _____ high school.
8. Jessica and Hector have been married _____ 25 years.

**B Pair work** Ask and answer the questions.

1. How long have you been in this class?
2. What haven't you done since you were a kid?
3. What have you wanted to do for a long time?

## 4 Speaking Three friends

**A** Think of three friends. Complete the chart.

| | Names | How long we've been friends | Their personality traits |
|---|---|---|---|
| 1. | | | |
| 2. | | | |
| 3. | | | |

**B Group work** Tell your group about your friends. Use your information from Part A. Ask and answer questions for more information.

   **A:** *I've known my friend Jesse since middle school.*
   **B:** *What's he like?*
   **A:** *He's very honest and reliable.*

## 5 Keep talking!

Go to page 138 for more practice.

*I can describe people's personalities.* ☑

# D What is your personality?

## 1 Reading 🔊

**A** When were you born? Read the description of your zodiac sign. Does it describe you well?

< > cambridge.org/thesignsofthezodiac

# THE SIGNS OF THE ZODIAC

**CAPRICORN** Dec. 22 – Jan. 20
You're ambitious and good at business, but you sometimes worry about things too much.

**AQUARIUS** Jan. 21 – Feb. 19
You're creative and care about other people's feelings, but you can sometimes be difficult to work with.

**PISCES** Feb. 20 – March 20
You're considerate, but sometimes you don't help yourself enough. You decide things quickly and rarely change your mind.

**ARIES** March 21 – April 20
You're optimistic and creative. You know what you want, but you sometimes have difficulty sharing your feelings.

**TAURUS** April 21 – May 21
You're talkative and always say exactly what you think. You work hard, but you can get angry quickly.

**GEMINI** May 22 – June 21
You like adventure. You love to try new things and can be very creative. You can sometimes be unreliable. ไม่น่าเชื่อถือ

**CANCER** June 22 – July 22
You're very patient and want everyone to get along, but you can have difficulty showing your feelings.

**LEO** July 23 – Aug. 23
You're a leader. You like to give, but you don't like to ask for things. You're not very patient.

**VIRGO** Aug. 24 – Sept. 22
You're ambitious and want things done with no mistakes. You are not always open to new ideas.

**LIBRA** Sept. 23 – Oct. 22
You get along with everyone and are curious about many things. You're always looking for something better.

**SCORPIO** Oct. 23 – Nov. 21
You're a reliable friend, but you can have difficulty sharing your feelings. You know exactly what you want.

**SAGITTARIUS** Nov. 22 – Dec. 21
You're honest – sometimes *too* honest. You don't always learn from your mistakes.

**B** Read the chart. Complete the sentences with the correct zodiac signs.

1. A ___LEO___ hates asking for things.
2. A ___TAURUS___ talks a lot.
3. A ___CAPRICORN___ is good at business.
4. A ___VIRGO___ wants everything perfect.

5. A _____ is adventurous.
6. A _____ is decisive. (เด็ดเดี่ยว)
7. A ___SAGITTARIUS___ always tells the truth.
8. A ___VIRGO___ is difficult to work with.

**C** **Group work** Think of three people you know. What is each person's zodiac sign? Does it describe their personalities well? Tell your group.

## 2 Listening Imagine you're in a forest . . .

**A** 🔊 Listen to the personality test. Number the questions from 1 to 7
in the order you hear them.

☐ What's it made of? _____

☐ Who are you with? _____

☐ What do you do with it? _____

☐ How big is it? _____

☐ What kind do you see? _____

☐ What's on the table? _____

☐ Is it open or closed? _____

**B** 🔊 Listen again. Now take the personality test. Answer
the questions with your own ideas.

**C Pair work** Compare your answers. Then turn to page 153 to see
what your answers mean.

## 3 Writing and speaking My personality

**A** Think about your personality. Answer the questions.

- What are your positive personality traits? _I like to adventurous_
- Are there any traits you'd like to change? _No I'm not_
- Has your personality changed through the years? If so, how? _Yes I have, I always change my mind_

**B** Write a paragraph about your personality, but do not write your name!
Use the model and your answers in Part A to help you.

> *What Am I Like?*
> *I'm a pretty easygoing and outgoing*
> *person. I'm also very optimistic about*
> *the future. I think people like to be*
> *around me. However, I can be stubborn*
> *sometimes. . . .*

**C Group work** Put your papers facedown on the table. Take one paper and read
the description. Your group guesses who it is and agrees or disagrees with the
description. Take turns.

A: *I think that paragraph describes Dana.*
B: *Yes, that's right. I wrote that one.*
C: *I agree you're easygoing, Dana, but I don't really think you're stubborn.*
B: *Yes, I am!*

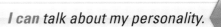

*I can talk about my personality.* ☑

# Wrap-up

## 1 Quick pair review

**Lesson A** **Test your partner!** Say an adjective. Can your partner write the adverb form correctly? Take turns. You have two minutes.

*"Careful."*

1.  ___carefully___
2.  ___quik___
3.  ___quikly___
4.  ___fairly___
5.  ___really___
6.  ___extremly___

**Lesson B** **Give your opinion!** Look at the two pieces of art. What do you think of them? Give two opinions about each one. You have two minutes.

**A:** *If you ask me, I think the sculpture is weird. Don't you think so?*
**B:** *In my opinion, it's very interesting.*

**Lesson C** **Brainstorm!** Make a list of positive and negative personality traits. How many do you know? You have two minutes.

**Lesson D** **Find out!** Who are two people that you and your partner know with the same personality traits? You have two minutes.

**A:** *My friend John is really stubborn. Do you know a stubborn person?*
**B:** *Yes. My little sister!*

## 2 In the real world

What's your zodiac sign? Find your horoscope from yesterday or last week in an English-language newspaper, magazine, or website. Was it true? Write about it.

> *My Horoscope*
> *I'm a Pisces. My horoscope last week said, "You are going to have a difficult day at work." It was true. I was very busy and nervous because I had to give a presentation. Luckily, it went very well!*

# The environment

## Warm-up

**A** Look at the "before" and "after" pictures. What do you see? What has changed?

**B** Which was the biggest improvement? Which was the easiest to do? Which was the most difficult?

# A Going green

## 1 Vocabulary Environmental impacts

**A** 🔊 Label the pictures with the correct words. Then listen and check your answers.

| | | | | |
|---|---|---|---|---|
| e-waste | hybrid car | organic food | pollution | solar energy |
| global warming | nuclear energy | plastic bags | recycling bin | wind farm |

1. global warming  2. e-waste  3. solar energy  4. plastic bags  5. pollution

6. wind farm  7. organic food  8. nuclear energy  9. recycling bin  10. hybrid car

**B** **Pair work** How do the things in Part A impact the environment?

## 2 Language in context Green products

**A** 🔊 Read the ads. What makes each product "green"?

GET GREEN GOODS!                    HOME   **PRODUCTS**   SERVICES   CONTACT

**Compact fluorescent lightbulbs**
Regular bulbs waste too much energy, so why not use compact fluorescent lightbulbs (CFLs)? They use less energy, and you save more money in the long term.
$20 for a pack of 3

**Cloth shopping bag**
Who needs paper or plastic? Bring your own cloth bag to the grocery store or mall. This bag makes an important statement and is made of 100% organic cotton.
$5

PUT AN END TO PLASTIC BAGS

**Recycled toothbrush**
Made from 100% recyclable plastic, each toothbrush comes with a reusable travel case. Junior toothbrushes feature endangered animals.
$20 for a pack of 6, or $18 for a pack of 6 Junior toothbrushes

**Steel water bottle**
Why should we use fewer plastic water bottles? Because too many of them end up in landfills and cause pollution. It's cool to carry your own reusable bottle.
$15

**B** What about you? Do you own any green products? Would you buy these?

## 3 Grammar 🔊 Quantifiers

| Quantifiers with count nouns | Quantifiers with noncount nouns |
|---|---|
| We need **more** wind farms. | You save **more** money with CFLs. |
| There are**n't enough** recycling bins. | People do**n't** buy **enough** organic food. |
| There are **too many** bottles in landfills. | Regular lightbulbs use **too much** energy. |
| People should buy **fewer** plastic bottles. | People should try to use **less** plastic. |

**A** Complete the opinions with quantifiers. Then compare with a partner.

1. "I think it's good that _____ people are buying hybrid cars. They help reduce global warming."
2. "In my opinion, there's _____ e-waste in our landfills. We need better and safer ways to recycle electronics."
3. "Farmers should grow _____ organic food. I prefer food without chemicals."
4. "Unfortunately, not _____ people use solar power. Is it because it's expensive?"
5. "I feel people should use _____ nuclear energy. Isn't it dangerous?"
6. "Some people say they don't have _____ time to recycle. That's crazy!"
7. "Maybe it's just me, but I think shoppers should take _____ plastic and paper bags from the supermarket. I always bring my own bags."
8. "_____ people throw plastic bottles in garbage cans. They should use recycling bins."

**B Pair work** Do you agree with the opinions in Part A? Why or why not? Tell your partner.

## 4 Pronunciation Stress in compound nouns

**A** 🔊 Listen and repeat. Notice how the first noun in compound nouns often receives stronger stress.

**land**fill     **light**bulb     **travel** case     **water** bottle

**B Pair work** Practice the compound nouns. Stress the first noun.

toothbrush     garbage can     recycling bin     wind farm

## 5 Speaking Our community

**A Pair work** What environmental problems does your community have? Complete the sentences.

1. There's too much _____ .
2. There isn't enough _____ .
3. We should have fewer _____ .
4. There are too many _____ .
5. There aren't enough _____ .
6. We should use less _____ .

**B Group work** Share your ideas with another pair. Did you identify the same problems? Which are the most important?

## 6 Keep talking!

Go to page 139 for more practice.

I can discuss environmental problems. ☑

# B | *I'd rather not say.*

## 1 Interactions Answering and avoiding answering

**A** Imagine these people are asking you questions. Are there any questions they might ask you that you think are too personal and that you would not answer?

| a doctor | a friend | a neighbor | a parent | a stranger | a teacher |

**B** 🔊 Listen to the conversation. What question doesn't Jim answer?
Then practice the conversation.

**Carl:** So, Jim, how's the new car?
**Jim:** Hey, Carl. It's great. I'm really happy with it.
**Carl:** It's a hybrid, isn't it?
**Jim:** Yeah. It causes less pollution. I'm trying to do my part to help the environment, you know?
**Carl:** That's great. How long have you had it?
**Jim:** I've only had it for a week.
**Carl:** Really? How many kilometers have you driven?
**Jim:** I'd say about 150.
**Carl:** So, how does it run?
**Jim:** Oh, it runs very well. I'll give you a ride later if you want.
**Carl:** OK, thanks. How much did it cost, exactly?
**Jim:** Actually, I'd rather not say. But I know I made a good purchase.

**C** 🔊 Read the expressions below. Complete each box with a similar expression from the conversation. Then listen and check your answers.

### Giving an approximate answer

_____
I'd say maybe . . .
Probably . . .

### Avoiding answering

_____
I'd prefer not to say.
I'd rather not answer that.

**D** Match the questions and the responses. Then practice with a partner.

1. How often do you drive? _____
2. How much do you drive every day? _____
3. How many people have you given rides to? _____
4. How much did you sell your old car for? _____

a. I'd say about ten.
b. Probably five or six times a week.
c. I'd rather not answer that.
d. I'd say about 30 minutes.

## 2 Listening Consumer research

**A** 🔊 Listen to a man answer survey questions in a grocery store. Number the questions from 1 to 9 in the order you hear them.

☐ Have your buying habits changed in the last year? _____

1️⃣ How often do you walk to the grocery store? *All the time.* _____

☐ Do you usually ask for paper or plastic bags? _____

☐ How much do you spend on groceries every month? _____

☐ How many people are there in your household? _____

☐ What is the highest level of education you've completed? _____

☐ What do you do for a living? _____

☐ Do you ever shop for groceries online? _____

☐ How often do you buy environmentally friendly products? _____

**B** 🔊 Listen again. Write the man's answers.

**C Pair work** Ask and answer the questions in Part A. Answer with your own information, or avoid answering.

## 3 Speaking Do you waste water?

**A** Read the survey. Are there any questions you would avoid answering, or is there any information you wouldn't share?

## WATER USE SURVEY

Name: _____    Phone number: _____

Address: _____    Email: _____

Age: _____    Education: _____

How many showers do you take in a week? _____

How long do you spend in the shower? _____

Do you ever leave the water running when you brush your teeth? _____

Do you wash dishes by hand or use a dishwasher? _____

When you wash dishes, do you leave the water running? _____

When you wash clothes, is the washing machine always completely full? _____

Do you flush the toilet after every use? _____

**B Pair work** Interview your partner. Complete the survey with his or her answers. Mark an ✗ if he or she avoids answering.

**C Pair work** Compare your answers. Who uses more water? How could you use less water?

*I can* give an approximate answer. ☑

*I can avoid answering.* ☑

# C  *What will happen?*

## 1 Vocabulary  Tips to help the environment

**A** ◀)) Match the tips and the pictures. Then listen and check your answers.

| | | |
|---|---|---|
| a. Buy local food. | d. Pay bills online. | g. Use cloth shopping bags. |
| b. Fix leaky faucets. | e. Take public transportation. | h. Use rechargeable batteries. |
| c. Grow your own food. | f. Use a clothesline. | |

 1. ☐
 2. ☐
 3. ☐
 4. ☐

 5. ☐
 6. ☐
 7. ☐
 8. ☐

**B Pair work** Which things in Part A do you do now? Which don't you do? Tell your partner.

## 2 Conversation  This is awful!

**A** ◀)) Listen to the conversation. When does Kendra want to start taking public transportation?

**Ina:** This is awful! It's taking forever to get to work.

**Kendra:** I know. There are just too many cars these days! The traffic seems to get worse and worse.

**Ina:** Maybe we should start taking public transportation. If we take the subway, we won't have to sit in traffic.

**Kendra:** And we might save money if we take the subway.

**Ina:** I think you're right. Also, if we take public transportation, we won't get stressed out before work. So, when do we start?

**Kendra:** How about tomorrow?

**B** ◀)) Listen to their conversation the next day. What are they unhappy about?

# 3 Grammar 🔊 | First conditional

*First conditional sentences describe real possibilities. Use the present tense in the* if *clause (the condition). Use* will *in the main clause.*

If we **take** public transportation, we**'ll save** money.

If we **take** public transportation, we **won't get** stressed out.

Air pollution **will get** worse if we **don't reduce** the number of cars.

*Use modals such as* may, might, *or* could *in the main clause when you're less certain about the results.*

If air pollution **gets** worse, more people **may get** sick.

If you **don't fix** your leaky faucet, you **might get** a high water bill.

You **could spend** money on other things if you **grow** your own food.

**A** Write first conditional sentences with the two clauses. Then compare with a partner.

1. you'll use 60 percent less energy / you replace your regular lightbulbs with CFLs

   *You'll use 60 percent less energy if you replace your regular lightbulbs with CFLs.*

2. you pay your bills online / you'll use less paper

   _____

3. we fix our leaky faucets / we'll save water

   _____

4. there won't be much air pollution / everyone uses hybrid cars

   _____

5. you use a clothesline / other people may start to do the same

   _____

6. we use rechargeable batteries / we could save a lot of money

   _____

**B Pair work** What else will or may happen for each condition in Part A? Discuss your ideas.

A: *What else will happen if you replace your regular lightbulbs with CFLs?*
B: *If I replace my regular lightbulbs with CFLs, I'll have cheaper electric bills.*

# 4 Speaking Around the circle

**A** Write a sentence about what will happen if you change a habit to become greener.

*If I grow my own food, I will eat better.*

**B Group work** Sit in a circle. Go around the circle and share your ideas. Repeat your classmates' main clauses as conditions, and add new ideas.

A: *If I grow my own food, I will eat better.*
B: *If you eat better, you will feel healthier.*
C: *If you feel healthier, you won't need to go to the doctor very often.*

# 5 Keep talking!

Go to page 140 for more practice.

*I can talk about future possibilities.* ☑

# D Finding solutions

## 1 Reading 🔊

**A** Look at the pictures. Which home would you prefer to live in? Why?

**B** Read the article. Write the captions under the correct pictures.

> The Recycled-Tire House    The Found-Object House    The Greenhouse

## One-of-a-Kind HOMES

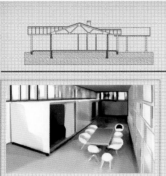

Shoichi wanted to live in an environmentally friendly home, and he always liked the greenhouses in his neighborhood in Tokyo, Japan. So he decided to create his own greenhouse-style home. Sunlight warms his new home, and a plastic cover around the house helps to keep the heat inside. There aren't any walls or rooms. The "rooms" are actually large boxes on wheels. He can move them anywhere he likes, even outside. He loves his home, but sometimes he would like to be able to move the whole house.

Ruth is an artist who lives in the Rocky Mountains in the U.S. state of Colorado. Over the years, she found and collected a lot of old objects for her art. When she decided she wanted to live in a more unusual home, she had a creative idea. She would use many of the old materials that she collected in the home's design. For example, she used old car parts in the front door and tire rubber as the roof. She also used the door of an old car as part of a wall, so she can still lower the window!

Wayne and Cate are a couple from the U.S. state of Montana. They wanted a new home that wasn't too expensive. Their solution was simple – they built their own home. They recycled and used 250 old tires as the base of the house and old glass for the windows. They even used 13,000 empty soda cans in the house. Their home also has large windows and lots of plants and flowers. Solar energy keeps the house warm, even on cold days.

**C** Read the article again. Answer the questions.

1. What warms the inside of Shoichi's home? _____
2. What would Shoichi like to be able to do? _____
3. What creative idea did Ruth have? _____
4. Where are there car parts in Ruth's home? _____
5. Why did Wayne and Cate build their own home? _____
6. What did Wayne and Cate use to build their home? _____

**D Pair work** Have you heard of or seen any unique homes or buildings? Were they environmentally friendly? Tell your partner.

## 2 Listening  Award winners

**A** 🔊 Listen to the conversations about two award winners, Gabriela McCall and Tayler McGillis. Who do the phrases below describe? Write T (Tayler) or G (Gabriela).

1. _T_ raised money for local charities.
2. _____ is a student in Puerto Rico.
3. _____ won an award at age 12.
4. _____ collects and recycles cans.
5. _____ helps birds.
6. _____ teaches children.
7. _____ speaks at schools about recycling.
8. _____ took photos to start a project.

Tayler McGillis    Gabriela McCall

**B** 🔊 Listen again. Correct the false sentences.

1. Tayler raised more than ~~$900~~ for local charities.                    _$9,000_
2. Tayler's new goal is to collect 175,000 bottles every year.             _____
3. Gabriela's project helps protect the ocean for birds in Puerto Rico.     _____
4. Gabriela teaches children about recycling so that they respect the environment. _____

## 3 Writing and speaking  Local concerns

**A** Write a letter to a local official about an environmental problem in your community. Use the questions and the model to help you.

- What is the problem?
- Who or what does the problem affect?
- Who or what is causing it?
- What's a solution to the problem?

*Dear City Councilman,*

*I am a student. I am writing to tell you about the amount of noise near our school. There is a lot of construction work and traffic near our school. It is very difficult for us to study and learn during the day.*

*I have an idea for a possible solution to this problem. If . . .*

**B Group work** Share your letters. Do you think the solutions will solve the problems? Can you offer other solutions?

**C Class activity** What are the most important concerns in your community? Who else can you write to or talk to about your concerns?

*I can discuss solutions to problems.* ☑

# Wrap-up

## 1 Quick pair review

**Lesson A** **Brainstorm!** Make a list of environmentally friendly products. How many do you know? You have two minutes.

**Lesson B** **Do you remember?** Is the sentence giving an approximate answer, or is it avoiding answering? Write AP (approximate answer) or AV (avoiding answering). You have one minute.

| **How much did your car cost?** | **How much trash do you throw away a week?** |
|---|---|
| I'd say about $3,000. _____ | I'd rather not answer that. _____ |
| I'd prefer not to say. _____ | I'd rather not say. _____ |
| I'd say maybe $6,000. _____ | Probably about five bags. _____ |

**Lesson C** **Give your opinion!** What do you think? Complete the sentences together. You have three minutes.

1. Our city will get cleaner if _____ .
2. If our school uses solar energy, _____ .
3. If we eat organic food, _____ .
4. We could recycle more if _____ .

**Lesson D** **Find out!** Who is one person you know who does each thing? You have two minutes.

- Who uses environmentally friendly products at home?
- Who takes public transportation to work?
- Who has taught you about an environmental issue?

**A:** *My aunt has solar panels on the roof of her house.*
**B:** *My father uses compact fluorescent lightbulbs.*

## 2 In the real world

How can we solve this? Go online and find information in English that gives solutions to one of these problems. Then write about them.

| | |
|---|---|
| pollution from cars | pollution from factories |
| global warming | too much garbage |

*Our Pollution Problem*
*If more people have hybrid cars, there will be less pollution. People can also carpool. If we share rides, there will be fewer cars on the road. Also, if we . . .*

# Relationships

| LESSON **A** | LESSON **B** | LESSON **C** | LESSON **D** |
|---|---|---|---|
| • Relationship behaviors<br>• Expressions with infinitives | • Apologizing<br>• Accepting an apology | • Inseparable phrasal verbs<br>• Modals for speculating | • Reading: "Addy's Advice"<br>• Writing: A piece of advice |

## Warm-up

**A** What is the relationship between the people? Number the pictures.

1. brother and sister    2. neighbors    3. co-workers    4. friends

**B** What do you think is happening in each picture? Do they all have good relationships?

# A Healthy relationships

## 1 Vocabulary Relationship behaviors

**A** 🔊 Match the words and the sentences. Then listen and check your answers.

| | |
|---|---|
| 1. apologize _____ | a. No! I'm not listening to you. |
| 2. argue _____ | b. I think we really need to talk about it. |
| 3. communicate _____ | c. I'm really sorry. I didn't mean to hurt your feelings. |

| | |
|---|---|
| 4. compromise _____ | d. I know you're sorry. It's OK. |
| 5. criticize _____ | e. Why don't I wash the dishes and you do the laundry? |
| 6. forgive _____ | f. You're being unfair. It's your turn to take out the garbage. |

| | |
|---|---|
| 7. gossip _____ | g. I told her I liked her new dress, but I didn't. |
| 8. judge _____ | h. Others may disagree, but I think what you said was awful. |
| 9. lie _____ | i. Did you hear about Wendy? You'll never guess what I heard. |

**B** **Pair work** Which actions from Part A should people do to have healthy relationships? Which shouldn't they do? Discuss your ideas.

## 2 Language in context Relationship tips

**A** 🔊 Read the relationship tips. Why is it a bad idea to criticize someone in front of others?

## 5 Tips for happy and healthy relationships

1. It's important to talk. It's good to communicate openly and listen carefully to others.

2. It's not a good idea to criticize someone in front of others. This can embarrass the person.

3. It's helpful to compromise in any relationship. It's not good to argue about little things.

4. It's good to forgive someone who apologizes. It's not easy to say you're sorry.

5. If you have a problem in a relationship, it's helpful to discuss it. Don't keep things inside.

**B** What about you? Do you agree with all the tips? Why or why not?

# 3 Grammar 🔊 **Expressions with infinitives**

*Use infinitives after* It's + *an adjective.*

It's good **to forgive** someone.     It's not good **to argue**.

It's important **to talk**.     It's never helpful **to judge** someone.

*You can also use infinitives after* It's + *a noun phrase.*

It's a good idea **to accept** an apology.     It's not a good idea **to criticize** someone.

**A** Circle the infinitives for the best relationship advice. Then compare with a partner.

1. It's important **to lie** / **to communicate** in a relationship.
2. It's helpful **to share** / **to forget** your feelings when you have a problem.
3. It's nice **to gossip** / **to think** about other people before making decisions.
4. It's a good idea **to judge** / **to meet** new people.
5. It's useful **to discuss** / **to accept** problems.
6. It's not a good idea **to argue** / **to compromise** with your friends a lot.

**B Pair work** Complete the sentences with your own ideas. Use *It's* expressions. Then discuss them.

1. _____ to be a reliable friend.
2. _____ to be honest with your parents.
3. _____ to apologize to someone but not really mean it.
4. _____ to say something if a friend is gossiping about you.

# 4 Pronunciation Sentence stress

**A** 🔊 Listen and repeat. Notice the stress on the important words in the sentences.

It's **important** to **talk**.     It's **not good** to **argue** about **little things**.

**B** 🔊 Listen to the sentences. Underline the stressed words.

It's helpful to compromise.     It's not easy to say you're sorry.

# 5 Speaking Good advice?

**A Pair work** Choose a relationship from the list below. Then make a list of the five most important tips to make the relationship happy and healthy. Discuss your ideas.

| | |
|---|---|
| best friends | co-workers |
| a brother and sister | a married couple |
| a child and parent | a teacher and student |

**B Group work** Share your tips with another pair. What's the best piece of advice you heard?

# 6 Keep talking!

Go to page 141 for more practice.

*I can discuss what's important in relationships.* ☑

# B I'm really sorry.

## 1 Interactions · Apologizing

**A** Is it difficult for you to say you're sorry? Can you remember the last thing you apologized for?

**B** 🔊 Listen to the conversation. What excuse does Susan give Gina? Then practice the conversation.

> **Gina:** Hello?
> **Susan:** Gina?
> **Gina:** Yeah.
> **Susan:** Hi. It's Susan.
> **Gina:** Hi, Susan.
> **Susan:** Listen, I know I missed your party last night. I'm sorry.
> **Gina:** Oh, that's OK. Is everything OK?
> **Susan:** Yeah, but you'll never believe what happened. It's kind of embarrassing. I mixed up the date.
> **Gina:** What do you mean?
> **Susan:** I thought the party was on the 31st, not the 30th.
> **Gina:** Oh, I see.
> **Susan:** So, how was the party?
> **Gina:** It was great. But we missed you!

**C** 🔊 Read the expressions below. Complete each box with a similar expression from the conversation. Then listen and check your answers.

| Apologizing |
| --- |
| _____ |
| I'm really sorry. |
| My apologies. |

| Accepting an apology |
| --- |
| _____ |
| Don't worry about it. |
| There's no need to apologize. |

**D** Number the sentences from 1 to 7. Then practice with a partner.

_____ **A:** I'm really sorry I didn't meet you at the café yesterday.

_____ **A:** Hi. It's Greg.

_____ **A:** Well, the repairs will be very expensive.

_____ **A:** My car broke down, and I forgot my phone.

_____ **B:** Is your car OK?

_____ **B:** Don't worry about it.

_____ **B:** Oh. Hi, Greg.

## 2 Listening What happened?

**A** 🔊 Listen to four people apologize over the phone. What happened? Where did they *not* go? Number the pictures from 1 to 4.

**B** 🔊 Listen again. Complete the excuses with the correct information.

1. I was at the _____ and completely forgot the _____ .
2. I washed my _____ last night, and the _____ was in my pocket.
3. I was out of _____ . My grandmother was in the _____ .
4. I'm in a _____ at work. I can't _____ right now.

**C Pair work** Are all the excuses good ones? Would you accept each person's apology? Discuss your ideas.

## 3 Speaking Explain yourself!

**A** Read the situations. Write an excuse for each one. Be creative!

| Situations | Excuses |
|---|---|
| You are 30 minutes late for your own wedding. | |
| You missed your dentist appointment. | |
| You didn't bring your résumé to a job interview. | |
| You forgot to pick up your friend. | |
| You didn't do your English homework. | |
| You broke your classmate's cell phone. | |

**B Pair work** Role-play the situations. Then change roles.

**Student A:** Apologize to Student B for each situation in Part A. Then make an excuse.

**Student B:** Ask Student A to explain each situation. Then accept the apology.

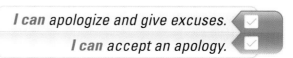
*I can apologize and give excuses.*
*I can accept an apology.*

# C That can't be the problem.

## 1 Vocabulary Inseparable phrasal verbs

**A** 🔊 Match the sentences. Then listen and check your answers.

1. It's awful when people **break up**. _____
2. I need friends that I can **count on**. _____
3. It's not nice when friends just **drop by**. _____

a. They should call before they visit.
b. It's always better to stay together.
c. My best friends are all reliable.

4. My family and I **get along** well. _____
5. My friends and I love to **get together**. _____
6. Most teenagers need to **grow up**. _____

d. They can be so immature.
e. We meet every Saturday.
f. We hardly ever argue.

7. People used to **pick on** me in class. _____
8. I love to **run into** old friends. _____
9. I **take after** my mother. _____

g. I sometimes see them at the coffee shop.
h. I'm just like her.
i. They were mean to me.

**B Pair work** Which sentences do you agree with or are true for you?
Tell your partner.

A: *I agree that it's awful when people break up, but I disagree that it's always better to stay together.*
B: *I agree with you. Some people shouldn't stay together when they argue a lot.*

## 2 Conversation He must be really busy.

**A** 🔊 Listen to the conversation. What is Evan probably doing right now?

**Ryan:** My friend Evan never seems to have time for me these days. I just can't count on him anymore.
**Katie:** Well, he started a new job, right? He must be really busy.
**Ryan:** Yeah, I'm sure he is. But he used to drop by or call me all the time.
**Katie:** He might be feeling stressed out from the job. Or he could be upset with you about something.
**Ryan:** No, that can't be the problem. I haven't done anything wrong. I think I'd better call him.
**Katie:** Yeah, I think you should.
**Ryan:** OK. . . . Well, there's no answer.
**Katie:** He must still be sleeping. It's only 6:30!

**B** 🔊 Listen to Ryan call Evan later in the day. What was the real problem with Evan?

# 3 Grammar ◀ )) Modals for speculating

**Speculating with more certainty**

He **must be** really busy. He started a new job.

He **must not leave** his house very often. He always seems to be busy.

He **can't be** upset with me. I haven't done anything to him.

**Speculating with less certainty**

He **could be** upset about something. Maybe you did something to him.

He **may not like** his new job. I haven't heard how he likes it.

He **might be feeling** stressed out. His new job may be a lot of work.

**A** Circle the correct words. Then compare with a partner.

1. I don't know his weekend plans. He **must / could** drop by on Saturday.
2. She didn't say much on the phone to him. They **must not / might** be getting along.
3. They **must / may not** come to the party. They're going out to dinner that night.
4. She **can't / could** take after her father. She's really tall, but he's pretty short.
5. You're coughing and sneezing so much. You **must / must not** be getting sick.
6. They **can't / might** be tired. Maybe they stayed up late to study for the test.

**B** Read the situations. Complete the sentences with your own ideas.
Then compare with a partner.

1. Pamela and Miguel don't get along anymore. She doesn't want to talk about it.
   Pamela must _____ .
2. Jeff just ran into his college friend Mary. He hasn't seen her for 20 years.
   Jeff could _____ .
3. Luis and Teresa arranged to get together at a restaurant, but she never came.
   Teresa may not _____ .
4. Brian dropped by and asked to copy your homework. You're not going to
   give it to him. Brian might _____ .

# 4 Speaking Look around!

**A Pair work** Look around the classroom. Speculate about your classmates.

A: *I think Tom must be playing tennis later. He has his tennis racket with him today.*
B: *And Carmen might be happy about something. She's smiling a lot.*

**B Class activity** Were your speculations correct? Ask your classmates.

A: *Tom, I see you have your tennis racket. Are you playing tennis later?*
B: *Actually, no. I played before class.*

# 5 Keep talking!

Go to pages 142–143 for more practice.

I can speculate about people. ☑

# D Getting advice

## 1 Reading 🔊

**A** Do you ever listen to talk shows on the radio or watch them on TV? What kind of problems do they usually discuss? Do people give good advice on the shows?

**B** Read the first few sentences of each email sent to the radio show *Addy's Advice*. Who does each person have a problem with?

○ ○ ○

# ADDY'S ADVICE

1. I have a big problem. It's my best friend. She doesn't really have any time for me these days. I call her, and she can't talk. I text her, and she doesn't answer right away. I think it's because of her cat, Peaches. She got this little cat for her 30th birthday, and now she takes it everywhere. She even dresses it in little sweaters and hats. I don't know what to do. Is it possible to be jealous of a cat? – **T. J.**

2. There's this new person at work. She works next to me and we get along, but she's always asking me to do things for her. For example, she asks me to get her coffee when I get some for myself. Or she drops by and asks me to copy things for her when she's "busy." She's not my boss! Should I just refuse to do things for her? I want to be nice, but I have to do my own work. Can you help me, please? – **Marcy**

3. My little brother is driving me crazy. I'm 15, and he's 10. He has his own friends, but he won't leave me and my friends alone. They come over a lot to study or just watch TV. He bothers me and sometimes tells my friends things that are personal about me. Maybe he just wants attention, but it's very annoying. He should just grow up! Anyway, I told my mom and dad, but they say I need to solve the problem. – **Kathy**

4. I'm a neat person, and I used to live alone. I got a roommate a few months ago to help with the rent. The problem is, my roommate is not like me at all. He never does any chores around the house. He just sits around playing video games and watching TV. The apartment is always a mess, and I'm the one who has to clean it up. I can't count on him for anything. Should I just clean the apartment myself? This is a big problem for me. – **Daniel**

**C** Read the emails again. Who is each question about? Check (✓) the correct answers.

| Who . . . ? | T. J. | Marcy | Kathy | Daniel |
|---|---|---|---|---|
| lives with a messy person | | | | |
| is a teenager | | | | |
| is jealous of an animal | | | | |
| is doing someone else's work | | | | |
| lived alone last year | | | | |
| mentions parents in the letter | | | | |

**D Pair work** Have you ever had similar problems? What did you do about them? Tell your partner.

## 2 Listening On the air

**A** 🔊 Listen to the radio show *Addy's Advice*. What advice does Addy give to each person from Exercise 1? Check (✓) the correct answers.

1. ☐ Show interest in the cat.
   ☐ Get a cat of your own.
2. ☐ Write your co-worker a note.
   ☐ Ask your co-worker to do things.
3. ☐ Go to someone else's house.
   ☐ Remind your parents of the situation.
4. ☐ Throw the roommate out.
   ☐ Communicate.

**B** 🔊 Listen again. Which statements does Addy probably agree or disagree with? Write A (agree) or D (disagree).

1. People never lose interest in things over time. _____
2. Most people have problems with co-workers at some time. _____
3. Parents don't always need to solve their children's problems. _____
4. Look for a new roommate if you have a problem. _____

## 3 Writing A piece of advice

**A** Choose an email from Exercise 1. Think of three pieces of advice.

**B** Write an email giving advice. Use the model and your ideas from Part A to help you.

**C** **Group work** Share your emails. Do you agree with the advice? What other advice can you give? Discuss your ideas.

> Dear T. J.,
>   I read your email, and I understand your problem. It _is_ possible to be jealous of a cat! I think it's important to find things that you can do with your friend and Peaches. It's a good idea to . . .

## 4 Speaking Take it or leave it.

**A** Imagine you have two relationship problems. Write two sentences about each one. Be creative!

**B** **Group work** Share your imaginary problems. Your group gives advice. Take turns.

1. My friends never remember my birthday. I always remember theirs!
2. My parents don't trust me. I need to call them every three hours.

A: *I have a problem. My friends never remember my birthday. I always remember theirs!*
B: *It's a good idea to help them remember. Why not send them reminders?*

**C** **Group work** Whose advice do you think you'd follow? Why? Tell your group.

I can give advice about relationships. ☑

# Wrap-up

## 1 Quick pair review

**Lesson A  Brainstorm!** Make a list of tips for healthy family relationships. How many can you think of? You have five minutes.

**Lesson B  Test your partner!** Apologize to your partner for three different things. Can your partner accept your apologies in three different ways? Take turns. You have two minutes.

**Lesson C  Guess!** Speculate about a celebrity, but don't say his or her name! Can your partner guess who it is? Take turns. You have two minutes.

**A:** *This person might win an award for his new movie.*
**B:** *Is it . . . ?*

**Lesson D  Find out!** What is the best relationship advice your partner has ever received? Who gave the advice? You have two minutes.

## 2 In the real world

What advice do the experts give? Go online and find advice in English about one of these topics. Then write about it.

| | |
|---|---|
| a jealous friend | a neighbor's noisy dog |
| a friend who talks too much | an annoying boss |
| a lazy husband or wife | an inconsiderate neighbor |

*Dealing with Jealous Friends*
*I found a website that gives advice about jealous friends. If you have a jealous friend, try to find out why the friend is jealous. Try to understand how your friend feels. It's a good idea to tell your friend about a time when you felt jealous, too. That way she will not feel alone or embarrassed. Tell your friend what you did to feel better. Another piece of advice on the website is . . .*

# Living your life

| LESSON **A** | LESSON **B** | LESSON **C** | LESSON **D** |
|---|---|---|---|
| • Qualities for success<br>• Reflexive pronouns | • Advising against something<br>• Considering advice | • Separable phrasal verbs<br>• Second conditional | • Reading: "A Walk Across Japan"<br>• Writing: An accomplishment |

## Warm-up

**A** Look at the pictures. What have the people accomplished?

**B** What are some of your accomplishments? What other things would you like to accomplish in your life?

# A He taught himself.

## 1 Vocabulary Qualities for success

**A** 🔊 Match the words and their meanings. Then listen and check your answers.

1. bravery _____     a. the ability to develop original ideas
2. confidence _____   b. the belief that you can succeed
3. creativity _____    c. a commitment to something
4. dedication _____    d. the quality of showing no fear

5. enthusiasm _____   e. the ability to change easily
6. flexibility _____    f. a strong interest in something
7. talent _____       g. the ability to make good decisions
8. wisdom _____       h. the natural ability to do things well

**B** 🔊 Complete the chart with the correct adjective forms for the nouns. Then listen and check your answers.

| Noun | Adjective | | Noun | Adjective |
|------|-----------|---|------|-----------|
| bravery | *brave* | | enthusiasm | |
| confidence | | | flexibility | |
| creativity | | | talent | |
| dedication | | | wisdom | |

**C Pair work** Which qualities in Part A do you think people are born with? Which do they develop from experience or by watching others? Discuss your ideas.

## 2 Language in context A success story

**A** 🔊 Read the story of Yong-eun Yang. What did he do in 2009?

**WEB ENCYCLOPEDIA**

**Yong-eun Yang**

In his late teens, South Korea's Yong-eun Yang, or "Y. E.," enjoyed lifting weights and hoped to own his own gym someday. But that dream died when he hurt himself in the gym. So at age 19, he took a part-time job at a golf course. He picked up golf balls and began to observe other players. He started to practice the game by himself late at night, and he even forced himself to get up early to be at the course by 5:00 a.m. for more practice. This is how Y. E. taught himself to play golf. His dedication and patience paid off. He became a professional golfer in 1995, and, in 2009, this talented man won his first championship, beating Tiger Woods.

**B** What other qualities for success do you think Y. E. has?

# 3 Grammar 🔊 Reflexive pronouns

*Use reflexive pronouns when the subject and object of a sentence refer to the same person or thing.*
I hurt **myself** at work.
He taught **himself** to play golf.
They consider **themselves** brave.

*By with a reflexive pronoun means "alone."*
She traveled **by herself** to the United States.
Do you like to practice with another person or **by yourself**?

| Personal pronouns | Reflexive pronouns |
|---|---|
| I | myself |
| you | yourself |
| he | himself |
| she | herself |
| it | itself |
| we | ourselves |
| you | yourselves |
| they | themselves |

Complete the sentences with the correct reflexive pronouns.
Then compare with a partner.

1. I drew a picture of _____ in art class.
2. I like your new hairstyle. Did you cut it _____ ?
3. If you and Joe have problems, you need to help _____ .
4. They had a great time. They really enjoyed _____ .
5. My brother doesn't consider _____ brave, but he is.
6. Heather wrote that by _____ . Nobody helped her.
7. We taught _____ Spanish before we moved to Peru.
8. I hurt _____ at the gym last week. My arm still hurts.
9. I took a trip by _____ . It helped me be more confident.

# 4 Pronunciation Stress shifts

🔊 Listen and repeat. Notice the stress shifts when some words change from nouns to adjectives.

| crea**ti**vity | dedi**ca**tion | en**thu**siasm | flexi**bi**lity |
|---|---|---|---|
| cre**a**tive | **de**dicated | enthusi**a**stic | **flex**ible |

# 5 Speaking Self talk

**A Pair work** Interview your partner. Ask questions for more information.
Take notes.

- Have you ever hurt yourself?
- Do you consider yourself brave?
- Have you ever traveled by yourself?
- Have you ever taught yourself something?
- Are you enjoying yourself in this class?
- Do you consider yourself a flexible person?

**B Pair work** Tell another classmate about your partner.

*"William hurt himself once. He broke his foot."*

# 6 Keep talking!

Go to page 144 for more practice.

*I can talk about myself and my experiences.* ☑

# B I'll give it some thought.

## 1 Interactions    Giving and considering advice

**A** What do you do if you have too much work or studying to do?
Do you talk to anyone?

**B** 🔊 Listen to the conversation. What is Bryan thinking about doing?
Then practice the conversation.

**Marta:** What's wrong, Bryan?
**Bryan:** Well, my job is just really stressful
right now. My boss just seems to
give me more and more work. It's
not fair.
**Marta:** That's not good.
**Bryan:** Actually, I'm thinking about quitting
and looking for another job.
**Marta:** Really? I wouldn't recommend that.
**Bryan:** Why not?
**Marta:** Well, because you may not find
something better. And that would
just give you more stress. Have you
thought about talking to your boss?
**Bryan:** Not really.
**Marta:** Why don't you try that? Maybe
there is something he can do.
**Bryan:** I'll see.

**C** 🔊 Read the expressions below. Complete each box with a similar expression from
the conversation. Then listen and check your answers.

| *Advising against something* | *Considering advice* |
|---|---|
| _____ | _____ |
| I don't think you should do that. | I'll think about it. |
| I'm not sure that's the best idea. | I'll give it some thought. |

**D** How would you respond? Write A (advise against it) or C (consider it). Then practice
with a partner.

1. I think you should call the doctor. _____

2. I plan to study all night before my test. _____

3. I recommend that you stay home tomorrow if you don't feel well. _____

4. I think you should visit your grandmother this weekend. _____

5. I'm going to paint my house bright pink. _____

6. I'm not going to class tomorrow because I want to watch a soccer game. _____

## 2 Listening  Maybe I'll do that.

**A** ◀》 Listen to Tim give advice to three friends. What is each friend's problem?
Check (✓) the correct answers.

| Problems | Recommendations |
|---|---|
| 1. ☐ She needs to get a full-time job.<br>☐ She wants to take more classes.<br>☐ She's thinking about quitting her job.<br>☐ She's not going to graduate. | |
| 2. ☐ He doesn't have the money.<br>☐ He doesn't have a credit card.<br>☐ The leather jacket doesn't fit.<br>☐ His friend won't lend him any money. | |
| 3. ☐ She takes too many breaks.<br>☐ She can't do a math problem.<br>☐ She drank too much coffee.<br>☐ Tim is driving her crazy. | |

**B** ◀》 Listen again. What does Tim tell each friend to do? Complete the chart with
his recommendations.

## 3 Speaking  Think about it!

**A** Imagine your friend wants to do the things below. What advice would you give?
Write notes.

- Your friend wants to buy a new, expensive car. He doesn't have the money, and he doesn't know how to drive!

- Your friend wants to take two more classes. He's already taking five classes, and he has a part-time job!

- Your friend wants to go camping in the mountains by himself for a week. He's never gone camping before!

**B Pair work**  Role-play the situations in Part A. Then change roles.

**Student A:** Imagine you want to do the things in Part A. Tell Student B what you want
to do and why. Consider his or her advice.

**Student B:** Advise Student A against doing the things in Part A and explain why.
Recommend something else. Use your ideas from Part A.

A: *I saw this really awesome car yesterday! I think I'm going to buy it.*
B: *I'm not sure that's the best idea.*
A: *Why not?*

*I can advise against something.* ☑
*I can consider advice.* ☑

# C What would you do?

## 1 Vocabulary Separable phrasal verbs

**A** 🔊 Match the phrasal verbs and their meanings. Then listen and check your answers.

1. He won't talk about his job, so don't **bring** it **up**. _____
2. I got a bad grade on this essay. I need to **do** it **over**. _____
3. I don't need these books. I might **give** them **away**. _____
4. This is Lynn's camera. I need to **give** it **back**. _____
5. Paul lent me some money. I need to **pay** him **back**. _____

a. donate
b. return money
c. mention
d. do again
e. return

6. Which one is Susan? Can you **point** her **out**? _____
7. We can't have this meeting now. Let's **put** it **off**. _____
8. This is serious. We need to **talk** it **over**. _____
9. I may buy that car, but I want to **try** it **out** first. _____
10. I have a job offer, but I plan to **turn** it **down**. _____

f. do later
g. identify
h. not accept
i. use
j. discuss

**B Pair work** What have you done over, talked over, paid back, tried out, or put off recently? Tell your partner.

A: *Have you done anything over recently?*
B: *Yes, I have. I did my English homework over last night. I made a lot of mistakes the first time!*

## 2 Conversation I'm kind of broke.

**A** 🔊 Listen to the conversation. What is Neil thinking about doing?

**Dana:** I really like your camcorder.
**Neil:** Actually, it's my friend Ben's. I'm just trying it out this week. I need to give it back to him tomorrow.
**Dana:** It looks really expensive.
**Neil:** It is. I'm thinking about buying one, but I can't right now.
**Dana:** Why not?
**Neil:** Well, I'm kind of broke. If I had more money, I'd buy it.
**Dana:** It would be nice to be rich, wouldn't it?
**Neil:** Tell me about it. What would you do if you were rich?
**Dana:** Hmm. . . . If I were rich, I'd travel. I'd give some money away, too.
**Neil:** That's nice.

**B** 🔊 Listen to the rest of the conversation. Why does Neil want a camcorder?

# 3 Grammar 🔊 Second conditional

*Second conditional sentences describe "unreal" or imaginary situations. Use a past tense verb in the* if *clause (the condition). Use* would *in the main clause.*

What **would** you **do** if you **had** more money?

   If I **had** more money, I **would buy** a camcorder.

*Use* were *for the past tense of* be *in the condition.*

**Would** you **travel** if you **were** rich?

| | |
|---|---|
| Yes, I **would**. | No, I **wouldn't**. |
| Yes. If I **were** rich, I**'d travel** a lot. | No. I **wouldn't travel** a lot if I **were** rich. |

**A** Complete the conversations with the correct words. Then compare with a partner.

1. **A:** What _____ you _____ (do) if you suddenly _____ (become) rich?

   **B:** I _____ (quit) my job. Then I _____ (travel) for a few months.

2. **A:** If a teacher _____ (give) you a good grade by mistake, what _____ you _____ (do)?

   **B:** I _____ (not / feel) right about it. I _____ (point) out the mistake.

3. **A:** How _____ you _____ (feel) if a friend _____ (call) you late at night?

   **B:** I _____ (be) surprised, but I _____ (not / feel) angry.

4. **A:** If you _____ (have) a relationship problem, who _____ you _____ (talk) to?

   **B:** I _____ (talk) about the problem with my best friend.

**B Pair work** Ask and answer the questions in Part A. Answer with your own information.

# 4 Speaking What would you do?

**A Pair work** Discuss the questions. Take notes.

- Where would you go if you had a lot of money?
- What would you give away if you were rich?
- What would you do if you saw your teacher or your boss at the supermarket?
- When would you turn down a job offer?
- Would you point out a mistake if a classmate made one? Why or why not?
- What would you do over if you had the chance?

**B Group work** Share your ideas with another pair. Are your ideas similar or different?

# 5 Keep talking!

Go to page 145 for more practice.

*I can* talk about imaginary situations. ✓

# D What an accomplishment!

## 1 Reading 🔊

**A** What do you think it would be like to walk across your country? Why?

**B** Read the interview. Why did Mary and Etsuko often have to walk between 30 and 40 kilometers a day?

## A Walk Across Japan

Mary King and Etsuko Shimabukuro completed a 7,974-kilometer walk across Japan. Mary takes our questions about their incredible accomplishment.

**Why did you walk across Japan?**
The mapmaker Ino Tadataka *inspired* me. He spent 17 years *on and off* walking through Japan. He drew the country's first real maps.

**How long did it take?**
A year and a half. We walked from the island of Hokkaido, in the north, down to Okinawa. In Hokkaido, we walked about 40 kilometers a day, and on the other islands, about 30. We often had no choice about the distance because we had to find a place to sleep.

**Describe a typical day.**
There really wasn't one, but we tried to start by 7:00 a.m. and walk for 10 to 12 hours. Sometimes we had breakfast on the road. We had to be careful in Hokkaido because the bears there could smell our food. We saw bears twice, which was terrifying!

**Did you walk every day?**
No. We needed to do our laundry, check our email, and rest. Also, I wanted to interview people for my blog.

**What were some of the best parts?**
There were many! We stayed in a *haunted* guesthouse, walked on fire at a festival, and visited many wonderful hot springs.

**Any low points?**
You know, overall, we really enjoyed ourselves, but there were a lot of aches and pains along the way. The traffic could be scary because there weren't always sidewalks for *pedestrians*.

**Did you ever think about *giving up*?**
No, we never wanted to stop. Actually, I was sad when it ended. I wanted to walk from Okinawa back to Tokyo, but Etsuko said we had to accept that we accomplished our goal. It was time to go home.

**Would you do it over again?**
Definitely. I'd love to *retrace* our steps when I'm 80. But I've also set myself the goal of walking across the U.K. or India someday.

*Source:* http://japanonfoot.blogspot.com

**C** Find the words in *italics* in the article. What do they mean? Write the words next to the correct definitions.

1. inhabited by ghosts __*haunted*__
2. quitting _____
3. people who walk _____
4. go back over a route again _____
5. with breaks _____
6. gave someone an idea _____

**D Pair work** How would you describe Mary's personality? Do you know anyone like her?

100

## 2 Listening Can I ask you . . . ?

**A** 🔊 Listen to four people talk about their biggest accomplishments this year. Write the accomplishments in the chart.

| | Accomplishments | Qualities for success |
|---|---|---|
| 1. | | |
| 2. | | |
| 3. | | |
| 4. | | |

**B** 🔊 Listen again. What quality led to each person's success? Complete the chart.

**C Pair work** Who do you think had the biggest accomplishment? Why? Discuss your ideas.

## 3 Writing An accomplishment

**A** Write a paragraph about something you accomplished in your lifetime. Use the questions and the model to help you.

- What did you accomplish?
- Why did you decide to do it?
- How did you accomplish it?
- What was challenging about it?
- Why was it important?

*A Healthy Change*
*I decided that I wanted to change something at our school. A lot of the vending machines had very unhealthy food, like chocolate, candy, and potato chips. Students wanted healthier food like fruits and yogurt. So I asked students and teachers to sign a petition to get healthier food. It was difficult at first . . .*

**B Group work** Share your paragraphs. How are your accomplishments similar or different?

## 4 Speaking What have you done?

**Class activity** Find people who have done these things. Write their names and ask questions for more information.

| Find someone who has . . . | Name | Extra information |
|---|---|---|
| helped someone with a challenging task | | |
| won an award for doing something | | |
| learned a new skill outside of school | | |
| solved a problem at school, home, or work | | |
| used technology to improve his or her English | | |

*I can ask and talk about accomplishments.* ☑

# Wrap-up

## 1 Quick pair review

**Lesson A** **Test your partner!** Say three personal pronouns. Can your partner use the correct reflexive pronouns in sentences? Take turns. You have two minutes.

**A:** *He.*
**B:** *Himself. My neighbor introduced himself to me yesterday.*

**Lesson B** **Do you remember?** Which sentences are advising against something? Check (✓) the correct answers. You have one minute.

☐ I don't think you should do that.      ☐ I'll give it some thought.
☐ Please don't worry about it.           ☐ I'd rather not answer that.
☐ I'm not sure that's the best idea.     ☐ I wouldn't recommend that.

**Lesson C** **Find out!** What is one thing both you and your partner would do in each situation? You have three minutes.

• Where would you go if you won a free vacation?
• What would you buy if you received money for your birthday?
• What would you do if you lost your cell phone?

**Lesson D** **Brainstorm!** Make a list of accomplishments. How many can you think of? You have two minutes.

## 2 In the real world

Which country would you like to travel across? Go online and find information in English about one of these trips or your own idea. Then answer the questions and write about it.

| a car trip across the United States | a train trip across Canada |
|---|---|
| a bike trip across France | a walking trip across England |

• How far is it?
• How long would it take?
• How much would it cost?
• What would you need to take?
• Where would you stay?

> *A Road Trip in the U.S.A.*
> *I'd take a car trip across the United States. I'd start in Ocean City, Maryland, and drive to San Francisco, California. The trip is about 3,000 miles. The first place I would stop is . . .*

# Music

| LESSON **A** | LESSON **B** | LESSON **C** | LESSON **D** |
|---|---|---|---|
| • Compound adjectives<br>• Past passive | • Giving instructions | • Verb and noun formation<br>• Present perfect with *yet* and *already* | • Reading: "Richie Starr"<br>• Writing: A music review |

## Warm-up

### Music Sales in the U.S.A.

other* 16%

jazz 1%
classical 2%
gospel 7%

pop 9%

R & B 10%

hip-hop 11%

rock 32%

country 12%

* Includes new age, soundtracks, electronic, ethnic, folk, etc.

*Source:* The Recording Industry Association of America, 2008

**A** Label the pictures with the correct types of music from the chart.

**B** What do you think are the most popular kinds of music where you live? What's your favorite kind of music? What's your least favorite? Why?

# A Music trivia

## 1 Vocabulary Compound adjectives

**A** 🔊 Complete the compound adjectives with the correct participles.
Then listen and check your answers.

| Compound adjective | | Present participle | | Compound adjective | | Past participle |
|---|---|---|---|---|---|---|
| award-_winning_ | video | selling | | high-_____ | ticket | downloaded |
| best-_____ | artist | winning ✓ | | oddly _____ | group | priced |
| nice-_____ | voice | breaking | | often-_____ | performer | named |
| record-_____ | hit | sounding | | well-_____ | singer | known |

**B Pair work** Ask and answer questions with each phrase in Part A.
Answer with your own ideas.

A: *Can you name an award-winning video?*
B: *Yes. Michael Jackson's video for "Thriller" won a lot of awards.*

## 2 Language in context Musical firsts

**A** 🔊 Read about these musical firsts. Which were downloaded?

# Milestones in Music History

The first rap recording was made by the Sugarhill Gang. In 1979, the band's song "Rapper's Delight" became the first rap song to make the U.S. pop charts.

The song "Crazy" by Gnarls Barkley was leaked in 2005, months before its release. When it was finally released in March 2006, it became the first song to reach number one from downloaded sales.

The band Radiohead was the first to sell their album online for whatever people wanted to pay. Over a million albums were downloaded before the CD was released in December 2007.

The well-known band Aerosmith was the first to have a video game created around their music. People can play the guitar and sing along to 41 of their songs. The game was released in June 2008.

**B** What else do you know about these musical firsts? Do you know of any others?

*"The band Run-DMC also recorded the song 'Rapper's Delight.'"*

104

# 3 Grammar 🔊  Past passive

*The passive voice places the focus of a sentence on the receiver of an action instead of the doer of the action.*

*Active voice (simple past)*
Fans **downloaded** <u>over a million albums</u>.

*Passive voice (past of* be *+ past participle)*
<u>Over a million albums</u> **were downloaded**.

*Use the passive voice when the doer of the action is not known or not important.*
The game **was released** in 2008.

*When the doer of the action is important to know, use the passive voice with* by.
The first rap recording **was made** <u>by</u> the Sugarhill Gang.

**A** Complete the sentences with the past passive forms of the verbs.
Then compare with a partner.

1. All of the high-priced tickets to the concert _____ (sell) online.
2. The best-selling artists of the year _____ (give) a special award.
3. The singer's record-breaking hit _____ (write) by her mother.
4. The performer's biggest hit song _____ (use) in a TV commercial.
5. The band's award-winning video _____ (see) by millions of people.
6. The songs on her album _____ (play) with traditional instruments.

**B Pair work** Say the trivia about the music group the Beatles.
Your partner changes the sentences to use the past passive. Take turns.

1. In 1960, John Lennon suggested the name "the Beatles."
2. Ringo Starr replaced the original drummer, Peter Best, in 1962.
3. Paul McCartney wrote "Hey Jude" for John Lennon's son Julian.
4. Many people called George Harrison "the quiet Beatle."
5. *Rolling Stone* magazine chose the Beatles as the best artists of all time.

A: *In 1960, John Lennon suggested the name "the Beatles."*
B: *In 1960, the name "the Beatles" was suggested by John Lennon.*

# 4 Speaking  Name it!

**A** Write three sentences in the past passive about the same song, singer, musician, band, or album, but don't use the name!

**B Group work** Share your sentences. Your group guesses the name of the song, singer, musician, band, or album. Take turns.

1. *This singer's first album was called* **The Fame.**
2. *She was born in New York City.*
3. *She was made famous by her music and fashion statements.*
*(answer: Lady Gaga)*

# 5 Keep talking!

Go to page 146 for more practice.

I can *talk about music.* ☑

# B The first thing you do is . . .

## 1 Interactions   Giving instructions

**A** What kinds of things do you use a computer for? How did you learn to do those things?

**B** 🔊 Listen to the conversation. What steps does Roger follow to download and play a song? Then practice the conversation.

> **Roger:** This is so frustrating!
> **Dena:** What are you doing, Dad?
> **Roger:** I'm trying to download a song, but I'm not having much luck. What am I doing wrong?
> **Dena:** It's not that hard. Here, let me show you.
> **Roger:** Thanks.
> **Dena:** First, type in the name of the artist or the title of the song in this search box and hit "search."
> **Roger:** OK. Ah, here we go.
> **Dena:** Next, choose the song you want and click "download."
> **Roger:** Oh, look at that. It's so fast! Is that it?
> **Dena:** Well, no. Finally, click "play."

**C** 🔊 Read the expressions below. Complete each box with a similar expression from the conversation. Then listen and check your answers.

| **Beginning instructions** | **Continuing instructions** | **Ending instructions** |
|---|---|---|
| _____ | _____ | _____ |
| To start, . . . | Then . . . | To finish, . . . |
| The first thing you do is . . . | After that, . . . | The last thing you do is . . . |

**D Pair work** Number the instructions from 1 to 5. Then have a conversation like the one in Part B.

*How to download a ringtone:*

_____ Select the ringtone that you want.

_____ Register with the site that you chose.

_____ Send the ringtone to your phone by text.

_____ Listen to the ringtones that are available.

_____ Find websites that offer ringtones.

## 2 Listening  How does it work?

**A** 🔊 Listen to people give instructions on how to use three different machines. Number the machines from 1 to 3. There is one extra machine.

**B** 🔊 Listen again. Each person makes one mistake when giving instructions. Write the mistakes.

1. She said _____ instead of _____ .
2. He said _____ instead of _____ .
3. She said _____ instead of _____ .

**C Pair work** Choose one of the machines above, and give instructions on how to use it. Add any additional instructions.

*"To use a record player, first plug it in. Then . . ."*

## 3 Speaking  Step-by-step

**A Pair work** Choose a topic from the list below or your own idea. Make a list of instructions about how to do it.

| |
|---|
| attach a file to an email |
| burn a CD or DVD |
| create a playlist |
| download a podcast |
| make an international call |
| send a text message |
| upload a video |

*How to* _____

1.

2.

3.

4.

5.

**B Pair work** Give your instructions to another classmate. Answer any questions.

A: *To attach a file to an email, first open your email account.*
   *After that, click "compose." Next, . . .*

*I can give instructions.* ☑

# C Music and me

## 1 Vocabulary Verb and noun formation

**A** 🔊 Match the phrases and the pictures. Then listen and check your answers.

| | | | |
|---|---|---|---|
| a. **announce** a tour | c. **compose** music | e. **perform** a song | g. **record** a song |
| b. **appreciate** music | d. **entertain** an audience | f. **produce** a song | h. **release** a new album |

 1. ☐
 2. ☐
 3. ☐
 4. ☐

 5. ☐
 6. ☐
 7. ☐
 8. ☐

**B** 🔊 Write the noun forms of the verbs in Part A. Then listen and check your answers.

a. _announcement_    c. _____    e. _____    g. _____

b. _____    d. _____    f. _____    h. _____

**C Pair work** Do you know any friends, artists, or other people who do or have done the things in Part A? Tell your partner.

## 2 Conversation I'm his biggest fan!

**A** 🔊 Listen to the conversation. What does Andy tell Miranda to listen to?

**Andy:** Oh, look! Richie Starr is going to perform here.
**Miranda:** Yeah, I know. I'm planning to go.
**Andy:** Really? Have you gotten a ticket yet?
**Miranda:** Not yet. But I think you can still get them. I didn't know you were a fan.
**Andy:** Are you kidding? I'm his biggest fan!
**Miranda:** Have you heard his new album?
**Andy:** He hasn't released it yet. But I've already downloaded his new single. Here, listen.
**Miranda:** Nice! I hear he has a cool online fan club.
**Andy:** He does. It gives information about new album releases and announces all upcoming performances.

**B** 🔊 Listen to the rest of the conversation. Why didn't Andy know about the concert?

# 3 Grammar 🔊 | Present perfect with *yet* and *already*

| In questions, use *yet* when you expect the action to have happened. | In responses, *already* means the action has happened earlier. | In responses, *yet* means the action hasn't happened, but you expect it to. |
|---|---|---|
| **Have** you **gotten** a ticket **yet**? | Yes, I**'ve already gotten** a ticket. | No, I **haven't gotten** a ticket **yet**. |
| **Has** he **released** his album **yet**? | Yes, he**'s already released** it. | No, **not yet**. He **hasn't released** it **yet**. |

**A** Write sentences in the present perfect with *already* and *yet* about Richie Starr's goals. Then compare with a partner.

1. <u>Richie has already written four new songs.</u>
2. _____
3. _____
4. _____
5. _____
6. _____

> *Richie Starr's Goals*
> ✓ write four new songs
>   record two songs for his album
>   release his new album
> ✓ entertain children at the hospital
> ✓ give a free performance in the park
>   announce his retirement

**B Pair work** Look at Richie's list in Part A. Ask questions with *yet* and answer them.

# 4 Pronunciation Syllable stress

**A** 🔊 Listen and repeat. Notice how the stress stays on the same syllable when these verbs become nouns.

| an**nounce** | enter**tain** | per**form** | pro**duce** |
|---|---|---|---|
| an**nounce**ment | enter**tain**ment | per**form**ance | pro**duc**tion |

**B** 🔊 Listen. Circle the verb-noun pairs if the stress stays the same.

| appreciate | compose | record | release |
|---|---|---|---|
| appreciation | composition | recording | release |

# 5 Speaking The latest

**A Class activity** Complete the questions with your own ideas. Then find someone who has already done each thing, and ask questions for more information.

- Have you heard _____ (a new album or song) yet?
- Have you played _____ (a new video game) yet?
- Have you seen _____ (a new TV show or movie) yet?
- _____ ?

**B Group work** Share your information.

# 6 Keep talking!

Student A go to page **147** and Student B go to page **148** for more practice.

> *I can talk about things I've done recently.* ☑

# D Thoughts on music

## 1 Reading 🔊

**A** What are "fan sites"? Who usually has them? What kind of information do the websites usually include?

**B** Look at the fan site. What things can fans do on this site?

**C** Read the fan site. Answer the questions.

1. Who has concert tickets? _____
2. Who can't get concert tickets? _____
3. Who wants advice? _____
4. Who is unhappy with a song? _____
5. Who has Richie's music helped? _____
6. Who has all of Richie's music? _____

**D Pair work** Do you ever look at fan sites of musicians, actors, or athletes?
Why or why not? Tell your partner.

## 2 **Writing** A music review

**A** Write a review of an album (or a song) you'd recommend. Use the questions and the model to help you.

- What's the name of the album / song?
- When was it released?
- What do you like about the album / song?
- Is there anything you don't like about it?
- Why would you recommend it?

**B Class activity** Post your reviews around the room. Read your classmates' reviews. Which songs or albums have you heard?

### Momento

*Bebel Gilberto's album Momento was released in 2007. All of the songs are good, but the title song is excellent. On the album, she blends Brazilian bossa nova with electronica and has a beautiful-sounding voice. The only thing I don't like about it is that there aren't enough songs! I'd recommend it because it was recorded with Japanese guitarist Masa Shimizu and . . .*

## 3 **Listening** Song dedications

**A** ◀)) Listen to five people call a radio show to dedicate songs to their friends and family members. Who do they dedicate songs to? Write the people in the chart.

|     | People | Song titles |
|-----|--------|-------------|
| 1.  | friend |             |
| 2.  |        |             |
| 3.  |        |             |
| 4.  |        |             |
| 5.  |        |             |

**B** ◀)) Listen again. What are the song titles? Complete the chart.

**C Pair work** Imagine you can dedicate a song to someone. What song would you dedicate and to whom? Why? Tell your partner.

## 4 **Speaking** Soundtrack of my life

**A** Make a list of three songs that remind you of particular times or events in your life.

|     | Song titles | Memories |
|-----|-------------|----------|
| 1.  |             |          |
| 2.  |             |          |
| 3.  |             |          |

**B Group work** Discuss your songs and memories. Ask and answer questions for more information.

**A:** *The song . . . reminds me of middle school. It was my favorite song when I was 14.*
**B:** *I know that song! How do you feel now when you hear it?*
**A:** *Oh, I feel totally embarrassed. I can't stand it now!*

*I can talk about memorable songs.* ☑

# Wrap-up

## 1 Quick pair review

**Lesson A** **Brainstorm!** Make a list of words and phrases related to music. How many do you know? You have two minutes.

**Lesson B** **Do you remember?** Complete the sentences with words or phrases to give instructions. You have one minute.

*How to install software:*

_____ turn on your computer.

_____ insert the CD and click "install."

_____ to do is restart your computer.

*How to get money out of an ATM:*

_____ put your ATM card in the machine.

_____ type in your code.

_____ select how much money you want.

**Lesson C** **Find out!** What are two things both you and your partner have already done today? What are two things you both haven't done yet? You have three minutes.

**Lesson D** **Test your partner!** Say (or sing) the words to a song you know in English. Can your partner guess the title and singer? You have two minutes.

## 2 In the real world

Who is your favorite singer? Go to the singer's website, and find information about his or her albums. Then write about them.

- What was the singer's first album? When was it released?
- When was the singer's last album released? Did it have any hit songs?
- What's your favorite song by this singer? What's it about?

> ### Taylor Swift
> My favorite singer is Taylor Swift. Her first album was called Taylor Swift. It was released in 2006. I love it. My favorite song on the album is called "Tim McGraw", who is a famous country music singer himself. Taylor was only sixteen years old when the song was released. The song is about how one of Tim McGraw's songs always reminds her of . . .

# On vacation

| LESSON **A** | LESSON **B** | LESSON **C** | LESSON **D** |
|---|---|---|---|
| • Vacation activities<br>• Gerunds | • Asking about preferences<br>• Reminding someone of something | • Extreme sports<br>• Modals for necessity and recommendations | • Reading: "A Taste of Cairo"<br>• Writing: A walking tour |

# Warm-up

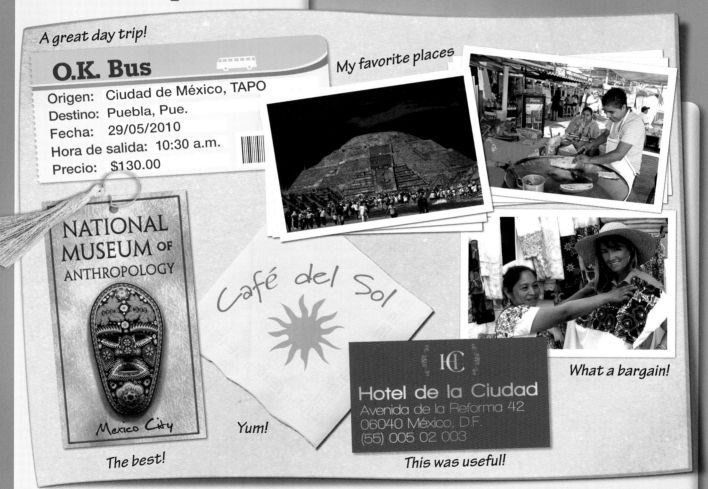

A great day trip!

**O.K. Bus**

Origen: Ciudad de México, TAPO
Destino: Puebla, Pue.
Fecha: 29/05/2010
Hora de salida: 10:30 a.m.
Precio: $130.00

NATIONAL MUSEUM OF ANTHROPOLOGY

Mexico City

The best!

Café del Sol

Yum!

My favorite places

What a bargain!

HC
Hotel de la Ciudad
Avenida de la Reforma 42
06040 México, D.F.
(55) 005 02 003

This was useful!

**A** Look at Julie's scrapbook. Where did she go on her vacation? What do you think she did there?

**B** What do you like to do on vacation? What kinds of things do you usually bring back with you?

# A Travel preferences

## 1 Vocabulary Vacation activities

**A** 🔊 Match the phrases and the pictures. Then listen and check your answers.

| | | | |
|---|---|---|---|
| a. buy handicrafts | c. listen to live music | e. speak a foreign language | g. visit landmarks |
| b. go to clubs | d. see wildlife | f. try local food | h. volunteer |

 1. ☐

 2. ☐

 3. ☐

 4. ☐

 5. ☐

 6. ☐

 7. ☐

 8. ☐

**B Pair work** Which things in Part A have you *never* done on vacation? Tell your partner.

## 2 Language in context Three types of tours

**A** 🔊 Read the ads for three tours. Which tour is best for someone who likes volunteering? someone who likes eating? someone who dislikes planning?

### Cuisine Adventures

Trying local foods is a great way to learn about a culture. Call today if you are interested in joining our "Eat and Learn" tour.

### ENVIRONMENTAL EXPERIENCES

Are you concerned about protecting the environment? Volunteering is a rewarding way to spend a vacation. Choose from over 20 tours.

### No Worries Tours

Do you enjoy traveling by bus but dislike planning the details? We specialize in organizing tours with no stress.

**B** What about you? Which tour interests you? Why?

# 3 Grammar ◄)) **Gerunds**

*A gerund is an -ing word that acts like a noun. Gerunds may be the subject of a sentence, or they may appear after some verbs or prepositions.*

As subjects: **Trying** local foods is a great way to learn about a culture.
**Volunteering** is a rewarding way to spend a vacation.

After some verbs: I **enjoy traveling** by bus.
I **dislike planning** the travel details.

After prepositions: I'm interested **in joining** the "Eat and Learn" tour.
I'm concerned **about protecting** the environment.

**A** Complete the conversations with the gerund forms of the verbs. Then compare with a partner.

| be | buy | get | go | help | lose | meet | ✓travel | try | volunteer |

1. **A:** Do you enjoy ___*traveling*___ alone or in a group?
   **B:** I prefer _____ in a large group. It's more fun.

2. **A:** Are you interested in _____ handicrafts when you travel?
   **B:** Not really. I like _____ to markets, but just to look.

3. **A:** _____ local food is the best way to learn about a culture. Don't you agree?
   **B:** I'm not really sure. _____ local people is also good.

4. **A:** Are you worried about _____ sick when you travel abroad?
   **B:** Not really. I'm more concerned about _____ my passport!

5. **A:** Do you think _____ on vacation would be fun?
   **B:** I do. _____ other people is a great thing to do.

**B Pair work** Ask and answer the questions in Part A. Answer with your own information.

# 4 Speaking Travel talk

**A** Complete the questions with your own ideas. Use gerunds.

- Do you enjoy _____ when you're on vacation?
- Are you interested in _____ on vacation?
- Which is more interesting on vacation, _____ or _____ ?
- Are you ever concerned about _____ when you travel?
- As a tourist, is _____ important to you?
- _____ ?
- _____ ?

**B Group work** Discuss your questions. Ask and answer questions to get more information.

# 5 Keep talking!

Go to page 149 for more practice.

*I can discuss travel preferences.* ☑

# B Don't forget to . . .

## 1 Interactions    Preferences and reminders

**A** Where do you usually stay when you travel? A hotel? A youth hostel?

**B** 🔊 Listen to the conversation. What doesn't the guest need help with?
Then practice the conversation.

**Clerk:** Can I help you?
**Guest:** Yes. I'm looking for a room for two nights.
**Clerk:** Do you have a reservation?
**Guest:** No, I don't.
**Clerk:** Let me see what we have. Would you like a single room or a double room?
**Guest:** A single is fine. I only need one bed.
**Clerk:** I can give you room 13A. Please sign here. And there's a free breakfast from 7:00 to 9:00.
**Guest:** Oh, great. Thank you very much.
**Clerk:** Here's your key. Do you need help with your bag?
**Guest:** No, that's all right.
**Clerk:** OK. Remember to leave your key at the front desk when you go out.
**Guest:** No problem.
**Clerk:** Enjoy your stay.

**C** 🔊 Read the expressions below. Complete each box with a similar expression from the conversation. Then listen and check your answers.

| *Asking about preferences* |
| --- |
| _____ |
| Would you prefer . . . or . . . ? |
| Would you rather have . . . or . . . ? |

| *Reminding someone of something* |
| --- |
| _____ |
| Don't forget to . . . |
| Let me remind you to . . . |

**D** Match the sentences and the responses. Then practice with a partner.

1. May I help you? _____
2. Would you like a single room? _____
3. Would you prefer a garden or an ocean view? _____
4. Please remember to lock your door at night. _____
5. Don't forget to check out by 11:00. _____

a. I don't know. Which one is cheaper?
b. Eleven? I thought it was by noon.
c. Actually, we need a double.
d. Yes. I have a reservation for one night.
e. I will. Thanks for the reminder.

## 2 Listening At a hostel

**A** 🔊 Listen to a backpacker check into a hostel. Complete the form with the correct information.

**Sydney Backpackers**

**Type of room:**
☐ single   ☐ double   ☐ triple   ☐ dorm

**Number of nights?** _____

**Bathroom?** ☐ yes ☐ no   **Breakfast?** ☐ yes ☐ no

**Method of payment:**
☐ cash   ☐ credit card

**Room number:** _____

**B** 🔊 Listen again. Answer the questions.

1. Why doesn't she get a single room? _____
2. What time is breakfast? _____
3. What floor is her room on? _____
4. What does the receptionist remind her to do? _____

## 3 Speaking Role play

**Pair work**  Role-play the situation. Then change roles.

**Student A:** You want a room at a hotel. Student B is the clerk at the front desk. Circle your preferences. Then check in.

- You want a **single** / **double** room.
- You want to stay for **two** / **three** / **four** nights.
- You **want** / **don't want** your own bathroom.
- You **want** / **don't want** breakfast.

**Student B:** You are the clerk at the front desk of a hotel. Check Student A in. At the end, remind him or her of something.

B: *Can I help you?*
A: *Yes, thank you. I'd like a room, please.*
B: *All right. Would you prefer a single or a double?*
A: *I'd prefer . . .*
B: *How many nights would you like to stay?*
A: *. . .*
B: *. . . And please don't forget . . .*

*I can ask about preferences.* ✓
*I can remind someone of something.* ✓

# C Rules and recommendations

## 1 Vocabulary Extreme sports

**A** 🔊 Label the pictures with the correct words. Then listen and check your answers.

| | | | |
|---|---|---|---|
| bungee jumping | paragliding | skydiving | waterskiing |
| kite surfing | rock climbing | snowboarding | white-water rafting |

1. _____  2. _____  3. _____  4. _____

5. _____  6. _____  7. _____  8. _____

**B** **Pair work** Which sports would you consider trying? Which wouldn't you do? Why not? Tell your partner.

## 2 Conversation First-time snowboarder

**A** 🔊 Listen to the conversation. Why does Sarah tell Kyle to stay in the beginners' section?

**Kyle:** Hi. I'd like to rent a snowboard, please.

**Sarah:** OK. Have you ever been snowboarding?

**Kyle:** Um, no. But I've skied before.

**Sarah:** Well, we offer lessons. You don't have to take them, but it's a good idea. You'll learn the basics.

**Kyle:** All right. When is your next lesson?

**Sarah:** At 11:00. You've got to complete this form here to sign up.

**Kyle:** No problem. What else do I need to know?

**Sarah:** After your lesson, you should stay in the beginners' section for a while. It's safer for the other snowboarders.

**Kyle:** OK. Anything else?

**Sarah:** Yes. You must wear a helmet. Oh, and you ought to wear sunscreen. The sun can be very strong.

**B** 🔊 Listen to the conversation between Kyle and his instructor. Why is Kyle uncomfortable?

# 3 Grammar 🔊 Modals for necessity and recommendations

**Necessity**
You **must** wear a helmet.
You**'ve got to** complete this form.
You **have to** listen to your instructor.

**Lack of necessity**
You **don't have to** take a lesson.

**Recommendations**
You**'d better** be back before dark.
You **ought to** wear sunscreen.
You **should** stay in the beginners' section.
You **shouldn't** go in the advanced section.

**A** Circle the best travel advice. Then compare with a partner.

1. You **should / must** get a passport before you go abroad. Everybody needs one.
2. You **don't have to / 've got to** visit every landmark. Choose just a few instead.
3. You **should / don't have to** book a hotel online. It's often cheaper that way.
4. You **ought to / shouldn't** get to your hotel too early. You can't check in until 2:00.
5. You **shouldn't / 'd better** keep your money in a safe place. Losing it would be awful.
6. You **have to / should** pay for some things in cash. Many places don't take credit cards.
7. You **must / don't have to** show your student ID to get a discount. Don't forget it!
8. You **ought to / shouldn't** try some local food. It can be full of nice surprises!

**B Pair work** What advice would you give? Complete the sentences with modals for necessity or recommendations. Then compare answers.

1. You _____ go paragliding on a very windy day.
2. You _____ have experience to go waterskiing.
3. You _____ have special equipment to go bungee jumping.
4. You _____ be in good shape to go kite surfing.

# 4 Pronunciation Reduction of verbs

**A** 🔊 Listen and repeat. Notice the reduction of the modal verbs.

You've **got to**     You **have to**        You **ought to**
pay in cash.     check out by noon.     try the food.

**B Pair work** Practice the sentences in Exercise 3. Reduce the modal verbs.

# 5 Speaking Rules of the game

**A Group work** Choose an extreme sport from Exercise 1.
What rules do you think there are? What recommendations
would you give to someone who wanted to try it?

A: *You must sign a form before you go bungee jumping.*
B: *Yeah. And you should wear a helmet.*
C: *Oh, and you shouldn't be afraid.*

**B Class activity** Share your ideas.

# 6 Keep talking!

Go to page 150 for more practice.

*I can talk about rules and recommendations.* ✓

# D Seeing the sights

## 1 Reading ))

**A** Do you ever read food or travel blogs? Do you ever watch food or travel TV shows?

**B** Read the blog. Write the headings above the correct paragraphs.

> A Delicious Dinner    Juice Break    The Market    Sweet Shop

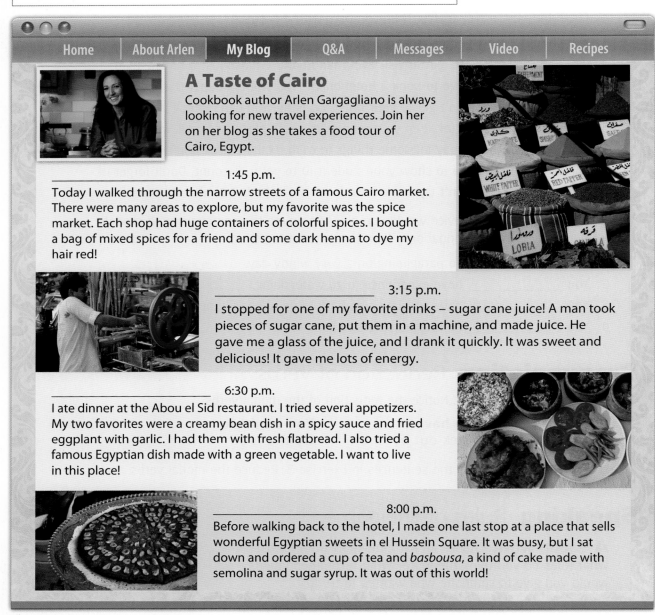

| Home | About Arlen | **My Blog** | Q&A | Messages | Video | Recipes |

### A Taste of Cairo

Cookbook author Arlen Gargagliano is always looking for new travel experiences. Join her on her blog as she takes a food tour of Cairo, Egypt.

_____ 1:45 p.m.

Today I walked through the narrow streets of a famous Cairo market. There were many areas to explore, but my favorite was the spice market. Each shop had huge containers of colorful spices. I bought a bag of mixed spices for a friend and some dark henna to dye my hair red!

_____ 3:15 p.m.

I stopped for one of my favorite drinks – sugar cane juice! A man took pieces of sugar cane, put them in a machine, and made juice. He gave me a glass of the juice, and I drank it quickly. It was sweet and delicious! It gave me lots of energy.

_____ 6:30 p.m.

I ate dinner at the Abou el Sid restaurant. I tried several appetizers. My two favorites were a creamy bean dish in a spicy sauce and fried eggplant with garlic. I had them with fresh flatbread. I also tried a famous Egyptian dish made with a green vegetable. I want to live in this place!

_____ 8:00 p.m.

Before walking back to the hotel, I made one last stop at a place that sells wonderful Egyptian sweets in el Hussein Square. It was busy, but I sat down and ordered a cup of tea and *basbousa*, a kind of cake made with semolina and sugar syrup. It was out of this world!

**C** Read the blog again. Write the initials of the blog headings (D, J, M, or S) in which Arlen did the activities below. (More than one answer is possible.)

1. ate a meal _____
2. bought a gift _____
3. drank something _____
4. had something sweet _____
5. saw spices _____
6. tried vegetables _____

**D Pair work** Would you enjoy a tour like this? Why or why not? Discuss your ideas.

## 2 Writing A walking tour

**A Pair work** Choose a topic for an interesting walking tour in your town or city. Use one of the topics below or your own idea.

| | | |
|---|---|---|
| architecture and design | historical sights | parks and nature |
| food and drink | nightlife | shopping |

**B Pair work** Write a description of your walking tour.

*Historic Old San Juan*
*To really learn about the history of Puerto Rico, you have to walk through Old San Juan. You should start your walking tour at the city walls. Follow these walls along the sea to San Juan Gate, which was built around 1635. Go through the gate, turn right, and walk uphill. At the end of the street you can see La Fortaleza. . . .*

La Fortaleza
Old San Juan, Puerto Rico

**C Group work** Present your tour to another pair. Did you include any of the same places?

## 3 Listening An adventure tour

**A** 🔊 Listen to a guide talk to some tourists before a Grand Canyon rafting trip. What does the guide tell the tourists to do? Check (✓) the correct answers.

- ☐ wear a safety vest
- ☐ drink a lot of water
- ☐ bring water
- ☐ bring food
- ☐ wear sunscreen
- ☐ wear a hat
- ☐ leave your camera
- ☐ bring plastic bags
- ☐ bring your cell phone
- ☐ wear a swimsuit
- ☐ wear tennis shoes
- ☐ listen to your guide

**B** 🔊 Listen again. Are the statements true or false? Write T (true) or F (false).

1. The most important thing to remember is to have fun. _____
2. The tourists need to wear safety vests at all times on the raft. _____
3. There is no eating or drinking allowed. _____
4. The tourists shouldn't leave their phones on the bus. _____

## 4 Speaking Dream trip

**A** Imagine you can go anywhere in the world for three weeks. Answer the questions.

- What kind of trip are you interested in taking?
- What places would you like to visit? Why?
- What would you like to do in each place?
- How long do you plan to spend in each place?
- How can you get from place to place?

**B Pair work** Tell your partner about your dream trip. Ask and answer questions for more information.

*I can describe my dream trip.*

# Wrap-up

## 1 Quick pair review

**Lesson A** **Test your partner!** Say four vacation activities. Can your partner use the gerund form of the phrase in a sentence correctly? You have three minutes.

**A:** *See wildlife.*
**B:** *I'm not interested in seeing wildlife on vacation.*

**Lesson B** **Give your opinion!** Ask your partner which vacation he or she prefers from each pair of pictures. Then remind your partner to do or take something on the trip. Take turns. You have two minutes.

**A:** *Would you prefer going to an island or to the mountains?*
**B:** *I'd prefer going to an island.*
**A:** *OK. Remember to take sunscreen.*

**Lesson C** **Brainstorm!** Make a list of extreme sports people do in the water, in the air, and on land. How many do you know? You have one minute.

**Lesson D** **Guess!** Describe your dream trip to your partner, but don't say where it is. Can your partner guess where it is? Take turns. You have two minutes.

## 2 In the real world

Would you like to try a new sport? Go online and find recommendations in English for people who want to try a new sport. Use one of the sports below or your own idea. Then write about it.

| sandboarding | downhill mountain biking | base jumping | bodyboarding |

> *Sandboarding*
> *Sandboarding is like snowboarding, but you do it on sand, not snow. You must have a sandboard for this sport. You should wear glasses so that you don't get sand in your eyes.*

## Finding out more

**A** Read the chart. Then add two more questions.

| Find someone who . . . | Name | Extra information |
|---|---|---|
| is saving money for something special | | |
| is in a good mood today | | |
| has one brother and one sister | | |
| is reading an interesting book | | |
| wants to get a pet | | |
| is taking a difficult class | | |
| works on weekends | | |
| thinks English is fun | | |
| hates to talk on the phone | | |
| | | |
| | | |

**B Class activity** Find classmates who do or are doing each thing in Part A.
Write their names. Ask questions for more information.

    **A:** *Are you saving money for something special?*
    **B:** *Yes, I am.*
    **A:** *Oh, really? What do you want to buy?*

**C Class activity** Share the most interesting information.

## Similar behaviors

**A** Write your answers to the questions in the chart.

| Questions | Me | Name: _____ |
|---|---|---|
| 1. What do you do when you can't sleep at night? | | |
| 2. What do you do if you forget to do your homework? | | |
| 3. When you feel really happy about something, what do you do? | | |
| 4. What do you do if someone tells you something that isn't true? | | |
| 5. If a friend calls you and you don't want to talk, what do you do? | | |
| 6. What do you do when you are extremely angry at someone? | | |

**B** **Pair work** Interview your partner. Complete the chart with his or her answers.

A: *What do you do when you can't sleep at night?*
B: *I usually read a book. How about you?*
A: *When I can't sleep at night, I always listen to music.*

**C** **Pair work** Compare your information. Do any of your partner's answers surprise you? Do you and your partner have any similar behaviors?

# What was happening?

**A** Look at this picture for two minutes. What was happening when it started to rain? Try to remember as many details as you can.

**B** **Pair work** Cover the picture. Ask the questions and answer with the information you remember.

1. Where was the couple sitting when the rain started? What were they doing?
2. What was the police officer holding? What was she wearing?
3. What was the name of the café? What was on the café table?
4. What was the waiter holding? Where was he standing?
5. What was the young boy holding? What was he watching on TV?
6. What was the taxi driver doing? What was the name of the cab company?

**C** **Pair work** Check your answers. How many answers did you remember correctly?

# How does it end?

**A** **Pair work**  Imagine you are the people in one of the sets of pictures below.
Tell a story that explains what happened. Choose your own ending to the story.

### Story 1

### Story 2

**B** **Group work**  Tell your story to another pair. Can they think of another ending
to your story? Which ending do you like better?

*"This really happened to us. We were driving down the road in our car. The weather
was very nice, and we were enjoying the ride. We were going to our friend's house.
We had a map, but suddenly . . ."*

**C** **Class activity**  Share your stories. Vote on the best one.

# Then and now

## Student A

**A** **Pair work** You and your partner have pictures of Chuck. You have an old picture of what he used to look like, and your partner has a new picture of what he looks like now. Describe Chuck to find the differences between then and now.

Chuck – then

A: *Chuck used to have long black hair.*
B: *He doesn't have long hair now.*
A: *So that's different. He used to . . .*

**B** **Pair work** You and your partner have pictures of Amy. You have a new picture of what she looks like now, and your partner has an old picture of what she used to look like. Describe Amy to find the differences between then and now.

Amy – now

# Then and now

## Student B

**A** **Pair work** You and your partner have pictures of Chuck. You have a new picture of what he looks like now, and your partner has an old picture of what he used to look like. Describe Chuck to find the differences between then and now.

Chuck – now

> **A:** *Chuck used to have long black hair.*
> **B:** *He doesn't have long hair now.*
> **A:** *So that's different. He used to . . .*

**B** **Pair work** You and your partner have pictures of Amy. You have an old picture of what she used to look like, and your partner has a new picture of what she looks like now. Describe Amy to find the differences between then and now.

Amy – then

# What's hot?

**A** Write your own example of each thing in the chart.

| Give an example of . . . | Me | Name: _____ |
|---|---|---|
| something which looks tacky on young people | | |
| an area of town that's extremely trendy | | |
| a store that's very popular with young people | | |
| a male celebrity who's really fashionable | | |
| a female celebrity who's very glamorous | | |
| a fashion trend that was very weird | | |
| a fashion that you really like | | |
| someone that has influenced fashion | | |

**B** **Pair work** Interview your partner. Complete the chart with his or her answers.

A: *What is something which you think looks tacky on young people?*
B: *Well, I don't like those big sunglasses that some young girls wear. I think they're tacky.*

**C** **Class activity** Compare your information. Do you agree with everyone's opinion? Why or why not?

A: *I think . . . is a celebrity who's very glamorous.*
B: *Really? I think her clothes are kind of weird.*
C: *I like most of the clothes that she wears. I think she has a lot of style.*

# I've never . . .

**A** Write examples of things you've never done.

a sport I've never played:

_____

a TV show I've never watched:

_____

a food I've never eaten:

_____

a famous movie I've never seen:

_____

a restaurant I've never been to:

_____

a place I've never visited:

_____

**B Group work** Tell your group about the things you've never done. Ask and answer questions for more information.

> **A:** _I've never played cricket._
> **B:** _Yeah, that's not popular here at all._
> **C:** _I've never played basketball._
> **D:** _You're kidding! Never? Not even in school?_

**C Class activity** Share your information. Which answers surprised you the most?

# No kidding!

**A** Add two more questions about experiences to the chart.

| Have you ever . . . ? | Name | Extra information |
| --- | --- | --- |
| seen a solar eclipse | | |
| watched three movies in one day | | |
| gone swimming in the rain | | |
| gotten a postcard from overseas | | |
| cooked a vegetarian dinner | | |
| seen a shooting star | | |
| had a really bad haircut | | |
| forgotten to pay an important bill | | |
| eaten in a French restaurant | | |
| lost something very special to you | | |
| | | |
| | | |

a solar eclipse

a shooting star

**B** **Class activity** Find classmates who have done each thing. Write their names and ask questions for more information.

> **A:** *Have you ever seen an eclipse?*
> **B:** *Yes, I have. I saw a solar eclipse once.*
> **A:** *No kidding! When did you see it?*

**C** Share the most interesting information.

# Impressive places

### Student A

**A** You and your partner have information about impressive places. Do you know the answers to the questions on the left? Circle your guesses.

1. Which is taller?
   a. Eiffel Tower
      (Paris, France)
   b. CN Tower
      (Toronto, Canada)

a. ☐ 300.5 meters tall      b. ☐ _____ meters tall

2. Which is longer?
   a. Golden Gate Bridge
      (San Francisco, the
      U.S.A.)
   b. Harbor Bridge
      (Sydney, Australia)

a. ☐ _____ meters long      b. ☐ 1,149 meters long

3. Which is bigger?
   a. Red Square
      (Moscow, Russia)
   b. Tiananmen Square
      (Beijing, China)

a. ☐ 23,100 square meters      b. ☐ _____ square meters

4. Which has more riders?
   a. São Paulo subway
      system
      (Brazil)
   b. London subway system
      (the U.K.)

a. ☐ _____ riders a day      b. ☐ 4,250,000 riders a day

**B** **Pair work** Ask and answer questions to fill in the missing information. Then check (✓) the correct answers in Part A.

How tall is . . . ?

How long is . . . ?

How big is . . . ?

How many riders does . . . have?

| **Saying large numbers** | |
| --- | --- |
| 100.2 | "one hundred point two" |
| 3,456 | "three thousand four hundred (and) fifty-six" |
| 78,900 | "seventy-eight thousand nine hundred" |
| 120,000 | "one hundred (and) twenty thousand" |
| 3,450,000 | "three million four hundred (and) fifty thousand" |

**C** **Class activity** How many of your guesses were correct? Can you make more comparisons?

# Planning a visit

**A** **Pair work** Imagine that a friend from another country is planning to visit you and asks you the questions in the email below. Discuss your responses.

| To: | Beth <bettybeth@email.com> | | **Send** |
| --- | --- | --- | --- |
| From: | Jane <jgal@email.com> | | |
| Date: | March 17, 2010 | | |
| Subject: | **Re: Planning my trip . . .** | | |

Hey!
Before I visit, I have some questions for you:

- What's the best way to travel around? Is it the fastest? Is it the cheapest?
- Which part of town has the best nightlife? When is the best time to go out?
- What's the most popular place for a tourist to visit? Have you been there?
- What's the most interesting traditional food to try? Where should I try it?
- What would make a nice day trip? Is it easy to get to?
- What's the best museum? What's it like? Should I go there?
- Which time of year has the nicest weather? Which has the worst?

I'm sorry that I'm asking so many questions. I'm just very excited, and I want to plan as much as I can!

Thanks in advance for the information. See you soon!

Take care,
Jane

A: *The best way to travel around is by subway.*
B: *I think it's better to go by bus. It's faster than the subway.*

**B** **Group work** Share your ideas with another pair. Do you have similar answers?

# Impressive places

### Student B

**A** You and your partner have information about impressive places. Do you know the answers to the questions on the left? Circle your guesses.

1. Which is taller?
   a. Eiffel Tower (Paris, France)
   b. CN Tower (Toronto, Canada)

a. ☐ _____ meters tall    b. ☐ 553.3 meters tall

2. Which is longer?
   a. Golden Gate Bridge (San Francisco, the U.S.A.)
   b. Harbor Bridge (Sydney, Australia)

a. ☐ 2,737 meters long    b. ☐ _____ meters long

3. Which is bigger?
   a. Red Square (Moscow, Russia)
   b. Tiananmen Square (Beijing, China)

a. ☐ _____ square meters    b. ☐ 440,000 square meters

4. Which has more riders?
   a. São Paulo subway system (Brazil)
   b. London subway system (the U.K.)

a. ☐ 3,500,000 riders a day    b. ☐ _____ riders a day

**B** **Pair work** Ask and answer questions to fill in the missing information. Then check (✓) the correct answers in Part A.

How tall is . . . ?
How long is . . . ?
How big is . . . ?
How many riders does . . . have?

| **Saying large numbers** | |
|---|---|
| **100.2** | "one hundred point two" |
| **3,456** | "three thousand four hundred (and) fifty-six" |
| **78,900** | "seventy-eight thousand nine hundred" |
| **120,000** | "one hundred (and) twenty thousand" |
| **3,450,000** | "three million four hundred (and) fifty thousand" |

**C** **Class activity** How many of your guesses were correct? Can you make more comparisons?

# The next two weeks

**A** Complete the calendars for next week and the week after it with the correct dates and any plans you have.

**Next week:**

| Monday | Tuesday | Wednesday | Thursday | Friday | Saturday | Sunday |
|--------|---------|-----------|----------|--------|----------|--------|
|        |         |           |          |        |          |        |

**The week after next:**

| Monday | Tuesday | Wednesday | Thursday | Friday | Saturday | Sunday |
|--------|---------|-----------|----------|--------|----------|--------|
|        |         |           |          |        |          |        |

**B** **Pair work** Ask and answer questions about your plans. Find a time to do something together.

A: *What are you doing next Thursday afternoon?*
B: *Oh, I have my karate lesson then. What are you doing the day after that?*
A: *Nothing. Do you want to get together?*

**C** **Group work** Tell another pair about the plans you made in Part B. Invite them to join you. Are they free?

A: *Barry and I are getting together on Friday.*
B: *We're meeting at Mr. Freeze for some ice cream. Do you want to join us?*
C: *I'm sorry, but I can't. I have a job interview on Friday.*
D: *I'm not free, either. I have to go grocery shopping.*

# A helping hand

**A** **Pair work** Imagine you're the people in the pictures. Role-play the situations.

**Student A:** Ask Student B for a favor.
**Student B:** Agree to Student A's request. Offer to help, and continue the conversation.

**A:** *Could you do me a favor? Could you please take my picture?*
**B:** *No problem. I'll take it for you.*

**B** **Pair work** Change roles. Role-play the new situations.

**C** **Pair work** Ask each other for two more favors.

# Left brain / right brain

**A** **Pair work** Interview your partner. Check (✓) his or her answers.

## Left Brain vs. Right Brain

Do you use your right or left brain more often? Try this fun quiz and find out.

1. **How do you remember things?**
   - ☐ a. with words
   - ☐ b. with pictures
   - ☐ c. both

2. **Which can you remember easily?**
   - ☐ a. names
   - ☐ b. faces
   - ☐ c. both

3. **Which math subject do you like?**
   - ☐ a. algebra
   - ☐ b. geometry
   - ☐ c. both

4. **How do you like to work in class?**
   - ☐ a. alone
   - ☐ b. in groups
   - ☐ c. both

5. **How do you like to study alone?**
   - ☐ a. quietly
   - ☐ b. with music playing
   - ☐ c. both

6. **Which activity do you enjoy?**
   - ☐ a. writing
   - ☐ b. drawing
   - ☐ c. both

7. **What kinds of tests do you like?**
   - ☐ a. multiple choice
   - ☐ b. essay
   - ☐ c. both

8. **How do you like things explained to you?**
   - ☐ a. with words
   - ☐ b. with actions
   - ☐ c. both

9. **What do you use to make decisions?**
   - ☐ a. the facts
   - ☐ b. my experience
   - ☐ c. both

10. **How do you like to solve problems?**
    - ☐ a. one at a time
    - ☐ b. at the same time
    - ☐ c. both

11. **How do you manage your time?**
    - ☐ a. very carefully
    - ☐ b. not very carefully
    - ☐ c. both

12. **Which animals do you like?**
    - ☐ a. dogs
    - ☐ b. cats
    - ☐ c. both

*Source:* library.thinkquest.org

**B** **Pair work** Score your partner's answers. Is he or she left-brained or right-brained? (More *c* answers or the same number of *a* and *b* answers means your partner has traits for both.)

| More *a* answers: Left-brained | More *b* answers: Right-brained |
| --- | --- |
| More verbal than visual | More visual than verbal |
| Likes to do things step by step | Likes to do things at the same time |
| Very organized | Not always organized |
| Follows rules without questioning | Often asks why |
| Strong sense of time | Little sense of time |
| Learns by seeing | Learns by doing |
| Uses few gestures when talking | Talks with hands |
| Listens to what is said | Listens to how something is said |

**C** **Group work** Do your results in Part B describe you well? What do you think your results say about your personality?

# People on my mind

**A** Write the name of someone you know for each description. Then think about answers to the questions.

Someone I miss very much:

_____

- How long have you known this person?
- When did you last see him or her?
- When will you see each other again?

Someone who gave me a special gift:

_____

- What was the gift?
- How long have you had it?
- What made the gift special?

Someone I'd like to know better:

_____

- How long have you known this person?
- When was the last time you spoke?
- What's he or she like?

Someone I've admired since I was a child:

_____

- When did you first meet this person?
- What do you admire about him or her?
- Do you share any of the same qualities?

**B Pair work** Interview your partner about each person. Ask questions for more information.

    **A:** *Who is someone you miss very much?*
    **B:** *I miss my grandmother very much.*
    **A:** *How long have you known her?*
    **B:** *I've known her since I was born! But I haven't seen her since April.*

# A green quiz

**A** **Pair work** Interview your partner. Circle his or her answers.

## HOW GREEN ARE YOU?
### Try this quiz to find out.

1. You're leaving for the weekend, but you're not taking your computer. What do you do?
   a. Put it to "sleep."
   b. Shut it down.
   c. Turn it off and unplug it.

2. You're planning to go to a movie with several friends. What do you do?
   a. Go in separate cars.
   b. Meet and go in one car.
   c. Take public transportation.

3. You're walking and see some empty bottles on the sidewalk. What do you do?
   a. Leave the bottles there.
   b. Put them in a garbage can.
   c. Put them in a recycling bin.

4. Your office has a watercooler with plastic cups for people to use. What do you do?
   a. Use a different plastic cup each time.
   b. Use the same plastic cup all day.
   c. Use your own regular cup.

5. You're buying a magazine, and the cashier starts to put it in a bag. What do you do?
   a. Take the bag and throw it away later.
   b. Take the bag, but reuse it.
   c. Just take the magazine.

6. You have some old, unused medicine that you don't need. What do you do?
   a. Flush it down the toilet.
   b. Throw it in the garbage.
   c. Return it to a pharmacy.

7. You're making a salad and realize you don't have enough lettuce. What do you do?
   a. Get any lettuce at the nearest store.
   b. Buy organic lettuce at a farmer's market.
   c. Pick some lettuce from your own garden.

8. A company in your neighborhood is harming the environment. What do you do?
   a. Nothing.
   b. Tell your friends.
   c. Write a letter to the local newspaper about it.

**B** **Pair work** Score your partner's answers. How green is he or she? Are the results accurate?

a answers = 0 points
b answers = 1 point
c answers = 2 points

11–16 Congratulations! You lead a very green life.
 6–10 You're green in some ways, but not in others.
 0–5  You're not very green. It's not too late to change!

**C** **Pair work** What other things do you do to help the environment? Tell your partner.

# Be an optimist!

**A** **Pair work** Add two situations to the chart. Then discuss what will, could, or might happen in each situation. Take notes.

| If we . . . , | we will . . . | we might . . . |
|---|---|---|
| eat too much fast food | | |
| spend all day at the beach | | |
| use cell phones in class | | |
| read the news every day | | |
| never study English | | |
| watch too much TV | | |
| don't get enough sleep | | |
| spend too much time online | | |
| | | |
| | | |

**A:** *What do you think will happen if we eat too much fast food?*
**B:** *If we eat too much fast food, we'll gain weight.*

**B** **Group work** Share your ideas with another pair. Which ideas are the best? Do you have any other ideas?

# What to do?

**A Group work** Imagine you have one of the relationship problems below. Your group gives you advice. Take turns.

My friend texts me constantly and then gets angry if I don't answer right away. Is it important to answer every text? I'm not sure what to do about this. I prefer to communicate by phone.

My sister has a new hairstyle, and I think it looks pretty awful. I don't really want to criticize her, but I think it's a good idea to say something to her. But what exactly do I say?

My co-worker won't talk to me. She says I gossiped about her. I guess I did, but it wasn't anything serious. It feels like she's judging me. I hope she can forgive me. After all, we need to work together.

My classmate always tries to copy my answers when we are taking tests or working on our own. It makes me angry. I don't want the teacher to think I'm cheating, too. Should I tell my teacher?

> **A:** *My friend texts me constantly and then . . .*
> **B:** *It's not important to answer every text. Just ignore them.*
> **C:** *But it's not good to ignore them. Say something to your friend about it.*
> **D:** *That's good advice. It's also a good idea to . . .*

**B Group work** Which advice was the best? Why? Tell your group.

*"Maria gave the best advice. It's important to tell the truth."*

**C Group work** Have you ever given relationship advice to someone? Who? What was the advice? Tell your group.

# What do you think?

**A** **Pair work** Look at the picture. Make one speculation about each person. Use
*must, could, can't, may,* or *might.*

A: *Diego is buying a dress, but it can't be for his wife. It's too small.*
B: *Right. He might be buying it for his daughter.*
A: *Yeah. And he must be rich. The store looks very expensive.*

**B Group work** Compare your speculations with another pair. Did you make any of the same ones?

# Reflections

**A Class activity** Find classmates who answer "yes" to each question. Write their names and ask questions for more information.

| Questions | Name | Extra information |
|---|---|---|
| 1. Have you ever eaten an entire pizza by yourself? | | |
| 2. Do you learn better by studying in a group than by yourself? | | |
| 3. Did you teach yourself how to cook? | | |
| 4. Do you see yourself living in another country in five years? | | |
| 5. Have you ever traveled anywhere by yourself? | | |
| 6. Would you like to change something about yourself? | | |
| 7. Have you ever lived by yourself? | | |
| 8. Do you know someone who taught himself or herself a foreign language? | | |

A: *Have you ever eaten an entire pizza by yourself?*
B: *Yes, I have!*
A: *Wow! That's a lot of pizza. What kind of pizza was it?*
B: *It had cheese, pepperoni, onions, and peppers on it.*

**B** Share your information. What's the most interesting thing you learned? Who else in the class answered "yes" to each question?

# Imagine that!

**A** Guess your partner's answers to the questions. Write your guesses in the chart.

| Questions | My guesses | My partner's answers |
|---|---|---|
| 1. What would you do if you saw your favorite celebrity? | | |
| 2. What would you do if your best friend moved to another country? | | |
| 3. How would you feel if someone brought up something embarrassing about you at a party? | | |
| 4. What would you do if you broke something expensive in a store? | | |
| 5. Where would you go if you had one week to travel anywhere in the world? | | |
| 6. What would you do if a friend borrowed some money from you and then didn't pay you back? | | |
| 7. What would you do if your grades in this class suddenly dropped? | | |

**B Pair work** Interview your partner. Complete the chart with his or her answers. How many of your partner's answers did you guess correctly?

**C Class activity** Do any of your partner's answers surprise you? Would you and your partner do any similar things? Tell the class.

# Facts and opinions

**A** **Group work** Add two sets of questions about music to the list. Then discuss the questions. Ask follow-up questions to get more information.

1. What bands were formed in the 1960s? '70s? '80s? '90s? What was their music like?
2. What male singer do you think has a nice-sounding voice? What female singer?
3. What well-known singers or bands do you not like very much? Why not?
4. Were any record-breaking hits released last year? What did you think of the songs?
5. Was any truly awful music released in the past few years? What made it so terrible?
6. What was the last music awards show you saw on TV? Who was on it?
7. Who are the best-selling singers from your country? Do you enjoy their music?
8. What are some easily learned songs in your native language? Do you know all the words?
9. _____ ? _____ ?
10. _____ ? _____ ?

The Rolling Stones, 1960s

ABBA, 1970s

R.E.M., 1980s

The Spice Girls, 1990s

**A:** *The Rolling Stones were formed in the 1960s.*
**B:** *How was their music?*
**A:** *Their music was fantastic. It still is.*
**C:** *Can you name the band members?*

**B** **Class activity** Share any interesting information.

# Find the differences

### Student A

You and your partner have pictures of Monica and Victor, but they aren't exactly the same. Ask questions with *yet* to find the differences. Circle the items that are different.

see a movie

get a new stereo

download a song

send a text

buy a CD

sing a song

**A:** *Have Monica and Victor seen a movie yet?*
**B:** *No, they haven't. In my picture, they haven't seen it yet. They're going inside.*
**A:** *So that's different. In my picture, they're leaving the movie theater.*

# Find the differences

### Student B

You and your partner have pictures of Monica and Victor, but they aren't exactly the same. Ask questions with *yet* to find the differences. Circle the items that are different.

see a movie

get a new stereo

download a song

send a text

buy a CD

sing a song

**A:** *Have Monica and Victor seen a movie yet?*
**B:** *No, they haven't. In my picture, they haven't seen it yet. They're going inside.*
**A:** *So that's different. In my picture, they're leaving the movie theater.*

# Travel partners

**A** Add three questions about travel preferences to the chart. Then check (✓) your answers.

| When you travel, . . . | Me | | Name: _____ | |
| --- | :---: | :---: | :---: | :---: |
| | Yes | No | Yes | No |
| 1.  do you like being in a large group? | ☐ | ☐ | ☐ | ☐ |
| 2.  are you interested in meeting new people? | ☐ | ☐ | ☐ | ☐ |
| 3.  is saving money important to you? | ☐ | ☐ | ☐ | ☐ |
| 4.  do you like trying new foods? | ☐ | ☐ | ☐ | ☐ |
| 5.  is asking directions embarrassing to you? | ☐ | ☐ | ☐ | ☐ |
| 6.  do you like knowing your schedule in advance? | ☐ | ☐ | ☐ | ☐ |
| 7.  is camping more fun than staying in hotels? | ☐ | ☐ | ☐ | ☐ |
| 8.  do you enjoy shopping for souvenirs? | ☐ | ☐ | ☐ | ☐ |
| 9.  do you like big cities? | ☐ | ☐ | ☐ | ☐ |
| 10.  do you like going to clubs? | ☐ | ☐ | ☐ | ☐ |
| 11.  is seeing everything possible important to you? | ☐ | ☐ | ☐ | ☐ |
| 12. | ☐ | ☐ | ☐ | ☐ |
| 13. | ☐ | ☐ | ☐ | ☐ |
| 14. | ☐ | ☐ | ☐ | ☐ |

**B** **Pair work** Interview your partner. Complete the chart with his or her answers.

**C** **Pair work** Compare your answers. Would you make good travel partners? Why or why not?

A: *We wouldn't make good travel partners. You like being in a large group. I don't.*
B: *Yes, but we're both interested in meeting new people.*
A: *Well, that's true. And saving money is important to us.*

# A backpacking trip

**A Pair work** Imagine someone is planning a two-week backpacking trip to your country. What rules and recommendations would you give for each category? Take notes.

| Packing | Communication |
|---|---|
|  |  |
| **Health and safety** | **Places to stay** |
|  |  |
| **Transportation** | **Money** |
|  |  |
| **Food** | **Other** |
|  |  |

**B Group work** Share your ideas with another pair. Did you have any of the same rules or recommendations? Can you think of any other rules or recommendations?

A: *You shouldn't pack too many clothes.*
B: *Yes, but you have to have enough clothes!*
C: *Also, you ought to bring your cell phone.*

# Irregular verbs

| Base form | Simple past | Past participle |
|---|---|---|
| be | was, were | been |
| become | became | become |
| break | broke | broken |
| build | built | built |
| buy | bought | bought |
| choose | chose | chosen |
| come | came | come |
| do | did | done |
| draw | drew | drawn |
| drink | drank | drunk |
| drive | drove | driven |
| eat | ate | eaten |
| fall | fell | fallen |
| feel | felt | felt |
| fly | flew | flown |
| forget | forgot | forgotten |
| get | got | gotten |
| give | gave | given |
| go | went | gone |
| hang | hung | hung |
| have | had | had |
| hear | heard | heard |
| hold | held | held |
| know | knew | known |
| leave | left | left |

| Base form | Simple past | Past participle |
|---|---|---|
| lose | lost | lost |
| make | made | made |
| meet | met | met |
| pay | paid | paid |
| put | put | put |
| read | read | read |
| ride | rode | ridden |
| run | ran | run |
| say | said | said |
| see | saw | seen |
| sell | sold | sold |
| send | sent | sent |
| sing | sang | sung |
| sit | sat | sat |
| sleep | slept | slept |
| speak | spoke | spoken |
| spend | spent | spent |
| stand | stood | stood |
| swim | swam | swum |
| take | took | taken |
| teach | taught | taught |
| think | thought | thought |
| wear | wore | worn |
| win | won | won |
| write | wrote | written |

# Adjective and adverb formations

| Adjectives | Adverbs | Adjectives | Adverbs |
|---|---|---|---|
| agreeable | agreeably | immature | immaturely |
| amazing | amazingly | impatient | impatiently |
| ambitious | ambitiously | inconsiderate | inconsiderately |
| angry | angrily | indecisive | indecisively |
| brave | bravely | interesting | interestingly |
| careful | carefully | late | late |
| confident | confidently | lucky | luckily |
| considerate | considerately | mature | maturely |
| creative | creatively | nervous | nervously |
| curious | curiously | optimistic | optimistically |
| decisive | decisively | patient | patiently |
| disagreeable | disagreeably | quick | quickly |
| dishonest | dishonestly | rare | rarely |
| early | early | reliable | reliably |
| easy | easily | sad | sadly |
| enthusiastic | enthusiastically | serious | seriously |
| extreme | extremely | similar | similarly |
| fair | fairly | strange | strangely |
| fashionable | fashionably | stubborn | stubbornly |
| fast | fast | sudden | suddenly |
| fortunate | fortunately | surprising | surprisingly |
| glamorous | glamorously | unfair | unfairly |
| good | well | unfortunate | unfortunately |
| hard | hard | unreliable | unreliably |
| honest | honestly | wise | wisely |

# Answer key

## Listening

This personality test is just for fun. Don't take the answers *too* seriously!

1. This person is the most important person in your life.

2. If you see a big animal, you think you have big problems.

3. If you have a big house, you are very ambitious.

4. If the door is open, you're happy for people to visit anytime. If it's closed, you prefer people to call first.

5. If there is food or flowers on the table, you are very optimistic.

6. If the material is strong (like metal or plastic), you have a strong relationship with the person in number 1.

7. If you keep the cup, you want to keep a good relationship with the person in number 1.

# Credits

# Four Corners

## Jack C. Richards · David Bohlke

## Video Activity Sheets

CAMBRIDGE
UNIVERSITY PRESS

# A busy schedule

## Before you watch

**A** Complete the sentences with the correct jobs. Then compare with a partner.

an artist

a doctor

a journalist

1. _____ studies chemistry.

2. _____ writes stories for newspapers.

3. _____ can draw and paint very well.

4. _____ makes creative things.

5. _____ interviews people a lot.

6. _____ takes a lot of science classes.

**B Pair work** Interview your partner. Take notes.

1. How many classes are you taking?

2. Why are you taking each class?

3. Do you like the subject(s) you are studying? Why or why not?

4. What job would you like to have someday?

**C Class activity** Share your information. Who is taking a lot of classes? Who is taking a fun class?

## While you watch

**A** Circle the correct answers.

1. Danielle and Amy are _____.

   a. friends    b. neighbors    c. roommates

2. Danielle and April are studying _____.

   a. art    b. chemistry    c. journalism

3. Danielle and April are making a _____ for their class.

   a. picture    b. poster    c. video

4. Amy is taking _____ classes.

   a. five    b. six    c. seven

5. Danielle feels like she has a really _____ schedule.

   a. busy    b. easy    c. hard

**B** Check ( ✓ ) the correct answers.

| | Amy | Danielle |
|---|---|---|
| 1. Who thinks chemistry is difficult? | ☐ | ☐ |
| 2. Who isn't hungry? | ☐ | ☐ |
| 3. Who eats a lot before a big exam? | ☐ | ☐ |
| 4. Who thinks art class looks stressful? | ☐ | ☐ |
| 5. Who is learning to write stories for newspapers? | ☐ | ☐ |
| 6. Who is preparing for medical school exams? | ☐ | ☐ |

**C** Write T (true) or F (false). Correct the false sentences.

*Amy*

1. ~~Danielle~~ has a big exam this week. ___F___

2. Amy drinks a lot of coffee. _____

3. When Danielle is nervous about something, she exercises. _____

4. Amy wants to be an artist. _____

5. Amy is late for class. _____

## After you watch

**A** Why do you think Amy is so sleepy? Write your answers on the lines. Then compare with a partner.

Amy is sleepy because she . . .

is preparing for medical
school exams.

_____ .

_____ .

**B** **Group work** Discuss the questions. Do any of you do the same things as Danielle or Amy?

• When you have a big exam, what do you do?

• If you're nervous about something, what do you do?

• What do you do if you feel sleepy in class?

# An awful, terrible, embarrassing, really bad day!

## Before you watch

**A** Look at the pictures. Complete the phrases with the correct verbs. Then compare with a partner.

| get | lose | make | miss | spill | wait |
|---|---|---|---|---|---|

1. _____ a drink

2. _____ an animation project

3. _____ in line

4. _____ a job

5. _____ a bad grade

6. _____ the bus

**B Pair work**  When was the last time you did each thing in Part A? Are there some things you've never done? Tell your partner.

*"I spilled coffee on my shirt this morning! I've never made an animation project."*

## While you watch

**A** What happened? Number the events from 1 to 9.

_____  April missed the bus to school.

_1_  April woke up late.

_____  April made an animation project.

_____  April's dog ate her homework.

_____  April went to the store for laundry detergent.

_____  April was late for her biology class.

_____  April sat next to Zach on the bus.

_____  April was late for work and lost her job.

April

**B** Circle the correct answers.

1. April spilled _____ on her shirt.

    a. orange juice     b. yogurt     c. coffee

2. April spilled _____ on Zach's shirt.

    a. orange juice     b. yogurt     c. coffee

3. Zach was _____ when April said she was sorry.

    a. angry     b. not amused     c. disgusted

4. The biology teacher's suggestion for April is to _____.

    a. do her homework again     b. come to class on time     c. give her dog some food

5. April didn't get the laundry detergent because _____.

    a. she didn't have enough money     b. there was a long line     c. there was none in the store

6. The one good thing that happened was that _____.

    a. Zach became April's boyfriend

    b. April found a new job after she lost her old one

    c. April had time to make an animation project for her art class

**C** Match the phrases to complete the sentences.

1. April was late for school _____
2. She was excited _____.
3. April was embarrassed when she lost her job _____.
4. She was late for work _____.
5. April got an "F" _____

a. because no one was sitting next to Zach.
b. because her dog ate her homework.
c. because there was a long line at the market.
d. because Zach was in the restaurant.
e. because her alarm clock didn't go off.

# After you watch

**A Pair work**  What was embarrassing about April's day? Do you know anyone who has had similar experiences to April? Tell your partner.

**B** Think about one very bad day in your life or the life of someone you know. Write three things about that day – two things that *really* happened, and one that *didn't* really happen.

1. _____

2. _____

3. _____

**C Pair work**  Tell your partner about the bad day. Your partner guesses what didn't really happen. Take turns.

    A: I broke my elbow and lost my cell phone. Then someone stole my laptop.

    B: I don't think you really broke your elbow.

    A: That's not right. I *did* break my elbow, but no one really stole my laptop.

unit **3** *What's your personal style?*

## Before you watch

**A** Complete the sentences with the correct words. Then compare with a partner.

| bright | comfortable | conservative | fashionable | flashy | tacky |

1. Many people think it is _____ to wear socks with sandals.

2. _____ clothing attracts attention and makes people stand out in a crowd.

3. People with a _____ style usually wear simple, plain clothes.

4. Orange and yellow are examples of _____ colors.

5. Models wear _____ clothing in magazines to help sell new items.

6. Most people think jeans, sneakers, and sweatshirts are _____.

**B Pair work** Make a list of ten words to describe clothing styles and fashion. Then give examples of each one.

A: *Glamorous is another word to describe clothing styles and fashion.*

B: *Yes, it is. Who or what do you think is glamorous?*

A: *I think actors and actresses always look glamorous at award shows.*

B: *So do I.*

## While you watch

**A** Check (✓) the correct answers. (More than one answer is possible.)

| | Jim | Lola | Officer Palone |
|---|---|---|---|
| 1. Who wears clothes that attract attention? | ☐ | ☐ | ☐ |
| 2. Who thinks black is always fashionable? | ☐ | ☐ | ☐ |
| 3. Who likes to wear comfortable clothes? | ☐ | ☐ | ☐ |
| 4. Who usually wears many different colors? | ☐ | ☐ | ☐ |
| 5. Who usually wears only two colors? | ☐ | ☐ | ☐ |
| 6. Who usually wears only one color? | ☐ | ☐ | ☐ |
| 7. Who used to wear flashy clothes? | ☐ | ☐ | ☐ |
| 8. Who doesn't like flashy clothes? | ☐ | ☐ | ☐ |

**B** Who is wearing each item in the video? Write E (Emi), J (Jim), L (Lola), or 0 (Officer Palone). (More than one answer is possible.)

1. a black jacket _____
2. a blue sweater _____
3. a gray shirt _____
4. a hat _____

5. a ponytail _____
6. a big bag _____
7. a red dress _____
8. a uniform _____

9. a white shirt _____
10. bracelets _____
11. earrings _____
12. sunglasses _____

**C** Correct the false sentences.

1. Jim wears a lot of blue and white clothing.
2. Jim likes to wear flashy and tacky clothes.
3. Lola doesn't like to stand out in a crowd.
4. Lola doesn't wear bright colors to work.
5. Officer Palone thinks his sunglasses are trendy.
6. Officer Palone's favorite color is red.

# After you watch

**A** What was your clothing style five years ago? Complete the diagram with your own ideas. In the circle, write the style (retro? trendy? etc.). On the lines, write examples of some favorite clothes you used to wear.

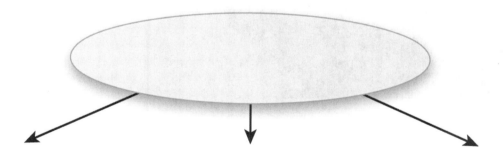

**B Pair work**  Ask and answer questions about your diagrams. Did you use to wear any of the same things that you saw in the video?

   A: *What was your clothing style?*
   B: *Well, I used to wear a lot of black and white, like Jim in the video. I used to have some really cool black jeans. I wore them with a white T-shirt and a black leather jacket. I thought it was really trendy.*

# unit 4 An interesting life

## Before you watch

**A** Complete the description with the correct words. Then compare with a partner.

| events | interview | newspapers | reporter | travel |
|---|---|---|---|---|

   A foreign correspondent is a type of _____. Many foreign correspondents write stories for _____, but they may also work for TV or radio news stations. They usually have to _____ to many different countries for their job. They _____ many different people for their stories. They tell us about important people and _____ from around the world that have an impact on our history.

**B Pair work** Read the description again. Can you name any foreign correspondents? How do you find out about people and events from around the world? Tell your partner.

## While you watch

**A** Circle the correct answers.

1. Danielle is making this video for her _____ class.

   a. journalism     b. world history     c. filmmaking

2. Irma was a _____ reporter.

   a. newspaper     b. TV     c. radio

3. She interviewed _____ in England.

   a. Queen Elizabeth     b. Princess Diana     c. Tony Blair

4. James Brown was a famous _____.

   a. hip-hop artist     b. actor     c. soul singer

5. Irma reported on a historical event in _____.

   a. England     b. Germany     c. the United States

**B** What does Irma say about James Brown? Write T (true) or F (false). Correct the false sentences.

1. James Brown was very polite and funny. _____

2. James Brown wasn't very hardworking. _____

3. James Brown used to practice an hour each day. _____

4. A lot of hip-hop artists have used his music. _____

5. She saw James Brown at the Apollo Theater in New York City. _____

**C** What does Irma say about the Berlin Wall? Check (✓) the correct answers.

☐ The fall of the Berlin Wall was the end of the Cold War.

☐ She took a piece of the wall home as a souvenir.

☐ People were so happy when it fell.

☐ People in East Berlin crossed the wall and celebrated with people in West Berlin.

☐ She won an award for her story.

☐ She lived in Berlin for five years after the wall fell.

## After you watch

**A Group work** Irma described some memorable experiences. Discuss the questions.

• Which of Irma's experiences was your favorite? Why?

• Who is a famous person you would like to interview? Why?

*"The Berlin Wall experience was my favorite. It was a big, historical event."*

**B Pair work** Tell your partner about an interesting person you've met and a memorable experience you've had. Ask and answer questions for more information.

• Who was the person?

• Where did you meet him or her?

• Why was he or she interesting?

• When did you have this experience?

• Where were you?

• Why was it memorable?

*"I met a famous jazz musician at a club. He was a talented saxophone player."*

# Travels with Nick and Ben: Yosemite National Park

## Before you watch

**A** Label the pictures with the correct words. Then compare with a partner.

| a bear | a meadow | a mountain lion | a rattlesnake | a rock | a waterfall |

1. _____

2. _____

3. _____

4. _____

5. _____

6. _____

**B Pair work** Have you ever seen the animals or geographical features in Part A? Where can you find them? Tell your partner.

## While you watch

**A** Read the sentences about Nick and Ben's trip to Yosemite National Park. Write T (true) or F (false).

1. They ate in a fancy restaurant. _____

2. They drove to the park. _____

3. They enjoyed the sunset. _____

4. They saw a bear. _____

5. They saw a mountain lion. _____

6. They saw very old trees. _____

7. They walked through a tree. _____

8. They went camping. _____

9. They went hiking. _____

10. They went rock climbing. _____

11. They went swimming. _____

12. They went to a spa. _____

**B** Match the phrases to complete the sentences.

1. El Capitán is _____.
2. Yosemite Falls is _____.
3. Bridalveil Falls is _____.
4. Mariposa Grove is _____.
5. Grizzly Giant is _____.
6. The California Tunnel Tree is _____.
7. A Sequoia is _____.

a. a beautiful waterfall.
b. the highest waterfall in North America.
c. a tree that people can walk through.
d. the oldest Sequoia tree in Mariposa Grove.
e. a forest of Sequoia trees.
f. a type of tree.
g. a huge rock.

**C** Who says it? Check (✓) the correct answers.

| | Ben | Nick |
|---|---|---|
| 1. "Yosemite National Park – the most beautiful place on earth." | ☐ | ☐ |
| 2. "Yosemite National Park – the most dangerous place on earth." | ☐ | ☐ |
| 3. "I saw a rattlesnake while I was walking on the road." | ☐ | ☐ |
| 4. "Look at that! Don't you think that looks dangerous?" | ☐ | ☐ |
| 5. "It was exciting and challenging!" | ☐ | ☐ |
| 6. "It was stressful. It was frightening. And it was wet!" | ☐ | ☐ |
| 7. "Water can't hurt you!" | ☐ | ☐ |
| 8. "I left the food in the car." | ☐ | ☐ |

## After you watch

**A Pair work** How would you describe Nick and Ben's trip? Would you like to go to Yosemite National Park? Why or why not? Discuss your ideas.

**B Group work** Discuss these questions about trips you've taken.
- What was the most exciting trip you've ever taken? Where did you go?
- What was your favorite trip? What did you do?
- What was the worst trip you've ever taken? What was so bad about it?
- Have you ever been in a dangerous situation on vacation? What happened?

**C Class activity** Tell the class the most interesting information or stories from your group discussion.

# The time of your life

## Before you watch

**A** Check (✓) the problems you have managing your time. Then compare with a partner.

☐ committing to too much work
☐ doing other people's work
☐ doing too many favors for other people
☐ finding time for your personal life
☐ finding time to be with your family
☐ keeping your home clean

☐ planning your weekly schedule
☐ remembering important things
☐ saying no to other people
☐ studying for exams
☐ taking on too many school projects
☐ working and going to school

Other: _____

**B  Pair work**  Who do you talk to when you're stressed out? Does anyone help you manage your time? Tell your partner.

## While you watch

**A** Check (✓) the correct answers.

| | Wendy | Nick | Soon-mi |
|---|---|---|---|
| 1.  Who can't find a list of things to do this weekend? | ☐ | ☐ | ☐ |
| 2.  Who commits to too much work? | ☐ | ☐ | ☐ |
| 3.  Who does a lot of other people's work? | ☐ | ☐ | ☐ |
| 4.  Who doesn't have time to finish the show? | ☐ | ☐ | ☐ |
| 5.  Who has to pay bills this weekend? | ☐ | ☐ | ☐ |
| 6.  Who is busy all the time? | ☐ | ☐ | ☐ |
| 7.  Who is late for the show? | ☐ | ☐ | ☐ |
| 8.  Who is too busy this weekend? | ☐ | ☐ | ☐ |
| 9.  Who needs to study for an exam? | ☐ | ☐ | ☐ |
| 10.  Who takes on too many projects at school? | ☐ | ☐ | ☐ |

**B** Circle the correct answers.

1. Wendy's show is called _____.

    a. TV Time     b. The Time Saver     c. The Time of Your Life

2. Nick needs to shop for _____ this weekend.

    a. groceries     b. clothes     c. school supplies

3. Wendy tells Nick to _____.

    a. call his mother     b. breathe slowly and deeply     c. cancel the party

4. Wendy's advice to Nick is to _____.

    a. make a list     b. go to the movies     c. pay his bills first

5. Wendy tells Soon-mi to _____.

    a. do things one at a time     b. help her classmates     c. learn to say no

6. Wendy _____ Chris's question.

    a. answers     b. likes     c. never hears

**C** Write T (true) or F (false).

1. Wendy is very good at managing her own time. _____

2. Wendy doesn't have any children. _____

3. Nick is having a birthday party for someone this weekend. _____

4. If Nick follows Wendy's advice, he probably won't go to the movies this weekend. _____

5. If Soon-mi follows Wendy's advice, she'll probably do the grocery shopping for her roommate. _____

6. Soon-mi learns to say no. _____

## After you watch

**A Pair work** Do you ever have the same problems as Wendy, Nick, or Soon-mi? Do you know other people who do? How do you (or they) manage them? Tell your partner.

**B Pair work** Make a list of five things you plan to do this weekend. Then share them with a partner.

1. _____

2. _____

3. _____

4. _____

5. _____

**C Pair work** Now imagine that you have time to do only three things on your list. Which two plans will you decide *not* to do? Why? Tell your partner.

# Signs of the Zodiac

## Before you watch

**A** Label the pictures with the correct words. Then compare with a partner.

| a consultant | a graphic designer | a salesman | a student |

1. _____  2. _____  3. _____  4. _____

**B** Complete the sentences with the correct words. Then compare with a partner.

| adventurous | ambitious | creative | unreliable |

1. Often consultants are _____ people who work very hard to share their knowledge and advice with other people to help them succeed.

2. Graphic designers are usually _____ people. They use technology to make websites, magazines, and other things look very interesting and artistic.

3. Some people think that some salesmen can be _____ and that they don't always give you honest information about what you want to buy.

4. Students who study abroad in a different country are pretty _____. They're not afraid to go to new places, meet new people, and try new things.

## While you watch

**A** Match the people and their zodiac signs.

Aries      Capricorn      Gemini      Virgo

1. Danielle's mother is a(n) _____.     a. Aries
2. Danielle's brother is a(n) _____.     b. Gemini
3. Danielle's father is a(n) _____.     c. Capricorn
4. Danielle is a(n) _____.     d. Virgo

**B** What are some characteristics of each sign? Write V (Virgos), A (Aries), C (Capricorns), or G (Geminis). (More than one answer is possible.)

1. _____ have difficulty sharing their feelings.

2. _____ are adventurous.

3. _____ are ambitious.

4. _____ are creative.

5. _____ are good at business.

6. _____ are sometimes unreliable.

7. _____ aren't open to new ideas.

8. _____ know what they want.

9. _____ want things done with no mistakes.

10. _____ worry too much.

**C** Check (✓) the correct answers.

| | Danielle | Wendy | Max | Peter |
|---|---|---|---|---|
| 1. Who has been a graphic designer for two years? | ☐ | ☐ | ☐ | ☐ |
| 2. Who is taking a psychology class? | ☐ | ☐ | ☐ | ☐ |
| 3. Who doesn't want to talk about Andy's promotion? | ☐ | ☐ | ☐ | ☐ |
| 4. Who wants to put new wallpaper in the kitchen? | ☐ | ☐ | ☐ | ☐ |
| 5. Who has owned a car dealership since 2003? | ☐ | ☐ | ☐ | ☐ |
| 6. Who loves to try new things? | ☐ | ☐ | ☐ | ☐ |
| 7. Who has to get back work? | ☐ | ☐ | ☐ | ☐ |
| 8. Who has worked as a time management consultant for ten years? | ☐ | ☐ | ☐ | ☐ |

## After you watch

**A Pair work** Why does Danielle think her family members' personalities match the typical characteristics of their zodiac signs? Discuss and explain your ideas.

**B Group work** Discuss the questions.
- What do you know about zodiac signs?
- Do you know the characteristics of your zodiac sign? Do you think it matches your personality?
- Do you know anyone who matches the characteristics of his or her zodiac sign? How long have you known him or her?
- How do your family members and friends describe your personality? Do you agree with them?

## Before you watch

**A** Match the words and the pictures. Then compare with a partner.

| | | | |
|---|---|---|---|
| a. candle | c. landfill | e. plant | g. recycling bins |
| b. ice | d. lightbulb | f. plastic bottles | h. superhero |

 1. ☐
 2. ☐
 3. ☐
 4. ☐

 5. ☐
 6. ☐
 7. ☐
 8. ☐

**B Pair work** Complete the sentences with the correct words from Part A. Then compare with a partner.

1. A _____ is a place where a town or group of people collects its garbage.

2. _____ is frozen water.

3. A _____ may go inside a lamp and provide light in a room.

4. Many people buy water and soda in _____.

5. The small fire on top of a _____ is called a flame; it gives off light.

6. A _____ is an imaginary person that saves and protects people or the earth.

7. A _____ could grow into an herb, a flower, or a vegetable.

8. In many public places, there are separate _____ for paper and plastic products.

## While you watch

**A** What does Henry Green do to help the environment? Check (✓) the correct answers.

☐ He drives a hybrid car.
☐ He grows vegetables.
☐ He pays his bills online.
☐ He takes cloth bags to the supermarket.

☐ He uses an ice box to keep his food cold.
☐ He uses candles.
☐ He uses solar energy.
☐ He uses the recycling bins in his building.

**B** Circle the correct answers.

1. April is doing this video for _____

    a. her journalism class    b. her biology class    c. the school TV station

2. Henry Green is April's _____.

    a. grandfather    b. biology teacher    c. neighbor

3. April's nickname for Henry Green is _____.

    a. Environmental Man    b. Green Man    c. Environmental Impact Man

4. April says that compact fluorescent bulbs use _____ regular lightbulbs.

    a. less energy than    b. more energy than    c. the same energy as

5. April says that plastic bags and water bottles often end up in _____.

    a. landfills    b. schools    c. the ocean

6. April thinks Mr. Green is like a _____ to her.

    a. grandfather    b. friend    c. superhero

7. To thank Mr. Green, April gives him a _____.

    a. T-shirt    b. cloth shopping bag    c. candle

**C** Why does Mr. Green do these things? Match the things he does and the reasons.

1. He uses an ice box because _____.    a. he doesn't want chemicals in his food.

2. He uses candles because _____.    b. he thinks people use too much plastic.

3. He grows vegetables because _____.    c. refrigerators use too much energy.

4. He uses a cloth shopping bag because _____.    d. they use less energy than lightbulbs.

## After you watch

**Group work** What's your opinion of what Mr. Green is doing? Discuss why you think each of his actions is a good idea or a bad idea.

- having an ice box instead of a refrigerator
- using candles instead of compact fluorescent bulbs
- growing vegetables at home
- taking a cloth shopping bag to the store

A: *I think using candles is a good idea. You can save energy if you use candles.*

B: *That's true. But candles could cause a fire if you aren't careful.*

# She must be copying me!

## Before you watch

**A** Match the words and the fashion items. Then compare with a partner.

a. bag

b. belt

c. bracelet

d. jacket

e. scarf

f. shirt

g. shoes

h. skirt

**B** People often *compliment* each other on fashion items, or say something nice to express that they like it. Are these compliments? Write Y (yes) or N (no).

1. "That jacket looks great on you!" _____

2. "Where did you buy that new bag?" _____

3. "I love your dress. It's really fashionable." _____

4. "Nice shirt! What a cool design!" _____

5. "I saw those same shoes in the store yesterday." _____

6. "That's a really pretty scarf. The color matches your eyes." _____

**C Pair work** Compliment your partner on two different fashion items.

## While you watch

**A** What does Amanda have that's exactly like something Jessica or Beth has? Check (✓) the correct answers.

☐ bag           ☐ a denim skirt      ☐ a sweater

☐ bracelet      ☐ a jacket           ☐ a pair of red boots

☐ denim jeans   ☐ a scarf            ☐ a pair of red shoes

**B** Circle the correct answers.

1. Jessica's bag was a birthday present from _____.

   a. Amanda     b. her family     c. her mom

2. Beth thinks that Jessica's bag is beautiful and _____.

   a. retro     b. trendy     c. unusual

3. Beth _____ Amanda a few minutes ago.

   a. ran into     b. got together with     c. called

4. Mark is _____.

   a. Beth's friend     b. Amanda's boyfriend     c. Jessica's brother

5. Amanda thinks Jessica and Beth are _____ her.

   a. copying     b. lying to     c. helping

**C** Who thinks what? Check (✓) the correct answers.

| | Jessica | Beth |
|---|:---:|:---:|
| 1. Who thinks that Amanda must be copying her? | ☐ | ☐ |
| 2. Who thinks that Amanda's behavior is a little strange these days? | ☐ | ☐ |
| 3. Who thinks that they shouldn't judge Amanda too harshly? | ☐ | ☐ |
| 4. Who thinks that Amanda broke up with Mark? | ☐ | ☐ |
| 5. Who thinks that it's not good to criticize someone? | ☐ | ☐ |
| 6. Who thinks that Amanda might be feeling upset or stressed out? | ☐ | ☐ |
| 7. Who thinks that it's always good to forgive? | ☐ | ☐ |

## After you watch

**Group work** Discuss the questions. What do you think?

- Is Amanda copying Beth and Jessica?
- Are Beth and Jessica copying Amanda?
- Is it a coincidence? (No one is copying anyone; they all like the same things.)
- Has someone ever copied your clothes? How did you feel?
- Have you ever copied someone else's clothes, even a famous person's? What did you copy, exactly?
- What kinds of clothes (shirts, shoes, etc.) do you think people often copy? Why?

# A cool accomplishment

## Before you watch

**A** Complete the paragraph with the correct words. Then compare with a partner.

| | | |
|---|---|---|
| accomplished | busy | fashion designer |
| advice | college | studio |

Martina has _____ something pretty cool! She graduated from Alicia's _____ seven years ago, and now she's a _____. Martina is working in her design _____. She is very _____ preparing for a fashion show, but she agreed to talk to Alicia. Alicia hopes Martina can give her some _____, because Alicia would like to become a fashion designer, too.

**B Pair work** Have you ever asked anyone for advice about how to be successful at school, your job, or your future career? What did they say you needed to do? Tell your partner.

## While you watch

**A** Correct the false sentences.

1. Alicia is a high school student.

2. Martina had a lot of training when she started designing.

3. Martina's three words of advice to Alicia are: creativity, flexibility, and talent.

4. Alicia bought the dress she is wearing.

5. Martina thinks Alicia should plan a career in business.

**B** Circle the correct answers.

1. Martina says making her own clothes was a way to _____.

   a. make money      b. be creative      c. stay busy

2. Other students wanted to _____ the dresses and skirts Martina made.

   a. make      b. sell      c. buy

3. Martina describes the samples of fabric as chic, _____, and tacky.

   a. old-fashioned      b. trendy      c. retro

4. Martina had to do her first sketch over _____ times.

   a. three or four      b. five or six      c. ten or twelve

5. Martina says, "You have to be _____ and not afraid to say what you like."

   a. brave      b. patient      c. flexible

**C** Who makes each comment? Write A (Alicia) or M (Martina).

1. "I like the color." _____

2. "I could give this one some thought." _____

3. "That's terrible." _____

4. "We'll talk it over." _____

5. "I don't think we should do that." _____

6. "Your dress is lovely." _____

7. "I think you should give those shoes away." _____

8. "I'm not sure it's the best idea." _____

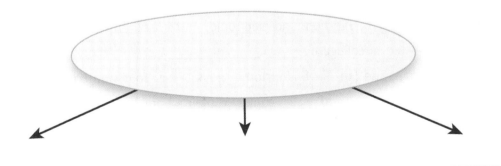

Alicia          Martina

## After you watch

**A Pair work**  How do you think Alicia felt after the interview with Martina? Why?
Do you think Alicia will become a fashion designer? Discuss your ideas.

**B** Write a job you have – or would like to have – in the circle. On the lines, write
three qualities that are necessary for success in that job.

**C Pair work**  Compare and discuss your diagrams in Part B.

*"I would like to become a teacher after I graduate. To be a successful teacher, I think
you need creativity, enthusiasm, and dedication."*

# I haven't made it yet.

## Before you watch

**A** Complete the sentences with the correct words. Then compare with a partner.

| bass | costumes | drums | guitar | lyrics | pets |
|------|----------|-------|--------|--------|------|

1. A _____ is a type of _____. It has four strings and plays very low musical notes.

2. The _____ are the words to a song.

3. Dogs and cats are common _____ in the U.S.A.

4. _____ are clothes people wear in theatrical plays and other performances to look like someone else.

5. _____ are musical instruments that often provide the beat, or rhythm, to a song.

**B  Pair work**  Do you know anyone who is (or was) in a band? What is (or was) the band like? What kind of music do (or did) they play? Tell your partner.

a bass

drums

## While you watch

**A** Circle the correct answers.

1. The Bulldogs are in the studio recording their _____ album.

   a. first     b. second     c. third

2. The band was named after their _____.

   a. pets     b. parents     c. favorite movie

3. The Bull Dogs describe their music as rock, hip-hop, _____.

   a. gospel, and jazz     b. hip-hop, and electronic     c. jazz, and pop

4. The band was started in college by _____.

   a. Chris, David, John, and Ian     b. four other guys     c. four women

5. They've sold _____ copies of their album.

   a. five     b. five hundred     c. five thousand

6. In college, they were given an award for _____.

   a. their record-breaking hit     b. best costume     c. worst-sounding band

7. Chris's song is about someone who _____.

   a. is in love     b. is a successful singer     c. wants to be a star

**B** Check (✓) the correct answers.

| | Chris | David | Ian | John |
|---|---|---|---|---|
| 1. Who hasn't finished his part on the last song yet? | ☐ | ☐ | ☐ | ☐ |
| 2. Who has a cat named Bull? | ☐ | ☐ | ☐ | ☐ |
| 3. Who says they're *not* a well-known band? | ☐ | ☐ | ☐ | ☐ |
| 4. Who says they have a lot of fun? | ☐ | ☐ | ☐ | ☐ |
| 5. Who is shopping? | ☐ | ☐ | ☐ | ☐ |
| 6. Who has "a way with words" and writes the lyrics? | ☐ | ☐ | ☐ | ☐ |

**C** Write T (true) or F (false).

1. John plays the drums. _____

2. Danielle doesn't really think "Dog" is a creative name for Chris's pet. _____

3. The band used to be called the Princesses. _____

4. The Bulldogs have sold many albums. _____

5. Chris finally sang his part of the song well, and the band recorded it. _____

## After you watch

**Group work** Discuss the questions.

- What qualities does a band need to become successful?
- How would you describe the members of the Bulldogs?
- Do you think they have the qualities to become successful? Why or why not?
- Who is your favorite band? Why? Are they successful?

*"I think you need talent to be a successful band. . . ."*

# Travels with Nick and Ben: Fish and chips

## Before you watch

**A** Label the pictures with the correct words. Then compare with a partner.

| fish and chips | ketchup | high tea | lamb kebabs | vegetable curry | vinegar |
|---|---|---|---|---|---|

1. _____

2. _____

3. _____

4. _____

5. _____

6. _____

**B Pair work** Have you ever had the food items in Part A? If so, did you like them? If not, would you like to try them? Why or why not? Tell your partner.

## While you watch

**A** Check (✓) the correct answers. (More than one answer is possible.)

|  | Ben | Nick |
|---|---|---|
| 1. Who likes trying local foods on vacation? | ☐ | ☐ |
| 2. Who likes to eat French fries with ketchup? | ☐ | ☐ |
| 3. Who had Indian food at a restaurant on Brick Lane? | ☐ | ☐ |
| 4. Who was only interested in eating fish and chips? | ☐ | ☐ |
| 5. Who got a stomachache? | ☐ | ☐ |
| 6. Who had high tea? | ☐ | ☐ |
| 7. Who made fish and chips in the microwave? | ☐ | ☐ |

**B** Write T (true) or F (false). Correct the false sentences.

1. When Nick goes on vacation, he loves visiting landmarks. _____

2. Nick and Ben prefer trying local foods when they travel. _____

3. French fries are called mashed potatoes in England. _____

4. People in England eat chips with ketchup. _____

5. Many people in London think of kebabs as British food. _____

**C** Circle the correct answers.

1. Nick says he does not like _____ on vacation.

   a. buying handicrafts     b. trying local food     c. traveling alone

2. Ben does *not* say the trip to London was _____.

   a. awesome     b. boring     c. delicious

3. Nick's lamb kebabs did *not* have any _____.

   a. fruit     b. lettuce     c. spicy sauce

4. Ben did *not* like the fish and chips from the _____.

   a. restaurant on Brick Lane     b. restaurant near Victoria Station     c. fast-food place

5. Ben and Nick do *not* say anything about _____ in the video.

   a. Buckingham Palace     b. Brick Lane     c. Hyde Park

## After you watch

**A Pair work** If you went to London, would you have a trip like Nick and Ben's? How would your trip be the same? How would be it be different? Tell your partner.

**B** Write a city you know or have visited in the circle. On the lines, write two foods that are very good in that city and a good place to eat each one.

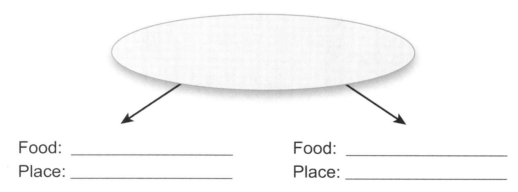

Food: _____     Food: _____

Place: _____     Place: _____

**C Pair work** Compare and discuss your diagrams in Exercise B.

*"You have to try the barbecue chicken in Ubon, Thailand. You can eat it at the night market."*

# Credits

# Four Corners

## Jack C. Richards · David Bohlke
### with Kathryn O'Dell

3

## Workbook

CAMBRIDGE
UNIVERSITY PRESS

# Contents

# Education

## A  *I'm taking six classes.*

**1** Look at the pictures. Write the correct school subjects.

1. c_hemistry___

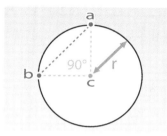

2. g_eometry___

3. w_orld___
   g_eography___

4. m_usic___

5. h_istory___

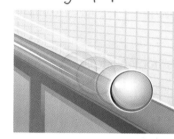

6. p_hysics___

7. b_iology___

8. a_rt___

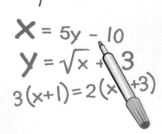

$$x = 5y - 10$$
$$y = \sqrt{x} + 3$$
$$3(x+1) = 2(x+3)$$

9. a_lgebra___

**2** Complete the sentences with the correct school subjects from Exercise 1.

1. Sandra's favorite classes are science classes: _____chemistry_____ ,
   _____ , and _____ .

2. John has two math classes: _____ and _____ .

3. Leo's favorite classes are in the arts: _____ and _____ .

4. Mi-hee is taking two social studies classes: _____
   and _____ .

**3** Check (✓) the correct sentences. Rewrite the incorrect sentences with the correct forms of the verbs. Use the simple present or the present continuous.

1. ☐ Dina reads her email right now.

   *Dina is reading her email right now.*

2. ☐ Tim is knowing a lot about biology.

   _____

3. ☐ Mateo and Alicia are taking a dance class together.

   _____

4. ☐ I'm wanting to study in Australia in the summer.

   _____

5. ☐ What is the word "engineer" meaning?

   _____

6. ☐ Do you go to class right now?

   _____

7. ☐ They don't remember the answers for the history test.

   _____

8. ☐ This homework isn't seeming difficult.

   _____

**4** Look at the schedule. Complete the sentences with the correct forms of *work*. Use the simple present or the present continuous.

| Officemart Summer Schedule | | | |
|---|---|---|---|
| **Name** | **Fridays** | **Saturdays** | **Sundays** |
| **Marcia** | 2:00 p.m. – 8:00 p.m. | 9:00 a.m. – 3:00 p.m. | ✗ |
| **Leo** | 10:00 a.m. – 5:00 p.m. | 9:00 a.m. – 5:00 p.m. | 12:00 p.m. – 4:00 p.m. |
| **Paul** | ✗ | 2:00 p.m. – 7:30 p.m. | ✗ |

1. Marcia and Leo _____work_____ on Fridays and Saturdays.

2. It's Sunday, and Marcia and Paul _____ .

3. It's 11:00 a.m. on Friday. Leo _____ .

4. It's 3:30 p.m. on Saturday. Leo and Paul _____ right now.

5. Leo _____ on Sunday afternoons.

6. Paul _____ on Fridays.

7. It's 6:00 p.m. on Friday. Leo _____ right now.

8. Marcia and Leo ____don't work____ on Saturday evenings.

**5** Complete the text messages with the correct forms of the verbs in parentheses.
Use the simple present or the present continuous.

> **J.Monk78:** Hi, Shelly. What _are you doing_ (do) right now?
> 1
> **SLP1980:** Hey, Jin-sung. I 'm writing (write) to you! 😊
> 2
> **J.Monk78:** Very funny! _are_ you _studying_ (study) for the chemistry test?
> 3                    8
> **SLP1980:** Yes, I am. Linda and I _are reading_ (read) the teacher's notes online.
> 4
> **J.Monk78:** I _don't understan_ (not / understand) those notes at all.
> 5
> **SLP1980:** _Do_ you _want_ (want) some help?
> 6          6
> **J.Monk78:** Yes, please!

> **Emmie:** Hey, Kate. What classes _do_ you _have_ (have) on Fridays?
> 7                7
> **KateM:** I _have_ (have) algebra in the mornings and geometry in the afternoons.
> 8
> **Emmie:** What time _is_ (be) your geometry class?
> 9
> **KateM:** At 2:00. Wait . . . my sister 's calling (call) me . . .
> 10
> **KateM:** OK. I'm back. My sister _is shoping_ (shop) right now. Let's go to the mall.
> 11
> **Emmie:** OK, but I 'm working (work) right now. How about at 11:30?
> 12
> **KateM:** Great! Let's meet in front of Los Zapatos Shoe Store.

**6** Answer the questions with your own information. Write complete sentences.

*Example:* _I'm taking English, physics, and music._

1. What classes are you taking? _I'm taking_
2. When do you study? _I study at C.I.U_
3. How often do you have English classes? _____
4. Where do you usually do your homework? _I usually do home at_
5. What school subjects do you like? _____
6. What school subjects do you hate? _____
7. What are you doing right now? _____
8. Where are you sitting? _I'm sitting at_

## B You're not allowed to . . .

**1** Complete the chart with the sentences from the box.

> ✓ You can't use your cell phone in the office.  ○ You need to have lunch at that time.
> ○ You have to come to work by 9:00.  ρ You're not permitted to eat in your office.
> ○ You must always wear a suit to work.  ꝗ You're not allowed to write emails to friends.

| Prohibition | Obligation |
|---|---|
| *You can't use your cell phone in the office.* | |
| You're not permitted to eat | |
| | |

**2** Complete the conversation with the correct sentences from the box in Exercise 1.

**Ms. Jones:** Welcome to Akron Accounting. This is your new office. Do you have any questions?

**Mr. Okada:** Yes. Can I make personal phone calls at work?

**Ms. Jones:** No, I'm sorry. *You can't use your cell phone in the office.*
1
You can make personal calls at lunch.

**Mr. Okada:** OK. What time is lunch?

**Ms. Jones:** It's from 1:00 to 2:00. you need to have lnch
2 .

**Mr. Okada:** Can I have lunch at my desk?

**Ms. Jones:** No, I'm sorry. _____
3 .
You can have lunch in our café, or you can go out to eat. There are a lot of good restaurants on Pine Street.

**Mr. Okada:** OK. Thanks. Is there anything else I need to know?

**Ms. Jones:** Yes. you must always
4 .
We try to dress for business here.

**Mr. Okada:** No problem.

# C  *My behavior*

**1** Look at the pictures. Complete the puzzle with the feelings and emotions you see. What's the mystery word?

 1.
 2.
 3.

```
        ¹T  H  I  R  S  T  Y
         2
     3
     4
     5
   ⁶S  l  e  e  p  y
```

 4.
 5.
 6.

**2** Complete the sentences with the correct words from the box.

| 2 | 4 | 5 | 3 |
|---|---|---|---|
| hungry | jealous | scared | ✓thirsty | upset |

1. Miguel wants some water. He's _____ *thirsty* _____ .

2. Carla didn't eat lunch today, and now she's very _____ .

3. John's team didn't win their soccer game. He's extremely _____ about it.

4. Paula is an actress. Mariana wants to be an actress, but right now she's a waitress. She's _____ of Paula.

5. When Peggy came home last night, her front door was open. She was _____ and called the police.

**3** Complete the conversation with *if* and the correct words from the box.

| I have a job interview | I'm prepared | there's a website |
| I'm nervous | she's home | ✓you're nervous |

**Carmen:** Hey, Danielle. What do you do

_if you're nervous_ ?

**Danielle:** ___I'm nervous___ about

something, I try not to think about it.

**Carmen:** Well, I have a job interview tomorrow, and

I have to think about it!

**Danielle:** Hmm . . . ___I have a job interview___ ,

I usually prepare before I go. It really helps.

**Carmen:** How do you prepare?

**Danielle:** _____ , I read about the place online.

**Carmen:** That's a good idea.

**Danielle:** Yes. I also practice the interview with my sister _____ .

**Carmen:** I can try that with my brother. What about during the interview?

**Danielle:** _____ , I usually don't get nervous. Good luck!

**4** Combine the sentences into one. Use *when*. Write it in two ways.

1. Emma has a test. → She studies a lot.

   _When Emma has a test, she studies a lot._

   _Emma studies a lot when she has a test._

2. I get bad news. → I get upset.

   When I get bad news, I get upset

   I get upset when I get bad news

3. Jordan gets up early in the morning. → He is sleepy.

   When Jordan gets up early in the

   _____

4. My sister is busy. → She doesn't call me.

   When

   _____

5. Lorena and Jessie have a soccer game. → They get nervous.

   _____

   _____

**5** Write sentences in the zero conditional. Use the words in the chart.

| Condition | Main clause | If / When |
|---|---|---|
| 1. Tonya's sister / go to a party | Tonya / always / get jealous | when |
| 2. Greg / be lonely | he / often / call a friend | when |
| 3. I / get scared | I / always / call my brother | if |
| 4. Kyle and Rick / be busy | they / sometimes / not eat | if |
| 5. Leticia / get angry | she / usually / not say anything | when |
| 6. I / be late for work | I / usually / say I'm sorry | if |

1.  *When Tonya's sister goes to a party, Tonya always gets jealous.*

2.  _____

3.  _____

4.  _____

5.  _____

6.  _____

**6** Write questions with the words in parentheses. Use *What* and the zero conditional.

1. (Charlie / do / if / be sleepy)     *What does Charlie do if he's sleepy?*

2. (you / do / when / get upset)     What do you do when you get upsent

3. (Frank and Julie / do / if / get angry)     What Frank and Julie do

4. (you / do / if / be hungry) _____

5. (you and your friends / do / when / be thirsty) _____

6. (Annette / do / when / feel nervous) _____

**7** Answer the questions with your own information. Write complete sentences with the zero conditional.

*Example:* *When I'm nervous about a test, I study really hard.*

1. What do you do when you're nervous about a test? _____

2. What do you do if you're sleepy in class? _____

3. How do you feel when you're too busy? _____

4. What do you do when you're lonely?     When I lonely , I always call to my friend

5. What do you drink if you're thirsty?     When I thirsty , I always drink water

6. What do you say when you're angry with a friend? _____

# D Alternative education

**1** Read the article. Answer the questions.

1. Who works for a magazine? _____Raul Gomez_____

2. Who works for an engineer? _____

## Work-Study Programs in High School

Many high schools in the United States have work-study programs. In their last year of high school, some students have a job for part of the day as one of their "classes." Some of these students make money and some don't, but all of them learn important things about having a job and being a good worker. Many people think that when students learn outside of the classroom in a real job, they prepare for life after high school. Work-study programs can really help students get a job or get into college.

There are many types of work-study programs. Most of the students work in offices, but not all of them do. Some students fix cars, and others work outside with environmental engineers. Big businesses, like computer companies and banks, often work with high schools to create work-study opportunities for students as well.

Raul Gomez usually goes to school from 9:00 a.m. to 4:00 p.m., but this year he works for a magazine from 7:00 a.m. to 11:00 a.m. He says, "I learn important things in my work-study program. I must be at work on time. And if I miss a day, they don't pay me!" At work, he reads stories and fixes spelling and grammar mistakes. He says, "At work, I use what I learn in my English class. And now I think that someday, I might want to write for a magazine or a newspaper."

*Raul Gomez at his work-study job*

Annie Miller works for an engineer in her work-study program. They design and help make bridges, roads, and buildings. She says, "It's great! I love learning math in school, but at work, I use algebra and geometry in the real world!"

Not all high schools offer work-study programs. But most of the schools that have them think they are a big success.

**2** Read the text again. Then write T (true), F (false), or NI (no information).

1. Work-study programs started in the United States. _NI_

2. Some students get money in work-study programs. _T_

3. Work-study programs rarely help students start their careers or further their education. _F_

4. Raul works at his job in the morning. _T_

5. Annie likes science classes. _T_

6. Not many of the work-study programs are a success. _NI_

# Personal stories

## A *What were you doing?*

**1** Put the letters in the correct order to make adverbs. Complete the sentences.

(y u o u t r n l f t a n e)

1. I was having a great day on Tuesday. Then, _____**unfortunately**_____ , I left my bag at a restaurant.

(l l i c y u k)

2. _____luckily_____ , someone found it.

(l y f e t o a n u t r)

3. And _____fortunately_____ , my cell phone was in the bag.

(l s y r u i n s g i p r)

4. _____surprisingly_____ , the person who found it called my home phone.

(a z n i g a y m l)

5. _____Amazingly_____ , the person was David, a boy I went to school with when I was six! We made plans to meet at a café.

(y e s t a r g l n)

6. _____strangely_____ , David looked the same! We ate lunch and talked a lot.

(s n u e y d d l)

7. Then David got a phone call, and he left the café _____Suddenly_____ .

(s a y l d)

8. _____sadly_____ , I never saw him again.

**2** What were they doing when the lights went out? Write sentences with the past continuous forms of the verbs.

1. (Mi-na / read / a book)

    _Mi-na was reading a book._

2. (Martin / wash / the dishes)

    Martin was washing the dishes.

3. (Brad and Kate / watch / TV)

    Brad and Kate were watching TV.

4. (I / talk / to Tom / on the phone)

    I was talking to Tom on the phone.

5. (Laura / play / video games)

    Laura was playing video games.

6. (Mr. and Mrs. Jones / eat / dinner)

    Mr. and Mrs Jones were eating dinner.

**3** Complete the sentences with *when* and the words in parentheses. Use the simple past forms of the verbs.

1. (their friends / arrive)

    Jane and Paul were making dinner on Friday _when their friends arrived_ .

2. (his brother / call)

    Martin was driving to the store when his brother called .

3. (the electricity / go off)

    What were you doing yesterday when the electricity went off ?

4. (Jill / send me / a text message)

    when Jill sent me a text message , I was talking to Tom on my cell phone.

5. (the ambulance / come)

    What were they doing when the ambulance came ?

6. (the storm / begin)

    When the storm began , I was walking home from work.

**4** Complete the conversation with the correct forms of the simple past or the past continuous of the verbs in parentheses.

**Rick:** Hi, Lisa. What _____*were*_____ you _____*doing*_____ (do)
1
when the electricity _____*went*_____ (go) off?
2

**Lisa:** Unfortunately, I _____*working*_____ (work)
3
on the computer! I couldn't finish my work. What
_____*were*_____ you _____*doing*_____ (do)?
4          4

**Rick:** Oh, I _____*was sleeping*_____ (sleep) when
5
everything _____*went*_____ (go) dark.
6
I didn't even know what happened.

**Lisa:** Really? It was only 7:30 p.m.

**Rick:** Well, I _____*was taking*_____ (take) a nap in the living room. I think I slept
7
for a long time. When I _____*woke*_____ (wake) up, it was really dark.
8
So I just went to bed. While everyone _____*was having*_____ (have) problems,
9
I _____*slept*_____ (sleep)!
10
*was sleeping*

**5** Complete the story with the verbs in the box. Use the past continuous or the simple past.

| ✓cook | go | make | stand | turn |
|-------|-----|------|-------|------|
| fall | hear | see | try | |

Terry and Wendy _____*were cooking*_____ in the kitchen when the electricity suddenly
1
_____*went*_____ off. Unfortunately, while Terry _____*was trying*_____ to find
2                                                 3
a light, he _____*fell*_____ down. He _____*was hearing*_____ a loud noise.
4                        5
When Wendy _____*heard*_____ the noise, she _____*was standing*_____ by the
6                            7
window. While she _____*was turning*_____ around, she _____*saw*_____
8                           9
something move outside the window. What was it?

**6** Answer the questions with your own information. Write complete sentences.

*Example:* *I took biology, history of China, and English last year.*

1. What classes did you take last year?   I took Law last year

2. What were you saying the last time you spoke?   I said, "Good bye."

3. Where did you eat breakfast today?   I ate breakfast at home

4. What did you do last night?   I did homework.

5. What were you doing at 6:00 a.m. today?   I watched a movie

6. What were you doing when class started?   I was studying when class started

## B Guess what!

**1** Write A (announcing news) or C (closing a conversation).

1. Listen, I've got to run. __C__
2. You'll never guess what happened! __A__
3. Sorry, I have to go. __C__

4. Hey, I need to get going. __C__
5. Guess what! __A__
6. Did you hear what happened? __C__

**2** Complete the conversations with the sentences from Exercise 1. Sometimes more than one answer is possible. Use each sentence once.

A. **Jim:** Hello, Pat. _Did you hear what_ 1 _happened?_

    **Pat:** No, I didn't.

    **Jim:** There was an accident on Main Street.

    **Pat:** That's terrible!

    **Jim:** Yes, it is. Fortunately, everyone is OK. _Sorry, I have to go_ 2 .

    **Pat:** OK. Bye.

a car accident

B. **Annie:** Hey, Tonya! _you'll never guess what happened_ 1 !

    **Tonya:** What?

    **Annie:** Martin got a promotion, and he's moving to Canada.

    **Tonya:** That's great.

    **Annie:** I know. _Listen, I've got to run_ 2 . I have a meeting in a few minutes.

    **Tonya:** No problem. Call me later!

C. **Beth:** Hi, Dan. _Guess what_ 1 !

    **Dan:** What?

    **Beth:** Our soccer team won the competition.

    **Dan:** That's fantastic! _Hey, I need to get going_ 2 . I have class now. But congratulations!

    **Beth:** That's OK. Thanks. See you tomorrow.

# C | I was really frightened!

**1** Put the letters in the correct order to make verbs that describe reactions.

1. i e t e c x    **excite** = ตื่นเต้น ✓
2. d u s s g i t    disgust = don't like
3. s o u n f c e    Confuse ✓
4. i t t n r s e e    Interest

5. g e t h f i r n    frighten = scare
6. a u e s m    amuse = enjoy
7. e c n l a g h l e    challenge = ท้าทาย
8. s m a e s a r b r    embarrass = อับอาย

**2** Complete the conversations with the correct forms of the verbs in Exercise 1.
Use the simple present.

1. **Nancy:** Hey, Karl. Did you do the homework for math class?

   **Karl:** No, I didn't. Geometry _____ **confuses** _____ me. I don't understand it.

2. **Po:** Jill. Try this sushi.

   **Jill:** No, thanks. Fish _____ disgust _____ me! I hate it!

3. **Larry:** My brother talks too loudly. He really _____ excite _____ me when he's with my friends.

   **David:** It's not so bad. He's very friendly.

4. **Tom:** What _____ you, Seth?

   **Seth:** Horror movies! I get really scared when I watch them.

5. **Ted:** Do you like animated movies?

   **Lea:** Yes, they usually _____ me. I think they're funny.

6. **Ahmet:** Chemistry _____ me, but I think physics is boring.

   **Andrea:** Really? I think physics is interesting.

7. **Miho:** What do you want to do this weekend? Anything exciting?

   **Karen:** Well, the idea of going to Chicago for the weekend _____ me!

8. **Eva:** You're pretty good at sports, Tim. What kind of sport _____ you?

   **Tim:** Golf, I guess. It's a lot more difficult than it seems.

**3** Complete the sentences with the present participles (-*ing*) or past participles (-*ed*) of the verbs in parentheses.

1. Amusement parks are _____*exciting*_____ (excite).

2. Can you help me? This physics problem is _____confusing_____ (confuse).

3. I want a new job because my work is too easy. I don't feel
   _____Challenged_____ (challenge).

4. I don't think your problem is _____embrrassing_____ (embarrass). A lot of people
   talk fast when they're nervous.

5. I'm _____frightening_____ (frighten) by our neighbor's dog! It's big and
   extremely loud.

6. I'm not _____interesting_____ (interest) in math, but I love science.

7. I don't think video games are _____amusing_____ (amuse), but many
   teenagers like them.

8. My brother is _____disgusting_____ (disgust) by reality shows, but I'd like
   to be on one!

**4** Circle the correct words to complete the conversation.

**Paul:** Hi, Wendy. Have you ever read *Life of Pi*? You
know . . . that story about a boy who is on the
ocean in a boat with a tiger.

**Wendy:** Yes, I have. I liked it, but I thought some parts
with the tiger were **disgusted** / **disgusting**.
1

**Paul:** Really? I thought it was **frightened** / **frightening**,
2
but I was **excited** / **exciting** when I read it.
3

**Wendy:** Well, yes, it was **excited** / **exciting**. But after a
4
while, I think Pi was probably **bored** / **boring** on
5
that boat. He was on it for 227 days!

**Paul:** Oh, I don't think so. I bet life on that boat wasn't
**bored** / **boring** at all! I loved how he became friends with the tiger. That was
6
really **interested** / **interesting**.
7

**Wendy:** Yeah. That part was **amused** / **amusing**, I guess, but it didn't seem like real life.
8

**Paul:** Maybe not, but I think the story shows that sometimes life is **challenged** / **challenging**.
9

**Wendy:** Yeah, you're right. And I guess the end was **surprised** / **surprising**.
10

**Paul:** Um, well . . . now I'm **embarrassed** / **embarrassing**. To be <u>honest</u>, I didn't
11
finish the book!

**14** **Unit 2** Lesson C

**5** Read Ron's online survey. Then complete the sentences about Ron's opinions.

# We want to hear from you!

**1** What kind of music are you interested in?

☑ rock  ☐ jazz  ☐ blues  ☑ techno

**2** What do you think of concerts?

☑ exciting  ☐ boring  ☑ amusing

**3** Who are you embarrassed by?

☐ your parents  ☑ your brothers and sisters  ☐ your friends

**4** What do think about technology?

☑ confusing  ☑ challenging  ☐ easy

**5** What kinds of foods do you think are disgusting?

☑ fish  ☐ meat  ☐ fruit  ☑ vegetables

1. Ron is _____*interested*_____ in _*rock and techno music*_____.
2. He thinks _____*concerts*_____ are __amusing_____.
3. He is ___embarrassing_____ by __his brothers and sisters_____.
4. He thinks ___technology_____ is __challenging_____.
5. He thinks ____vegetables_____ are ___disgusting_____.

**6** Write sentences about your opinions with a participial adjective from the box.

Example: _I think horror movies are amusing._ or _I'm frightened by horror movies._

| amused / amusing | disgusted / disgusting | frightened / frightening |
|---|---|---|
| bored / boring | embarrassed / embarrassing | interested / interesting |
| challenged / challenging | excited / exciting | surprised / surprising |
| confused / confusing | | |

1. horror movies: _____

2. history classes: _____

3. the news: _____

4. reading books: _____

5. reality shows: _____

6. math: _____

# D How embarrassing!

**1** Read the email. Then check (✓) the correct adjectives.

1. The hotel is _____ .
☐ interesting ☐ dirty ☐ embarrassing

2. The Japanese street names are _____ .
☐ amusing ☐ challenging ☐ disgusting

3. Angela did two things that were _____ .
☐ traditional ☐ interesting ☐ embarrassing

Hi George,

I'm having an amazing time in Japan! I'm in Kyoto visiting a lot of interesting places. I'm staying in a *ryokan*. It's a traditional Japanese hotel. It's really interesting. The hotel is part of a man and woman's home. Their names are Mr. and Mrs. Ito. I have breakfast by myself at the *ryokan*, and I eat lunch in the city, but I have dinner with the family in their part of the house. And their daughter brings me tea in the evening before I go to bed! (I feel like a very important person!)

I'm learning a lot about life in Japan, but I'm also doing some embarrassing things by mistake! In the *ryokan*, you take off your shoes before you go in the house so that the floor doesn't get dirty. You leave your shoes outside the door. On my first day, I took off my shoes, but I did it in my bedroom. I walked through the house first, and I got the floor dirty. How embarrassing! I hope Mr. and Mrs. Ito weren't disgusted with me. But they are nice and very friendly, and now I remember to take off my shoes before I come in the house.

I was also embarrassed while I was traveling around the city yesterday. I don't speak Japanese, but I speak Spanish. When I asked for directions, no one understood me! I was pronouncing the street names like Spanish words. They're very difficult to say! But it's easy to get around in Kyoto. The buses and trains are extremely modern and clean. Tomorrow I'm going to an art museum. I'm going to practice pronouncing the museum name and the street name in Japanese tonight!

It's really fun here. I don't want to go back home!

Your friend,

Angela

**2** Read the text again. Then answer the questions. Write complete sentences.

1. Where is Angela staying in Kyoto? _____

2. Who gives Angela tea? _____

3. What two embarrassing things did Angela do? _____

4. What is Angela's opinion of the buses and trains? _____

5. What is Angela doing tomorrow? _____

# Style and fashion

## A Fashion trends

**1** Look at the pictures. Complete the puzzle with fashion words.

**Across**

4.

5.

7.

8.

**Down**

1.

2.

3.

6.

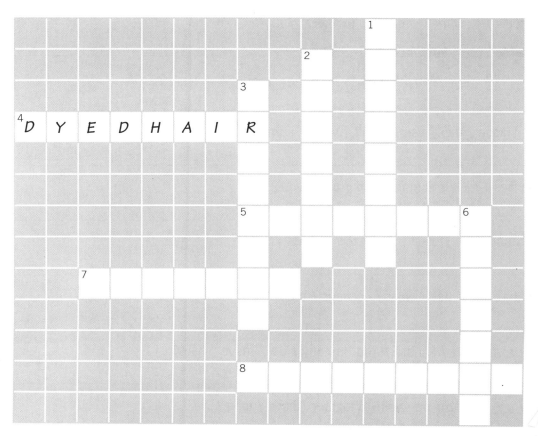

4. D Y E D H A I R

**2** Cross out the fashion word that doesn't belong in each list.

1. **Clothing:**     ~~a bracelet~~     a leather jacket     a uniform

2. **Hairstyles:**     a ponytail     dyed hair     sandals

3. **Jewelry:**     earrings     a bracelet     glasses

4. **Eyewear:**     contact lenses     earrings     glasses

5. **Shoes:**     sandals     a uniform     high heels

**3** Put the words in the correct order to make sentences.

1. high heels / to work / used / I / to / wear / .

   _I used to wear high heels to work._

2. wear / used / to / wig / My / mother / a / .

   My mother used to wear a wig

3. every / Jason / day / use / didn't / wear / suits / to / .

   _____

4. to / lenses / have / contact / Did / use / you / ?

   _____

5. on vacation / We / used / buy / to / T-shirts / .

   _____

6. to / Katia / Did / use / wear / earrings / big / ?

   _____

7. dyed / to / didn't / Sandra / and Bethany / use / have / hair / .

   _____

8. used / a / My / to / ponytail / daughter / have / long / .

   _____

**4** Circle the correct words to complete each conversation.

1. **A:** Did you _____ to have dyed hair?

   **B:** No, I _____ , but I do now.

   a. use, did    (b.) use, didn't    c. used, did    d. used, didn't

2. **A:** Did Leo _____ to wear a bracelet?

   **B:** Yes, he _____ ! But now he doesn't wear any jewelry.

   a. used, did    b. used, didn't    c. use, did    d. use, didn't

3. **A:** Where _____ Kelly and Margie use to shop?

   **B:** They _____ to shop at the mall.

   a. didn't, use    b. didn't, used    c. did, use    d. did, used

4. **A:** What kinds of clothes did Jake _____ to wear?

   **B:** He _____ to wear T-shirts and baggy jeans.

   a. use, use    b. used, use    c. use, used    d. used, used

5. **A:** Did you _____ to wear glasses?

   **B:** Yes. I didn't _____ to wear contact lenses.

   a. use, use    b. used, use    c. use, used    d. used, used

**5** Look at Emma's information. Then write sentences with the words in parentheses.
Use *used to* or *didn't use to*.

## What did you use to wear?

|  | 1970s | 1980s | 1990s | 2000s |
|---|---|---|---|---|
| **baggy jeans** | ✓ | ✗ | ✗ | ✓ |
| **tight jeans** | ✗ | ✓ | ✓ | ✓ |
| **bright T-shirts** | ✓ | ✓ | ✗ | ✗ |
| **high heels** | ✗ | ✗ | ✓ | ✓ |
| **big earrings** | ✓ | ✓ | ✓ | ✗ |

1. (bright T-shirts / the 1970s)   _Emma used to wear bright T-shirts in the 1970s._

2. (high heels / the 1970s)   _She didn't_ _____

3. (baggy jeans / the 1980s)   _____

4. (tight jeans / the 1980s)   _____

5. (big earrings / the 1990s)   _____

6. (big earrings / the 2000s)   _____

# B Does this come in . . . ?

**1** Write the conversation in the correct order.

| | |
|---|---|
| Can I help you? | Oh, thanks! Um, do you have this in brown? |
| ✓ Excuse me. | They're here, behind you. |
| No, I'm sorry. It only comes in black. | Yes. Where can I find the leather jackets? |

Renaldo: _Excuse me._

Clerk: _____

Renaldo: _____

Clerk: _____

Renaldo: _____

Clerk: _____

**2** Write a conversation for each picture with the words in the box and your own ideas. Use the conversation in Exercise 1 as a model.

| | |
|---|---|
| Can I get this in . . . ? | Does this come in . . . ? |
| Could you tell me where the . . . are? | Where are the . . . ? |

1. **Debbie:** Excuse me.

   **Clerk:** _____ ?

   **Debbie:** Yes. _____ ?

   **Clerk:** _____ .

   **Debbie:** Oh, thanks! _____ in red?

   **Clerk:** No, I'm sorry. _____ .

2. **Ichiro:** _____ .

   **Clerk:** _____ ?

   **Ichiro:** Yes. _____ ?

   **Clerk:** _____ .

   **Ichiro:** Oh, thanks! _____ in blue?

   **Clerk:** Yes. _____ .

**1** Read about the types of clothes. Then write the fashion word that matches each type.

1. clothes that people like right now but might not like next year: <u>t  r  e  n  d  y</u>

2. clothes that are the style that people want or like: __ __ __ __ __ __ __ __ __ __ __

3. clothes that used to be what people liked: __ __ __ - __ __ __ __ __ __ __ __ __ __

4. new clothes that look like old styles (in a good way): __ __ __ __ __

5. clothes that look expensive and exciting (in a good way): __ __ __ __ __ __ __ __ __

6. usually cheap clothes of bad quality or bad style: __ __ __ __ __

7. clothes that look very strange: __ __ __ __ __

8. clothes that attract a lot of attention because they're bright: __ __ __ __ __ __

**2** Look at the pictures. Complete the sentences with your own opinions. Use words from the box. Not all the words will be used.

| | | | |
|---|---|---|---|
| fashionable | glamorous | retro | trendy |
| flashy | old-fashioned | tacky | weird |

*Example:* <u>*Her dress is fashionable.*</u>  *or*  <u>*Her dress is flashy.*</u>

1. Her dress is _____ .

2. Her shoes are _____ .

3. Her sunglasses are _____ .

4. His shirt is _____ .

5. His pants are _____ .

6. His hat is _____ .

**3** Rewrite the sentences. Replace *that* with *which* or *who*.

1. I don't like clothes that are trendy.

   *I don't like clothes which are trendy.*

2. Tonya is the kind of person that buys things for other people.

   _____

3. I like the kind of store that has a lot of sales.

   _____

4. Is Jason someone that follows fashion trends?

   _____

5. We prefer salesclerks that give us their opinions.

   _____

6. Carla prefers shoes that are not high heels.

   _____

7. Is there a store in the mall that sells sunglasses?

   _____

8. Greg and Roberto are people that always wear retro clothes.

   _____

**4** Complete the conversation with *which* or *who*.

**Emily:** Mom, what is a fashion designer?

**Mom:** It's a person _____*who*_____ makes new
1
clothing styles.

**Emily:** And what is a tailor shop?

**Mom:** It's a store _____ has tailors.
2

**Emily:** OK . . . but what's a tailor?

**Mom:** Well, a tailor is a person _____
3
makes or fixes clothes.

**Emily:** Really? OK. And what does a stylist do?

**Mom:** That's a person _____ helps actors look good.
4

**Emily:** Thanks, Mom!

**Mom:** Why are you asking me all these questions?

**Emily:** I found this magazine _____ is about fashion. I'm taking a quiz in it.
5

**Mom:** You mean, *I'm* taking a quiz in it!

**5** Read the question. Then complete the response with *who*, *that*, or *which* and the correct forms of the verbs and other words in parentheses.

1. **A:** *Who is Ms. Young?*

   **B:** She is the chemistry teacher  <u>who wears</u>

   <u>flashy clothes</u> . (wear / flashy clothes)

2. **A:** Does Marvin buy all types of clothes?

   **B:** No, he doesn't. He usually buys clothes

   _____ .

   (be / fashionable)

3. **A:** What kind of malls do you like?

   **B:** I like malls _____ .

   (have / a lot of stores with trendy clothes)

4. **A:** Who is Jennifer X?

   **B:** She's a singer _____ .

   (wear / weird clothes at her concerts)

5. **A:** Who is Jacques?

   **B:** He's that famous designer _____ .

   (make / retro clothing)

6. **A:** What is *Viv?*

   **B:** It's a website _____ .

   (sell / old-fashioned jewelry)

**6** Complete the sentences with your own information.

*Example:* <u>*Black is a color that I wear a lot.*</u>

1. _____ is a color that I wear a lot.

2. _____ is a person who has a style that I really like.

3. _____ is a magazine or website that people read for information about fashion.

4. _____ is a clothing style that is trendy right now.

5. _____ is a place that sells clothes that I like to wear.

6. _____ is someone who wears clothes that are fashionable.

**1** **Read the article. Then match the two parts of each sentence.**

1. Coco Chanel was a woman _____        a. who made the first jeans.

2. Levi Strauss was the man _____        b. who wrote about fashion.

3. Richard Blackwell was a person _____        c. who designed hats and clothing for women.

# People Who Changed Fashion

Coco Chanel was a French fashion designer who changed fashion for women. She started making glamorous hats in her apartment. Then a famous actress wore Chanel's hats in a play, and suddenly many women wanted her hats. So Chanel started a business and opened a hat store in 1913. In the early 1900s, women used to wear uncomfortable skirts, but Chanel wanted to be comfortable. She often wore men's pants, jackets, and ties. She started making comfortable and fashionable clothing for women. She made pants and women's suits that were comfortable and trendy, and she began selling them in her store. By 1919, she opened a larger store and was famous in France and other parts of the world. She changed women's clothing, and she inspired other designers.

Levi Strauss had a clothing store in California in the 1870s. His store sold work clothes for men. At that time, working men wore pants that ripped or tore a lot. Strauss worked together with the tailor Jacob Davis to make better pants that were strong and that a man could wear for a long time. They made the pants with a heavy cloth called denim. At that time, there was another heavy cloth called jean. People started to call the denim pants *jeans*. Jeans used to be for work, but they became trendy in the 1950s when teenagers started wearing them. Now many people wear them, even when they aren't working.

Richard Blackwell was an American designer who wrote about fashion. In 1960, he wrote a "Ten Worst-Dressed Women" list in a magazine. People didn't use to talk badly about famous people's clothes, but Blackwell wrote about actresses who wore clothes that he thought were ugly or weird. Today, there are many TV shows with people who give opinions about the clothes that actors and actresses are wearing these days. There are also many websites that have "Worst-Dressed" lists about celebrities.

**2** **Read the article again. Answer the questions. Write complete sentences.**

1. What was the first item of clothing Coco Chanel made?   *She made hats.* _____

2. Why did Chanel sometimes wear men's clothing?   _____

3. Why did Levi Strauss make pants from denim?   _____

4. Who made jeans trendy?   _____

5. Who did Richard Blackwell write about?   _____

# Interesting lives

## A  *Have you ever been on TV?*

**1** Look at the pictures. Check (✓) the correct sentence for each picture.

1. ✓ I often get seasick.
   ☐ I often lose my phone.
   ☐ I often win an award.

2. ☐ I moved to a new city last week.
   ✓ I was on TV last week.
   ☐ I acted in a play last week.

3. ✓ I met a famous person in New York.
   ☐ I broke my arm in New York.
   ☐ I was on TV in New York.

4. ☐ I got seasick at work.
   ☐ I broke my arm at work.
   ✓ I won an award at work.

5. ✓ I used to act in plays.
   ☐ I used to be on TV.
   ☐ I used to win awards.

6. ☐ We're meeting a famous person.
   ☐ We're acting in a play.
   ✓ We're moving to a new city.

**2** Complete the chart. Write the past participles. Then write R (regular) or I (irregular).

| Base Form | Past Participle | Regular or Irregular | | Base Form | Past Participle | Regular or Irregular |
|---|---|---|---|---|---|---|
| 1. lose | lost | | | 9. try | | |
| 2. be | been | | | 10. break | broken | |
| 3. act | acted | | | 11. happen | | |
| 4. chat | chated | | | 12. do | done | |
| 5. see | see | | | 13. meet | met | |
| 6. win | won | | | 14. move | | |
| 7. have | had | | | 15. eat | eaten | |
| 8. go | gone | | | 16. get | gotten | |

**3** Complete the conversation with the present perfect forms of the verbs in parentheses. For answers to questions, use short answers.

Joe: Hey, Marta. _____Have_____ you ever
1
_____been_____ (be) on TV?
1

Marta: Yes, I _____have_____ . I was interviewed
2
about the Japanese language school I went to
in Tokyo. Hey, _____have_____ you ever
3
_____visited_____ (visit) Japan?
3

Joe: No, I _____have not_____ .
4

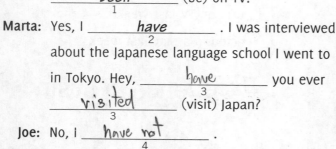

Marta: It's great. I studied there for a month.

Joe: What did you like the best?

Marta: The food! _____Have_____ you ever _____ (try) sushi?
5                                  5

Joe: Yes, I _____have_____ . I like Japanese food. I also like Korean
6
food. _____Have_____ you ever _____try_____ (try) Korean food?
7                          7

Marta: Yes. I _____have_____ . A few times. _____Have_____ you ever
8                                    9
_____gone_____ (go) to South Korea?
9

Joe: No, I _____haven't_____ . But my sister _____was_____ (be) there. She went to Seoul.
10                                11

Marta: I hear they have good food at the markets in Seoul. _____Has_____ she ever
12
_____eaten_____ (eat) at a night market?
12

Joe: Yes, she _____has_____ . She _____has_____ (have) food at
13                      14
night markets lots of times.

Marta: That's cool!

**4** Look at the chart. Then write questions and short answers with the words in parentheses. Use the present perfect.

| | play table tennis | do karate | break a bone | act in a play | be on TV | chat online |
|---|---|---|---|---|---|---|
| Emily | ✓ | | | ✓ | | ✓ |
| Ken | | ✓ | ✓ | | | ✓ |
| Sandra | | ✓ | | ✓ | | ✓ |
| Marcos | | ✓ | | ✓ | ✓ | ✓ |
| Julia | ✓ | | | ✓ | | |

**What have you done?**

1. (Emily / break a bone)

   Question: _Has Emily ever broken a bone_ ?  Answer: _No, she hasn't_ .

2. (Emily and Ken / be on TV)

   Q: _Have Emily and ken ever been on TV_ ?  A: _No, They haven't_ .

3. (Ken / play table tennis)

   Q: _Hes ken ever played table tennis_ ?  A: _No, he hasn't_ .

4. (Sandra / do karate)

   Q: _Has Sandra every done karate_ ?  A: _Yes, she has_ .

5. (Marcos / chat online)

   Q: _Has Marcos every chateq online_ ?  A: _Yes, she has_ .

6. (Marcos and Julia / act in a play)

   Q: _Have Marcos amd Julia acted in a play_ ?  A: _Yes, They have_ .

**5** Look at the chart in Exercise 4. Write sentences about what you have and haven't done. Use *never* for negative sentences.

   Example:  _I've played table tennis lots of times._

   _I've never done karate._

1. _____

2. _____

3. _____

4. _____

5. _____

6. _____

# B | What I mean is, . . .

**1** Cross out the expression that doesn't belong in each list.

| | | |
|---|---|---|
| 1. Are you saying . . . | Do you mean . . . | What I mean is, . . . |
| 2. Do you mean . . . | What I'm saying is, . . . | I mean . . . |
| 3. What I mean is, . . . | Does that mean . . . | What I'm saying is, . . . |
| 4. What I'm saying is, . . . | Does that mean . . . | Do you mean . . . |
| 5. Does that mean . . . | I mean . . . | Are you saying . . . |
| 6. What I'm saying is, . . . | Are you saying . . . | What I mean is, . . . |

**2** Circle the correct words to complete the conversation.

**Jenny:** I'm really sleepy.

**Amy:** Really? Why?

**Jenny:** I didn't sleep last night.

**Amy:** (Do you mean) / I mean you didn't get any sleep?
1

**Jenny:** Well, no. ~~What I mean is~~, / Does that mean I didn't get *much* sleep.
2

**Amy:** That's too bad. It was better for me. I couldn't stay awake!

**Jenny:** What I'm saying is, / (Are you saying) that you slept a lot?
3

**Amy:** Well, yes. (I mean) / Do you mean I slept all night . . . for about eight hours.
4

**Jenny:** Oh. What time do you usually go to bed?

**Amy:** I go to bed about 10:00 p.m., and I never use an alarm clock in the morning.

**Jenny:** What I mean is, / (Does that mean) you get up late in the morning?
5

**Amy:** No. . . . (What I'm saying is), / Are you saying I wake up early. I always wake up
6
at 6:00 a.m. I don't need an alarm.

**Jenny:** That's nice. I never wake up early without an alarm.

an alarm clock

**28 Unit 4** Lesson B

# C Life experiences

**1** Look at the pictures of Roger and Mary's trip. Then complete the email with the correct expressions from the box.

| | | |
|---|---|---|
| climbed a mountain *(2)* | tried an extreme sport *(4)* | went to a spa *(6)* |
| tried an exotic food *(5)* | ✓ went camping | went whale-watching *(3)* |

1.

2.

3.

4.

5.

6.

Hi Lorena and Bill,

We're having a lot of fun in Canada with our friends. Victoria is a beautiful city. Last weekend we

*went camping* near the ocean. It was great. We

Climbed a mountain *(2)* on Saturday, and we went whale watching *(3)*

on Sunday. Roger and I even tried an extreme sport *(4)* : zip-lining. You go through the

air from tree to tree! It was exciting!

This week, we're staying in a nice hotel. We had dinner at a very nice restaurant in the hotel last

night. I tried an exotic food *(5)* . I ate broiled rainbow trout with fiddleheads and rice.

Rainbow trout is a delicious fish. Fiddleheads are an exotic vegetable. I even

went to a spa *(6)* at the hotel with Barbara. Can you believe it? It was very

relaxing. Roger and Tim didn't go.

I have to say good-bye now. We're going to an amusement park in Vancouver, a big city near

Victoria. I can't wait to ride the roller coasters!

Write soon,

Mary

**2** Complete the sentences with the correct forms of the words in parentheses. Use the present perfect or the simple past.

1. I _'ve been_ (be) to Mexico lots of times.

2. My sister _ate_ (eat) at a Turkish restaurant yesterday.

3. Paulina _never go_ (never / go) to a spa, but I _went_ (go) to one last month.

4. _Have_ you ever _try_ (try) an extreme sport?

5. I _tried_ (try) skiing last year, but I _didn't like_ (not / like) it.

6. _Did_ Jorge and Vanessa _ride_ (ride) a roller coaster at the park yesterday?

7. What countries _have_ you _been_ (be) to in the past?

8. My cousins _went_ (go) camping last week, but I _never go_ (never / go) camping before.

**3** Write questions to complete the conversations. Use the present perfect and the simple past.

**A. Hyun-ju:** Hey, Matt. _Have you ever gone camping_ ?
   _1_

   **Matt:** No, I haven't. But my sister went camping last weekend.

   **Hyun-ju:** Really? _Did she go camping_ ?
   _2_

   **Matt:** Yes, she did. She had a lot of fun.

   **Hyun-ju:** _Did she climb a mountain_ ?
   _3_

   **Matt:** No. She didn't climb a mountain, but she went kayaking.

   **Hyun-ju:** Wow! _Have you ever gone kayaking_ ?
   _4_

   **Matt:** No, I have never gone kayaking. But I'd like to go sometime.

   **Hyun-ju:** Me too!

**B.    Josh:** How was your vacation, Nicky?

   **Nicky:** It was great! _Did you get my postcard_ ?
   _1_

   **Josh:** No, I didn't get your postcard. _When did you send_ ?
   _2_

   **Nicky:** I sent it on Monday. It's from Mexico City.

   **Josh:** Cool!

   **Nicky:** _Have you ever gone to Mexico_ ?
   _3_

   **Josh:** Yes, I have. I went to Mexico City last year.

   **Nicky:** _Did you see the pyramids_ ?
   _4_

   **Josh:** Yes, I saw the pyramids. They were amazing!

   **Nicky:** Great! You're going to like my postcard!

**4** Look at the chart. Write sentences about what Victor has done using the information in the chart. Use the present perfect or the simple past.

|  | never | last year | a few years ago | lots of times |
|---|---|---|---|---|
| 1. bowl |  | ✓ |  |  |
| 2. play golf |  |  | ✓ |  |
| 3. do yoga | ✓ |  |  |  |
| 4. join a gym |  |  | ✓ |  |
| 5. lift weights |  |  |  | ✓ |
| 6. climb a mountain | ✓ |  |  |  |
| 7. play soccer |  |  |  | ✓ |
| 8. try karate |  | ✓ |  |  |

1. _Victor bowled last year._
2. _He played golf last year_
3. _He has never done yoga_
4. _He joined a gym a fee years ago_

5. _He has lifted weights lot of times._
6. _He has never climbed a mountain_
7. _He has played soccer lot of time_
8. _He tried karate last year_

**5** Answer the questions with your own information. Write complete sentences. If your answer is no, add more information.

Example: _Yes, I have. I found it on the beach._ or
            _No, I haven't. I don't take my phone on vacation._

1. Have you ever lost your phone on vacation? If yes, did you find it?
   _No, I haven't_

2. Did you go on vacation last year? If yes, where did you go?
   _Yes I did. I went to Canada with my sons_

3. Have you ever tried an extreme sport? If yes, did you like it?
   _No, I have't_

4. Have you ever won an award? If yes, why did you win it?
   _No, I haven't_

5. Have you ever met a famous person? If yes, who did you meet?
   _Yes, I have, I met a movie star in korea_

6. Have you ever gotten seasick? If yes, where were you?
   _Yes, I have. I was in jejudo_

**1** Read the article. Write the correct question from the box before each answer.

Is it dangerous?     Are *caving* and *spelunking* different?     What is spelunking?

# The Life of a Spelunker

We interviewed Karen Osgood, a woman who has been spelunking for over 15 years. Read what she says about this interesting activity.

**Q:** _____
                                           1

**A:** *Spelunking* is another word for *caving*. It's an interesting activity. People go in caves and walk around in them. For example, I walk around and look at the rocks in caves, and I take pictures. I often have to walk through water, and I sometimes see waterfalls in caves. There is a lot of climbing, too.

**Q:** _____
                                           2

**A:** No, not really. Well, what I mean is that some people say *cavers* are serious about the activity and *spelunkers* aren't. They say *spelunkers* go in caves for sport or fun and *cavers* go in caves to explore and learn new things. But many people use the two words in the same way. Of course, scientists who study caves for their job are called speleologists. They know a lot about biology, physics, and chemistry. I'm not a speleologist, but I know a lot about caves. I'm serious about it, too, so I guess I'm a caver. But it's OK if you call me a spelunker!

**Q:** _____
                                           3

**A:** Yes, it is. People need to be very careful. Caves are often wet because of water, and you can fall down. You should also wear safe hats and good boots. You sometimes need to wear warm clothing because caves are usually cold. It's very important to take lights, too. You can't see anything without them. I have a light on my hat, so I don't have to hold one in my hand. Oh, and never go in a cave alone. I always explore caves with two or three other people.

**2** Read the article again. Then write T (true) or F (false).

1. Karen has been spelunking for many years. __*T*__

2. People don't climb in caves. _____

3. There's sometimes water in caves. _____

4. Spelunkers study caves as part of their job. _____

5. There isn't a lot of light in caves. _____

6. You should always go caving with other people. _____

# Our world

## A Older, taller, and more famous

**1** Label the things in the picture with the correct words.

1. c_anal_____

2. b_____

3. tu_hnel_____

4. p_laza_____

5. su_bway___sys_____
   sy_____

6. to_____

7. sk_____

8. st_____

**2  Put the words in the correct order to make sentences.**

1. is / the Akashi-Kaikyo Bridge in Japan / older / The Tower Bridge in England / than / .

   _The Tower Bridge in England is older than the Akashi-Kaikyo Bridge in Japan._

2. the Erie Canal in the United States / than / is / The Murray Canal in Canada / shorter / .

   The Murray Canal in Canada is shorter than the Erie Canal in the United States

3. more / The Sydney Harbor Bridge in Australia / is / than / modern / the Tower Bridge in England / .

   _____

4. as / long / the Channel Tunnel between England and France / The Lincoln Tunnel between New Jersey and New York City / is / not / as / .

   The Lincoln Tunnel between New jersey and

5. tall / the Sears Tower in the United States / is / The Jin Mao Tower in China / not / as / as / .

   _____

6. the London Underground / people on it / has / The New York City subway system / more / than / .

   _____

7. as / as / large / the Zócalo square in Mexico City / is / The Plaza Mayor in Madrid / not / .

   _____

**3  Circle the correct words to complete the paragraphs.**

There are many skyscrapers in Hong Kong. Two very tall skyscrapers are the Bank of China Tower and Central Plaza. Central Plaza is **more tall than / (taller than)** the Bank of China Tower. It also has
1
**more floors than / more floors** the Bank of China Tower. The Bank
2
of China Tower is **older than / older** Central Plaza. But it looks
3
**more modern / more modern than** Central Plaza.
4
I. M. Pei created the Bank of China Tower, and Dennis Lau and Ng Chun Man created Central Plaza. Some people say that I. M. Pei has created **(more famous buildings than) / more than famous buildings**
5
Dennis Lau and Ng Chun Man. He has made buildings around the world. For example, he made the John F. Kennedy Library in Boston and the pyramid at the Louvre Museum in Paris.

Bank of China Tower   Central Plaza

35-42

**4** Read about the bridges. Then write comparisons with the words in parentheses. Use *-er* endings or *more . . . than.*

The Brooklyn Bridge, New York City

The Golden Gate Bridge, San Francisco

1. The Brooklyn Bridge is 1,825 meters long. The Golden Gate Bridge is 2,737 meters long. (is / long)

   *The Golden Gate Bridge is longer than the Brooklyn Bridge.*

2. The Brooklyn Bridge is 26 meters wide. The Golden Gate Bridge is 27 meters wide. (is / wide)

   _____

3. The Brooklyn Bridge opened in 1883. The Golden Gate Bridge opened in 1937. (is / old)

   _____

4. The cost to build the Brooklyn Bridge was $15.5 million. The Golden Gate Bridge was $35 million. (was / expensive)

   _____

5. It took 13 years to build the Brooklyn Bridge. It took four years to build the Golden Gate Bridge. (took / time to build)

   _____

6. Each day, 145,000 people go on the Brooklyn Bridge. Each day, 118,000 people go on the Golden Gate Bridge. (has / people on it each day)

   _____

**5** Change sentences 1–4 from Exercise 3. Use *not as . . . as.*

1. *The Brooklyn Bridge is not as long as the Golden Gate Bridge.*
2. _____
3. _____
4. _____

# B  *I don't believe it!*

**1** Complete the conversation. Use expressions for expressing disbelief and for saying you don't know. The first letter of each word is given.

**Tyler:** Hey, Susana, look at this.

**Susana:** What is it?

**Tyler:** It's information about the plazas in Mexico. There are more plazas in Mexico than anywhere else in the world!

**Susana:** *I don't believe it!* _____
<br>1

**Tyler:** And we're in a very famous plaza – the Zócalo. Do you know another name for it?

**Susana:** I h_____ n_____ i_____ .
<br>2

**Tyler:** It's also called Constitution Plaza.

**Susana:** That's interesting. But I like the name Zócalo better. . . . How old is it?

**Tyler:** I r_____ d_____ k_____ . But the plaza is older than
<br>3
some of the buildings around it.

**Susana:** S_____ ?
<br>4

**Tyler:** Yeah. There used to be different buildings around the plaza, but over the years people built new buildings in place of some of the old ones.

**Susana:** N_____ w_____ ! I wonder why the old ones are gone. . . .
<br>5
Hey, do you know how big the square is?

**Tyler:** It says here it's 240 meters long and 240 meters wide.

**Susana:** That's pretty big! Hey, I'm hungry. Is there a restaurant near the plaza?

**Tyler:** I d_____ h_____ a c_____ ! Maybe there are some
<br>6
ideas in this book.

**2** Complete the conversations with one of the expressions from Exercise 1. More than one answer is possible.

1. **A:** Do you know how long the Channel Tunnel is?

   **B:** _____

2. **A:** Wow! Did you know the Weihe Grand Bridge is the longest bridge in the world?

   **B:** _____

# C  *World geography*

**1** Complete the puzzle with words for geographical features. What's the mystery word?

1.

2.

3.

4.

5.

6.

¹ R I V E R

2

3

4

5

6

**2** Complete the sentences with words for geographical features.

1. The Nile _____*River*_____ is 6,650 kilometers long.

2. A _____ is extremely dry and hot.

3. We swam in a small _____ on vacation.

4. The Indian _____ has less water than the Atlantic or Pacific.

5. Maui is a beautiful _____ surrounded by the Pacific Ocean.

6. I went to the Amazon _____ _____ last winter.
   The trees and other plants were beautiful, and I saw a lot of animals, but it
   really rained a lot!

7. When we went camping last summer, we put up our tent in a _____
   next to a river. Every morning, we looked up at the mountains all around us. It was great!

8. The most famous _____ in the United States is Niagara Falls.

**3** Complete the text with the correct superlative forms of the adjectives in parentheses.

# YOSEMITE NATIONAL PARK

Yosemite National Park is one of _the most beautiful_ (beautiful)
[1]
parks in the United States, and it's one of _____
[2]
(large) parks in California. There are many interesting geographical
features in Yosemite. Yosemite Valley is _____
[3]
(popular) place to visit in the park. It's easy to walk around in the
valley. Tuolumne River is _____ (long) river in the
[4]
park, and there are many river trips you can take. There are also many
waterfalls to see in the park. Yosemite Falls is _____ (high) waterfall.
[5]
Chilnualna Falls is one of _____ (difficult) to see because it's behind rocks.
[6]

January, February, and March are _____ (wet) months in Yosemite. Spring
[7]
is _____ (good) season to see waterfalls. Summer is
[8]
_____ (hot) season, and it's also the _____ (busy)
[9]                                                        [10]
season. There aren't many visitors in the park in the winter because it's very cold.

**4** Look at the chart. Write sentences with superlative nouns.

| In the Caribbean | | | |
|---|---|---|---|
| | **Aruba** | **Cuba** | **the Dominican Republic** |
| 1. land | 180 km$^2$ | 110,860 km$^2$ | 48,670 km$^2$ |
| 2. people | 104,589 | 11,477,459 | 9,794,487 |
| 3. rain (each year) | 21.3 inches | 52 inches | 54.5 inches |
| 4. official languages | 2 | 1 | 1 |
| 5. TV stations | 1 | 58 | 25 |

1. _Cuba has the most land._ _____
2. _____
3. _____
4. _____
5. _____

**5** Complete the sentences with the superlative forms of the underlined words.

1. **A:** We're going to New Guinea this year. It's an extremely large island.

   **B:** Yes, it is. But Greenland is *the largest* island in the world.

2. **A:** This street has a lot of cars. Is there always this much traffic?

   **B:** Yes, First Avenue gets *the most traffic* in the city.

3. **A:** My uncle does research in the Antarctic Desert, and he says it's really cold.

   **B:** I know. The Antarctic Desert is _____ desert in the world.

4. **A:** What a great day! Let's sit in the sunshine.

   **B:** OK. This is _____ we've had all summer!

5. **A:** Wow, this is beautiful! We're up so high. What a great view!

   **B:** Did you know Lake Titicaca is one of _____ lakes in the world?

6. **A:** I'm going to Japan. Where is a good place to see temples?

   **B:** I think Kyoto is one of _____ places to see temples in Japan.

7. **A:** I'm tired of being wet on this vacation! It has rained every day on this trip.

   **B:** Well, May is usually _____ month in this city.

8. **A:** How many people live in New York?

   **B:** Over 8 million. It's the city in the United States with _____ .

Greenland

**6** Answer the questions with your own information. Write complete sentences and use superlatives.

*Example:* *The longest bridge I've ever been on is the Golden Gate Bridge.*

1. What's the longest bridge you've ever been on? _____
2. Where's the highest place you've ever been? _____
3. What's the most beautiful place you've ever seen? _____
4. Where's the hottest place you've ever been? _____
5. What's the tallest building in your town? _____
6. What's the longest river in your country? _____
7. Which city in your country has the most people? _____
8. Which month gets the most rain in your town? _____

# D  *Natural wonders*

**1** Read the article. Then write the name of the correct natural wonder under each picture.

1. _____    2. _____    3. _____

## Canada's Seven Wonders

In 2007, the CBC TV and radio stations had a contest to choose the Seven Wonders of Canada. People sent their ideas to a website and voted for their favorites.

| People's Choices | Votes |
|---|---|
| **Sleeping Giant:** This is a long peninsula in Lake Superior, which means it has water on three sides. From across the lake, it looks like a big, sleeping person! | 177,305 |
| **Niagara Falls:** These amazing waterfalls are on the border of Canada and the United States. There are three waterfalls, but the largest and most beautiful is called Horseshoe Falls, and most of it is in Canada. | 81,818 |
| **Bay of Fundy:** This is a large body of water where the Atlantic Ocean meets part of Canada. It has the highest tides in the world. The water from the ocean comes in 17 meters higher than when it goes out! | 67,670 |
| **Nahanni National Park Reserve:** This beautiful national park in northern Canada has rivers, waterfalls, mountains, forests, birds, fish, and other animals. | 64,920 |
| **Northern Lights:** These are colorful moving lights in the sky. The best time to see them is on very dark, cool nights in March, April, September, and October. | 61,417 |
| **The Rockies:** The Canadian Rockies are beautiful, high mountains that have sharp peaks and wide valleys. They are cool and wet, but the tops have no trees because it is too cold and rocky for them to grow. | 55,630 |
| **Cabot Trail:** This 950-kilometer hiking trail through part of the Rockies has some of the most beautiful views in Canada. It is named after John Cabot, an Italian man who explored the land in 1497. | 44,073 |

**2** Read the article again. Then answer the questions.

1. When was the contest for the Seven Wonders of Canada? _____ *2007* _____

2. Which place had the most votes? _____

3. Which ocean's water goes into the Bay of Fundy? _____

4. What are the best months to see the northern lights? _____

5. How long is the Cabot Trail? _____

# Organizing your time

## A A busy week

**1** Complete the phone conversations with words from the box.

| ✓birthday | business | doctor's | soccer |
|---|---|---|---|
| blind | conference | job | violin |

**A.** **Jake:** Hey, Ramon. Can you come to my

_____**birthday**_____ party on Saturday?
   ₁

**Ramon:** I'm not sure. I have a _____
   ₂

   appointment at the hospital at 2:00 p.m. What

   time is the party?

**Jake:** It starts at 4:00 p.m. And there's someone

   I want you to meet. Her name is Olivia.

**Ramon:** Well, I can come to the party. But I don't know about Olivia. I've never

   been on a _____ date.
   ₃

**Jake:** It's not really a date. You're both just going to be at the party. It'll be fun!

**B.** **Yae-jih:** Hi, Don. How are you?

**Don:** OK. I'm a little nervous about my _____ interview at TGL Bank.
   ₁

**Yae-jih:** Oh, right. When is it?

**Don:** Today at 2:00. Mr. Lawrence and Mrs. Nelson have a lot of _____
   ₂

   meetings, so we are going to have a _____ call. I won't have an
   ₃

   interview face-to-face.

**Yae-jih:** Wow. That's different. Good luck!

**C.** **Laura:** Hello, Sibel. Do you want to have lunch tomorrow?

**Sibel:** I'm sorry. I can't. I have a _____ lesson tomorrow.
   ₁

   How about on Saturday?

**Laura:** I have _____ practice in the afternoon.
   ₂

   Let's have dinner on Saturday night.

**Sibel:** OK, great. And we can go to a movie after dinner, too.

**2** Circle the correct words to complete the email.

Hi Jim,

How are you? Thanks for your email. It will be great to see you next week. What (are you doing) / do you do on Thursday? I have tickets to a hip-hop concert, if you'd like to go with me. **It's starting** / **It starts** at 8:00 p.m. **I'm having** / **I have** soccer practice at 4:00, but **it's ending** / **it ends** at 5:30. If you can go to the concert, we could meet for dinner at 6:30 at Oh Boy Pizza. What do you think?

Are you busy on July 28th? **I'm moving** / **I move** that day. Could you help me move? Katie and Mike **are helping** / **help** me, too. They **are going** / **go** to a yoga class every Saturday from 8:00 to 10:00 a.m., so we'll start at 11:00. **I'm buying** / **I buy** lunch for everyone.

I hope you can go to the concert. Write soon or call me!

Raul

**3** Check (✓) the correct sentences. Rewrite the incorrect sentences with the correct forms of the verbs. Use the simple present or the present continuous.

1. ☐ Lorena is having a violin lesson every Thursday.

   *Lorena has a violin lesson every Thursday.*

2. ☐ Do you have any doctor's appointments next week?

   _____

3. ☐ Marvin picks up his sister in Miami at 3:30 p.m. on Saturday.

   _____

4. ☐ Brenda and Tom are staying at my house this weekend.

   _____

5. ☐ Naoki plans a conference call in meeting room B for Tuesday next week.

   _____

6. ☐ The movie starts at 9:00 and is ending at 11:30.

   _____

**4** Read the sentences. Check (✓) if the event is happening right now or in the future.

|   | | Now | Future |
|---|---|:---:|:---:|
| 1. | I can't have lunch now. I'm studying for my biology test. | ✓ | ☐ |
| 2. | I have a doctor's appointment on Friday. | ☐ | ☐ |
| 3. | Jen is working late next week. | ☐ | ☐ |
| 4. | I'm eating a great sandwich. Do you want to try it? | ☐ | ☐ |
| 5. | I'm sorry. Tae Jung isn't here. He has soccer practice. | ☐ | ☐ |
| 6. | Melanie can't go on a blind date on Saturday. She has a guitar lesson. | ☐ | ☐ |
| 7. | We're leaving for vacation in three days! | ☐ | ☐ |
| 8. | Larry isn't answering his cell phone. He is on a conference call. | ☐ | ☐ |

**5** Complete the calendar with your own plans for next week. Write sentences with the present continuous or the simple present.

*Example:* **Sunday:**  _I have gymnastics practice._  *or*  _I'm visiting my aunt and uncle._

WEEKLY CALENDAR

| Sunday | |
|---|---|
| **Monday** | |
| **Tuesday** | |
| **Wednesday** | |
| **Thursday** | |
| **Friday** | |
| **Saturday** | |

# *Can I take a message?*

**1** Put the words in the correct order to make sentences for leaving and offering to take phone messages.

1. leave / want / a / message / to / you / Do / ?       *Do you want to leave a message?*

2. Amber called / him / Please / tell / that / .       _____

3. is at 12:15 / the conference call / her /
   Can / you / tell / that / ?       _____

4. know / in the morning / that / you / her / Could /       _____
   let / we're leaving / ?

5. like / to / you / Would / leave / message / a / ?       _____

6. take / a / message / I / Can / ?       _____

**2** Complete the conversations with sentences from Exercise 1. Each sentence in Exercise 1 is used once. Sometimes, the first word is given.

**A.** **Brandon:** Hello?

    **Amber:** Hi. Can I speak to Jim?

    **Brandon:** I'm sorry. He's not here. Do

        _you want to leave a message_ ?
        <sub>1</sub>

    **Amber:** Sure. _____
                    <sub>2</sub>

    _____ .

| **While You Were Out** | |
|---|---|
| **For:** *Jim* | **Date:** *October 2* |
| **Message:** *Amber called.* | |
| *909-555-1234* | |
| | |
| | |

**B.** **Victoria:** Hello?

    **Marcos:** Hello. Can I speak to Tonya, please?

    **Victoria:** Um, she's busy right now. Can _____?
                                               <sub>1</sub>

    **Marcos:** Yes. We have a business meeting at work tomorrow.

    _____?
                              <sub>2</sub>

    **Victoria:** 12:15. OK. No problem.

**C.** **Emma:** Hello?

    **Asami:** Hi. Is Kendra there?

    **Emma:** No, she isn't. Would _____?
                                      <sub>1</sub>

    **Asami:** Oh, sure. I'm picking her up tomorrow for a camping trip.

    _____?
                              <sub>2</sub>

    **Emma:** OK. What time?

    **Asami:** About 10:00 a.m.

# C Can you do me a favor?

**1** Circle the correct phrase to complete each conversation.

1. **A:** Algebra is difficult.

   **B:** Do you want some help?

   **A:** Yes. Can you **help me with my résumé** / **check my homework**?

2. **A:** That restaurant is too expensive.

   **B:** I know, but the food is really good. Let's go.

   **A:** Well, OK. Could you **lend me some money** / **water my plants**?

3. **A:** Hi, Ed. It's Sherry.

   **B:** Hi, Sherry. You're calling me early. Is there a problem?

   **A:** Yes. My car isn't working. Can you **check my homework** / **give me a ride to work**?

4. **A:** Look at those flowers! Your garden is so beautiful!

   **B:** Thanks. Would you mind **watering the plants** / **getting the mail** with me?

5. **A:** Julia is so nice. She always wants to help.

   **B:** I know. She's **feeding my cat** / **giving me a ride** while I'm on vacation.

6. **A:** Do you want to go to a movie tonight?

   **B:** I'm sorry, I can't. I'm **getting my mail** / **picking up my parents at the airport**.

7. **A:** I need to find a job.

   **B:** My office needs some new workers.

   **A:** Really? That's great. Could you **help me with my résumé** / **pick me up**?

8. **A:** Does anyone stay at your house when you travel for work?

   **B:** No. My neighbor usually **gets my mail** / **checks my homework**.
   And he also feeds my fish.

**2** Complete the conversation with words from the box.

| ✓can you do | I'll clean | I won't forget | would you mind cleaning |
|---|---|---|---|
| could you take | I'll cook | Would you make | |

**Tina:** Matt, _can you do_ _____ me a favor?
                                  1

**Matt:** Sure, Tina. What is it?

**Tina:** I'm going to be home late tonight, around 7:00.

_____ dinner?
                    2

**Matt:** No problem. _____ tacos
                                        3

and rice and beans.

**Tina:** Oh, that sounds great! And _____
                                                      4

_____ out the garbage? It has to go out tonight.

**Matt:** Definitely. _____ . I promise!
                                        5

**Tina:** Thanks. Oh, and _____ the apartment? Our new
                                              6

neighbors, Jay and Camille, are coming over for dinner. Remember?

**Matt:** Um, OK. I guess _____ it before I make dinner.
                                            7

**Tina:** Thanks. You're the best!

**3** Rewrite the questions. Use *would you mind*. Then complete the responses with *will*.

1. Can you check my homework?

   **A:** _Would you mind checking my homework?_ _____

   **B:** No problem. _I'll check_ _____ it after dinner.

2. Could you pick me up at 10:30 a.m.?

   **A:** _____

   **B:** Not at all. _____ at any time you want me to.

3. Would you give me a ride to my doctor's appointment?

   **A:** _____

   **B:** No problem. _____ you a ride in my new car!

4. Would you tell Josh that the meeting is tomorrow?

   **A:** _____

   **B:** No, I don't mind. _____ him when I see him at lunch.

5. Could you water the plant in my office while I'm out next week?

   **A:** _____

   **B:** No problem. _____ it. How often should I do it?

**4** Look at Eric's notes. Then complete his conversation with each person.

| | |
|---|---|
| _give me a ride to the airport_ | Priscilla |
| _feed my fish_ | Chuck |
| _feed my cat_ | Chuck |
| _get my mail_ | Amira |
| _pick me up from the airport_ | Greg |

1. **Eric:** Can you give me a ride to the airport on Monday afternoon?

   **Priscilla:** No problem. _I'll give you a ride to_ _the airport._ What time?

2. **Eric:** Can _____ while I'm on a trip next week?

   **Chuck:** Sure. _____ them.

   **Eric:** And would you mind _____ , too?

   **Chuck:** No, I don't mind. _____ it, too.

3. **Eric:** Would _____ when I'm on my trip?

   **Amira:** All right. _____ it on Wednesday and Friday.

4. **Eric:** Could _____ at 4:30 on Sunday?

   **Greg:** Yeah, sure. _____ and _____ be late!

**5** People are asking you favors. Write their questions and your own answers.

1. **Ed:** _Can you take my picture_ ?

   **You:** _____ .

2. **Mai:** _____ ?

   **You:** _____ .

3. **Chris:** _____ ?

   **You:** _____ .

4. **Mara:** _____ ?

   **You:** _____ .

# Time management

Read the article. What are four ways that people waste time?

1. _the Internet_  2. _____  3. _____  4. _____

## A Waste of Time!

Many people don't manage their time well. They often find other things to do when they should be working. Some people don't even know they are wasting time. These are some of the top time-wasters. Do any of them sound like you?

**1.** The Internet is a very useful tool, but it's also the biggest way people waste time. Many people play games or chat online instead of working or doing research for school. Have you ever looked at a funny video online instead of working?

**2.** TV can be interesting and educational, but many people waste time by watching TV. Have you ever taken a short break from work to watch "just a little TV" and then hours later thought, "Oh, that's right. . . . I was doing laundry."?

**3.** People can actually waste a lot of time when they talk. At work, some people talk too much about personal things instead of doing their jobs. Other people have the same problem at home. They talk to friends and family on the phone instead of doing chores.

**4.** Believe it or not, thinking can be a waste of time. Some people think about work, but they don't do it. They even make to-do lists, but then they just think about all the things they have to do, and they never get them done!

**2** Read the article again and the sentences below. Did each person waste time? Check (✓) Yes or No.

|  | Yes | No |
|---|---|---|
| 1. Vicky researched information on the Internet for a work report. | ☐ | ✓ |
| 2. Dan played a game online for two hours at work. | ☐ | ☐ |
| 3. Ines watched TV for ten minutes and then finished her homework. | ☐ | ☐ |
| 4. Haluk talked to his boss about a business meeting. | ☐ | ☐ |
| 5. Sam talked to his boss about his son's soccer game. | ☐ | ☐ |
| 6. Jen made a to-do list, and then she thought about how she'd never finish all of it. | ☐ | ☐ |

# Personalities

## A You're extremely curious.

**1** Put the letters in the correct order to make words for personality traits.

1. i a t s m i u b o    _____ambitious_____
2. b n s u b r t o    _____
3. e a c f l r u    _____
4. i o c m i t t i s p    _____

5. r s c i u u o    _____
6. o t i g u g o n    _____
7. u d s r t o n u a e v    _____
8. a i e o y n g s g    _____

**2** Complete the sentences with the words for personality traits.

John sets high goals for himself. He's very

_____ambitious_____ . He's also extremely
         1

_____ . He loves learning
     2

about new things.

Celia is _____ , but she's also
           3

pretty _____ . She likes trying
        4

exciting sports, but she does them with attention

to detail.

Gina doesn't have a job right now, but she seems

OK. She always looks on the bright side, so she's

_____ about her future. She
    5

hardly ever worries. She's a very relaxed and

_____ person.
     6

Daniel can be very _____ .
             7

He never changes his mind about things! But

he's also very _____ .
           8

He's extremely friendly, so people like to be

around him.

**3** Circle the correct words to complete the conversation.

**Jane:** How do your children like college, Rob?

**Rob:** Very much, thanks. Don is **carefully** / ~~extremely~~

    ₁

ambitious. He sets high goals for himself. You

know, he wants to be a pilot.

**Jane:** Wow. That's great. And the others?

**Rob:** Well, Greg **fairly** / **really** likes college. He's

                              ₂

**early** / **very** outgoing. He works **early** / **well** in

    ₃                                       ₄

groups, but he thinks it's difficult to work alone, and you have do that a lot in college.

**Jane:** Well, it's good that he likes school.

**Rob:** And Ken is **pretty** / **slowly** curious. He likes to learn new things, so he loves school.

                        ₅

He's interested in many subjects, so he hasn't decided what career he wants yet.

**Jane:** That sounds like my son. And how's Brandon doing?

**Rob:** He's doing OK. He doesn't work **very** / **well** without direction, but if you tell him

                                            ₆

what to do, he does it **really** / **well**. Ken and Brandon go to the same college,

                          ₇

so they help each other.

**Jane:** That's nice.

**4** Rewrite the sentences to correct the mistakes in the order of the words.
Sometimes there is more than one mistake in the sentence.

1. Steven and Susan are curious extremely about the new student in class.

    *Steven and Susan are extremely curious about the new student in class.*

2. Mario doesn't play well the guitar when he's nervous.

    _____

3. Tae-ho's parents are important very to him.

    _____

4. Kendra is outgoing fairly, and she makes easily new friends.

    _____

5. Pam quickly drives, but she's careful pretty.

    _____

6. Jacob slowly is moving, so he'll be late for his doctor's appointment this morning.

    _____

**5** Look at the chart. Write sentences about Shan.

| | easily | very | fairly | hard |
|---|---|---|---|---|
| 1. make friends | ✓ | | | |
| 2. ambitious | | | ✓ | |
| 3. study during the week | | | | ✓ |
| 4. not stubborn | | ✓ | | |
| 5. not work on the weekends | | | | ✓ |
| 6. outgoing | | ✓ | | |
| 7. optimistic | | | ✓ | |
| 8. not share her feelings | ✓ | | | |

1. *Shan makes friends easily.* _____
2. *She is* _____
3. _____
4. _____
5. _____
6. _____
7. _____
8. _____

**6** Complete the sentences so they are true for you. Use some of the adverbs from the box.

Example: *I'm pretty ambitious.* or *I'm not very ambitious.*

| | | | |
|---|---|---|---|
| carefully | (not) extremely | pretty | slowly |
| completely | fairly | quickly | (not) very |
| easily | hard | (not) really | well |

1. I'm _____ ambitious.
2. I'm _____ serious about learning English.
3. I'm _____ optimistic about my future.
4. I make new friends _____ .
5. I'm _____ curious about math and science.
6. I work _____ when I do my homework.

## B  *In my opinion, . . .*

**1** Complete the conversations with phrases from the box. Use each expression once.
More than one answer is possible.

| | | |
|---|---|---|
| Don't you agree | Don't you think that's true | In my opinion, |
| Don't you think so | If you ask me, | Maybe it's just me, but I think |

**Olivia:** Heather, what do you think of this statue?

**Heather:** Oh, it's very interesting. _Don't you agree_ ?
<br>1

**Olivia:** No, not really. _____ it's ugly.
<br>2

**Olivia:** And look at this painting. What do you think of it?

**Heather:** I like it, but it's a little weird. _____ ?
<br>3

**Olivia:** _____ it's pretty amazing!
<br>4

**Olivia:** Wow. Look at this. It's great! _____ ?
<br>5

**Heather:** No, I don't. _____ it's disgusting!
<br>6

**2** What do you think? Complete the conversation with your own idea. Use an expression
for giving an opinion.

**Olivia:** Hey, what do you think of this painting?

**Heather:** Oh, it's nice. Don't you agree?

**You:** _____

_____

_____

# C  *We've been friends for six years.*

**1** Look at the dictionary definitions for personality traits. Write the correct words.

1. a *greeable* _____ (*adj*) friendly and pleasing

2. c_____ (*adj*) thinking of the needs of others

3. d_____ (*adj*) making decisions quickly

4. f_____ (*adj*) treating people equally or right

5. h_____ (*adj*) truthful

6. m_____ (*adj*) behaving in a responsible way

7. p_____ (*adj*) waiting without getting annoyed

8. r_____ (*adj*) doing what is expected or promised

**2** Complete the sentences with the correct words for personality traits.
Use the opposites of the words from Exercise 1.

1. John is sometimes _____*dishonest*_____ . He doesn't always tell the truth.

2. Some people in the group were _____ , so we didn't become friends.

3. Jack is pretty _____ . He didn't come to pick me up at the airport.
   I had to take a taxi home.

4. Amanda is 17, but she's pretty _____ . She acts like she's only
   12 or 13.

5. Please don't be _____ ! You don't have to wait much longer. I'm
   almost finished.

6. Bob and I are often _____ . We hardly ever make decisions quickly!

7. Peter is a very _____ and _____ person.
   He never thinks about other people's needs, and he doesn't treat people equally.

**3** Complete the chart. Write the words from the box in the correct column.

| ✓2010 | a few days | last night | two months |
|-------|-----------|-----------|-----------|
| 4:30 | five hours | a long time | Wednesday |
| December | I was 18 | quite a while | a year |

| I've lived here for . . . | I've known him since . . . |
|---------------------------|----------------------------|
|  | *2010* |
|  |  |
|  |  |
|  |  |
|  |  |

**4** Look at the calendar and the information about Vanessa. Today is Saturday. Complete the sentences with *since*. Then rewrite them with *for*.

| Monday | Tuesday | Wednesday | Thursday | Friday |
|--------|---------|-----------|----------|--------|
| got a new job | met Greg at work | had a blind date with Carlos | stopped talking to Greg | got sick |

1. Vanessa has had a new job  *since Monday* _____ .

   *Vanessa has had a new job for five days.* _____

2. She has known Greg _____ .

   _____

3. She has known Carlos _____ .

   _____

4. She's hasn't talked to Greg _____ .

   _____

5. She's been sick _____ .

   _____

**5** Write sentences with the words in parentheses. Use the present perfect with *for* or *since*.

1. (Yolanda / be / friends with Jenna / a long time)

   *Yolanda has been friends with Jenna for a long time.*

2. (I / not see / Jun / three days)

   _____

3. (I / not have / an argument with my parents / I was a kid)

   _____

4. (Tom and Melissa / be / married / three years)

   _____

5. (Matt / not eat / sushi / he was in Japan)

   _____

6. (Sandra / know / Katia / 2005)

   _____

**6** Read the email. Then answer the questions. Use *for* or *since*.

Dear Uncle Henry,

How are you? I'm great! As you know, I got married a week ago! I'm sorry you couldn't come to the wedding. Can you believe that I met Julie at your son's wedding in 2001?

Julie and I are on vacation now. We got to Hawaii four days ago. It's beautiful here! Unfortunately, Julie got sick on Wednesday, so we're in the doctor's office now. We got here at 1:00 p.m., and we have to wait a little longer to see the doctor. The office is pretty busy. Julie's mother called five minutes ago, and they're talking on the phone now. Julie's going to be OK. She probably had some bad seafood.

I have to go. They say I have to turn off my computer!

Take care,

Josh

1. How long has Josh been married?          *He's been married for a week.*

2. How long has Josh known Julie?          _____

3. How long have Josh and Julie been in Hawaii?   _____

4. How long has Julie been sick?          _____

5. How long have they been in the doctor's office?   _____

6. How long has Julie been on the phone?          _____

# D  *What is your personality?*

**1** **Read the article. Then answer the questions.**

1. Which color in the article do you like best? _____

2. Are you like (or not like) the personality description for that color? _____

## What does your favorite color say about your personality?

We all have a favorite color. But did you know that your favorite color might say something about your personality?

**WHITE.** White is a peaceful color. You like simple things. You are extremely fair, and you always tell the truth. You also want your friends to be truthful.

**RED.** Red is a strong color. You are outgoing and like meeting new people. You are optimistic and very ambitious. You are also decisive, and you are sometimes stubborn.

**ORANGE.** You are pretty easygoing and you like to be agreeable. You are curious about people and like to learn about them. You have a lot of friends. You want people to notice you, and you sometimes dress in flashy clothes!

**YELLOW.** Yellow is a happy color. You are very funny and have a lot of friends. You are pretty adventurous, too! But

sometimes you are not very responsible. That's not always a bad thing because taking risks is fun if you are careful.

**GREEN.** Green is the color of nature. You're fairly curious about the world. You like to be outdoors, and you are also adventurous. You are patient, kind, and easygoing.

**BLUE.** Blue is also a color in nature. Like "green" people, you are also very patient. You are reliable, and you want your friends to be considerate. You probably aren't very adventurous.

**PURPLE.** Purple is a color for creative people. You like music and the arts. You enjoy visiting museums and taking pictures.

**BLACK.** Black is a mysterious color. You have secrets. You are very curious about many different things.

**2** **Read the article again. Then circle the correct word to complete each sentence.**

1. People who like white are (honest)/ **dishonest**.

2. People who like yellow **like** / **don't like** trying new things.

3. People who like red are **good** / **bad** at making decisions.

4. People who like blue probably **like** / **don't like** trying new things.

5. People who like purple are usually **creative** / **boring**.

6. People who like black often **have** / **don't have** secrets.

# The environment

## A Going green

**1** Complete the text with one word from box A and one word from box B.

| A | e- | global | hybrid | ~~nuclear~~ | organic | plastic | recycling | solar | wind |
|---|----|--------|--------|----------|---------|---------|-----------|-------|------|
| B | bags | bin | car | ~~energy~~ | energy | farm | food | warming | waste |

## Easy Ways You Can Help the Environment

1. Many people don't like <u>*nuclear energy*</u> . They prefer to get their electricity from a _____ .

2. Buy and drive a _____ . They don't use as much gas as other cars, and they cause less pollution.

3. Take your own cloth bags to the supermarket. Don't use _____ .

4. Cook and eat _____ . It is safer for the environment.

5. Regular lightbulbs are not good for the environment. Use CFLs instead. This will help reduce _____ .

6. Put a large _____ in your house, and recycle paper, glass, and plastic.

7. When you buy a new computer, don't throw the old one away. If it still works, give it to a friend. This will help reduce _____ .

8. Use _____ to dry your clothes. Put your towels, blouses, shirts, pants, and even jeans on a clothesline to dry in the sun.

**2** Write C (count noun) or N (noncount noun).

1. energy  __N__
2. e-waste _____
3. lightbulb _____
4. recycling bin _____
5. pollution _____
6. plastic bag _____
7. bottle _____
8. landfill _____
9. plastic _____

**3** Complete the sentences with *fewer* or *less*.

1. The world would be a better place with _____*less*_____ e-waste.

2. People should use _____ plastic bags.

3. There should be _____ pollution in big cities.

4. There are _____ wind farms in the United States than in Europe.

5. Many people are trying to use _____ energy in their homes.

6. I'm sure you'll use _____ gas with your hybrid car.

**4** Complete the letter with *too many* or *too much*.

## LETTER TO THE EDITOR

June 17

I read the article *Building Goes Up Green* yesterday. It was very interesting, and I'm glad we're going to have a shopping mall that is better for the environment. There are

_____*too many*_____ buildings in this city that are bad for the environment. Most
        1

buildings use _____ energy, so it's important that the new
            2

buildings will use solar energy.

I think that the mall has a lot of creative ideas to help the environment in other ways, too. Using cloth bags is a wonderful idea. People will save money and help the

environment at the same time. There are _____ plastic bags in
                               3

landfills around the world, and every little bit helps! I also think there are

_____ landfills in this city, so I'm glad the shopping mall plans to
       4

have a recycling center, too. People throw away _____ garbage,
                                          5

and I hope this will help more people recycle.

I hope you write more articles about the mall.

Sincerely,

Dennis Armstrong

Environmental Student

**5** Look at the web post. Then write sentences about what Mi-yon has. Use *not enough* or *too many.*

Thank you, friends! I almost have enough recycled things for my art project, but I still need a few more. If you have any of them, please send them to me at 556 Claremont Street.

| | I needed | Now I have | I still need |
|---|---|---|---|
| 1. plastic bottles | 100 | 85 | 15 |
| 2. glass bottles | 25 | 30 | 0 |
| 3. plastic bags | 250 | 199 | 51 |
| 4. old lightbulbs | 50 | 40 | 10 |
| 5. old toothbrushes | 30 | 42 | 0 |
| 6. old CDs | 175 | 170 | 5 |

Thanks!

Mi-yon Kam, Green Artist

1. _Mi-yon doesn't have enough plastic bottles._
2. _She has too_ _____ .
3. _____
4. _____
5. _____
6. _____

**6** Answer the questions with your own information. Use quantifiers.

Example: _Yes, I do. I recycle paper. I could recycle more glass and plastic._ or
_No, I don't, and I don't use enough cloth bags._

1. Do you recycle? _____
2. Do you have recycling bins in your home? _____
3. Does your town have enough recycling centers? _____
4. Do you use things in your home to save energy? _____
5. How much pollution is in your town? _____
6. How could you make less garbage in your home? _____

# B  *I'd rather not say.*

Complete each conversation with the expressions in the box.

| I'd say about | I'd rather not answer that |
|---|---|

A. **Larry:** Hi, Kim. How's your new house?

**Kim:** It's great. We love the solar roof.

**Larry:** How much is your electric bill now?

**Kim:** I'd _____ $40 a month.
       <sub>1</sub>

**Larry:** Wow! That's cheap. How much did the solar roof cost?

**Kim:** _____ , but it was a
       <sub>2</sub>
good purchase. We save money each month, and we help the environment!

| I'd say maybe | I'd rather not say |
|---|---|

B. **Alice:** Hi, Hala. Where are you going?

**Hala:** I'm going to the mall.

**Alice:** What are you going to buy?

**Hala:** Actually, _____ . It's a surprise for
        <sub>1</sub>
my sister's birthday.

**Alice:** Oh, OK. Well, I'll see you at her party. What time should I get there?

**Hala:** Oh, _____ around 6:00 p.m.
        <sub>2</sub>

**Alice:** OK.

| probably | I'd prefer not to say |
|---|---|

C. **Peng:** Wow, Steve. I like your new car.

**Steve:** Thanks!

**Peng:** When did you get it?

**Steve:** Um, _____ about a month ago.
         <sub>1</sub>

**Peng:** Is it a hybrid car?

**Steve:** No, it isn't. The hybrid cars were too expensive.

**Peng:** Oh, that's too bad. How much do you spend on gas?

**Steve:** _____ , but definitely too much!
         <sub>2</sub>

# C  *What will happen?*

**1**  Circle the correct verb to complete each tip for helping the environment.

1. (Use) / Grow / Take a clothesline.

2. Fix / Buy / Use leaky faucets.

3. Take / Pay / Buy local food.

4. Grow / Take / Pay public transportation.

5. Use / Pay / Fix rechargeable batteries.

6. Pay / Fix / Use cloth shopping bags.

7. Grow / Pay / Use your own food.

8. Take / Fix / Pay bills online.

**2**  Look at the pictures. Complete each sentence with the simple present of one tip from Exercise 1.

1. Debbie _uses a_
   _clothesline_ .

2. Martin _____ .

3. Many people in big cities
   _____ .

4. Wesley _____
   _____ .

5. Rita _____ .

6. Andy _____ .

**3** Complete the story. Change the main clause of the last sentence to an *if* clause in the next sentence.

If I get a new car, I'll buy a hybrid car.

1. _If I buy a hybrid car_____, I'll save money on gas.

2. _If I save_____, I'll have more money to spend.

3. _____, I'll buy a new cell phone.

4. _____, I'll recycle my old cell phone.

5. _____, there will be less e-waste.

6. _____, the world will be a better place!

**4** Write sentences with the phrases in the chart. Use the first conditional and *will*. Write each sentence two ways.

|  | Who | The condition | The result |
|---|---|---|---|
| 1. | Robert | use rechargeable batteries | buy fewer batteries |
| 2. | Emma | take public transportation | use less gas |
| 3. | Tom and Jackie | have enough money | buy a hybrid car |
| 4. | You | buy local food | get good fruit and vegetables |
| 5. | We | recycle more bottles | help the environment |

1. _If Robert uses rechargeable batteries, he'll buy fewer batteries._

   _Robert will buy fewer batteries if he uses rechargeable batteries._

2. _____

   _____

3. _____

   _____

4. _____

   _____

5. _____

   _____

**5** Write the answers to the questions. Use the first conditional and the words in parentheses.

www.ecoblog.cup/Q&A

# We want your opinions! Please tell us what you think!

**What do you think will happen if more people recycle?**

Marc67: *If more people recycle, we might have less garbage* .
(have less garbage / we / might) 1

SSGreen: *If more people* .
(could / help the environment / it) 2

**What do you think will happen if our town starts a wind farm?**

EcoJoe: _____ .
(use less energy / we / may) 3

EvaR22: _____ .
(be more jobs / might / there) 4

**What do you think will happen if the big supermarket closes?**

SSGreen: _____ .
(we / may / buy more local food) 5

EvaR22: _____ .
(some people / get upset / might) 6

**6** Answer the questions with your own opinion. Use *will*, *may*, *might*, or *could*. Use each word at least once.

Example: *If people stop driving cars, there will be less pollution.* or

*Many people might lose their jobs if people stop driving cars.*

1. What will happen if people stop driving cars? _____

2. What will happen if everyone buys a bike? _____

3. What will happen if we don't have clean water? _____

4. What will happen if people don't fix leaky faucets? _____

5. What will happen if there is no more pollution? _____

6. What will happen if people have to pay for plastic bags in stores? _____

7. What will happen if you grow your own food? _____

8. What will happen if people buy new computers every year? _____

# D  Finding solutions

**1** Read the article. Then check (✓) the chapters that might be in Chelsea Thomson's book.

1. ☐ How to Use Less Energy
2. ☐ How to Waste Time
3. ☐ How to Recycle More
4. ☐ Buy More Than You Need

5. ☐ How to Have More Garbage
6. ☐ How to Use Your Car Less Often
7. ☐ Where to Buy Local Food
8. ☐ Kinds of Food You Can Grow at Home

Dear Readers,

My new book, *Going Completely Green*, is finished! As the title says, I decided to go completely green for a month – no electricity, no running water, no car, no phone, no computer! I didn't even use anything with batteries. It was very difficult, and I decided to write a book about my experience. During the day, I wrote on paper with a pencil. When I wanted to sharpen my pencil, I remembered my pencil sharpener uses electricity. I had to sharpen it with a knife! At night, I used a candle for light. I washed all of my clothes by hand with water from the river behind my house, and then I put them on a clothesline. I walked to a local farm to buy food. I ate mostly fruits and vegetables. I only ate meat about five times, and I cooked it over a fire in my yard. The hardest part was not talking to friends and family on the phone or emailing them. My best friend lives an hour away by car, so I didn't communicate with her at all.

In my opinion, it is impossible to live completely green for a long time, but there are many things you can do. Now, I try to work with the lights off for most of the day. I'm driving my car again, but I try to walk or ride my bike when I only have to go a short distance. I buy more local food now, too. I have to use my computer for work, but I use it for fewer hours each day. I also turn it off when I'm not home. There are many things you can do to use less energy and water. This book will help you learn how to live a greener life. If you follow the steps in my book, you'll really help the environment. Oh, and if you buy my book, you might want to read it by candlelight to save energy!

*Chelsea Thomson*

**2** Read the article again. Rewrite the sentences to correct the underlined mistakes.

1. Chelsea went green for <u>two months</u>.     *Chelsea went green for a month.*

2. She wrote <u>on a computer</u>. _____

3. She washed her clothes <u>on a clothesline</u>. _____

4. She thinks it's impossible <u>to work with the lights off</u>. _____

5. Now she <u>drives her car</u> for short distances. _____

6. She turns her computer off if <u>she's working</u>. _____

# Relationships

## A  *Healthy relationships*

**1** Complete the sentences and the puzzle with the correct words. Use words about relationship behaviors.

**Across**

3. Mr. Jenkins said I didn't do a good job. He always finds things in my work to _____ .

6. Don and Greg _____ all the time. They never listen to each other.

7. Gina is really sorry. She's going to _____ to Kate.

8. Kate knows Gina is sorry. She's going to _____ her.

**Down**

1. My mother likes to _____ my friends. She always tells me if they are good or bad friends.

2. Please don't _____ . I know you're not being honest.

3. Josh and Dan usually _____ by email, but they sometimes talk on the phone.

4. I want to go to a restaurant, and you want to go to the park. Let's _____ and eat food in the park!

5. Shannon talks about everyone! I hate when people _____ .

**2** Complete the advice column. Use the infinitive forms of the correct verbs from the box.

| apologize | argue | be | communicate | compromise | ✓lie |

# Ask Lee

Dear Lee,

Sometimes it's difficult to tell my parents the truth. I'm a pretty good son, but I make mistakes. I don't want my parents to get upset. I know that it's not good <u>to lie</u><sub>1</sub> , but sometimes it's hard to be honest. What's your advice?

         – Stressed-Out Son

   Dear Stressed-Out Son,

   It's not always easy

   _____<sub>2</sub> honest, but you should try. It's very important

   _____<sub>3</sub> with your parents. If you say you made a mistake, it might help them understand. They used to be young, and they made mistakes, too.

Dear Lee,

My friends and I are planning a vacation, and we're arguing. Two people want to go to the beach, and one person wants to go hiking. What should we do?

         – Ralph

Dear Ralph,

It's never a good idea

_____<sub>4</sub> with your friends. It's important

_____<sub>5</sub> . Why don't you go to a park with mountains near the ocean, like the Manuel Antonio National Park in Costa Rica? You can hike in the mountains and go to the beach!

Dear Lee,

I gossiped about my friend to some other people. I feel terrible, and now she won't talk to me. Please help!

         – Pamela G.

Dear Pamela,

When someone is upset with you, it's useful _____<sub>6</sub> . If she doesn't want to talk to you, tell her you're sorry in an email. If she knows how you feel, she may forgive you.

**3** Put the words in the correct order to make a sentence.

1. It's / to help / your neighbors / a good idea / .

   _It's a good idea to help your neighbors._

2. to apologize / It's / nice / when you're wrong / .

   _____

3. with your teacher / not good / It's / to argue / .

   _____

4. It's / to compromise / important / with your friends / .

   _____

5. helpful / It's / in class / to listen carefully / .

   _____

6. never a good idea / about your friends / It's / to gossip / .

   _____

**4** Complete the sentences with your own ideas. Use expressions from the box.

| It's (not) a good idea | It's (not) helpful | It's (not) useful |
|---|---|---|
| It's (not) good | It's (not) important | |

*Example:* **At school:** _It's important to be on time._

**At school:**

1. _____ (be) on time.

2. _____ (use) a dictionary in class.

**With your friends:**

3. _____ (communicate) dishonestly
   or impatiently.

4. _____ (plan) activities that
   everyone enjoys.

**At a library:**

5. _____ (talk) quietly.

6. _____ (write) in the books.

## B I'm really sorry.

**1** Circle the correct phrase to complete each conversation.

A.

**Kelly:** Hi, Doug. **That's OK** / (**I'm really sorry**) I missed your birthday.
          ¹

**Doug:** **There's no need to apologize.** / **I'm sorry.**
                                          ²

**Kelly:** Well, it's not nice to miss a friend's birthday.

**Doug:** Please, Kelly. **I'm sorry.** / **Don't worry about it.**
                       ³

**Kelly:** OK. But let's celebrate on Friday.

**Doug:** Great!

B. **Kelly:** Hi, Doug. **There's no need to apologize** / **I'm sorry**, but I can't make it on Friday.
                                               ¹

**Doug:** **That's OK.** / **My apologies.**
                        ²

**Kelly:** No, it's not. I feel terrible. **My apologies.** / **Don't worry about it.** Can you come over on Saturday? I'll make dinner!
                                                          ³

**Doug:** OK. That sounds great.

**2** Complete the conversations. Use some of the expressions from Exercise **1** and your own ideas.

A. **You:** I missed your party. _____ .
                                              ¹

**Friend:** Oh, _____ . What happened?
                                   ²

**You:** _____ .
                      ³

**Friend:** That's too bad.

B. **Friend:** I am very late. _____ .
                                          ¹

**You:** _____ . Is everything all right?
                              ²

**Friend:** Not really. _____ .
                                    ³

**You:** Oh. Too bad!

# C  *That can't be the problem.*

**1** Complete each question with the correct word from the box.

| | | |
|---|---|---|
| ✓after | into | together |
| along | on | up |
| by | on | up |

1. Do you take _____ *after* _____ anyone in your family? Who?

2. Have you ever been picked _____ in school? By whom?

3. Do you get _____ well with your friends?

4. Have you ever broken _____ with a boyfriend or girlfriend? Who?

5. How often do you get _____ with friends each month? What do you do?

6. Do you like it when friends drop _____ and don't call first? Who does this?

7. Who is the last person you ran _____ when you were shopping?

8. Do you know anyone who is immature and needs to grow _____ ? Who?

9. Who is the person you count _____ the most?

**2** Answer the questions in Exercise 1 with your own information. Use phrasal verbs, and add more information when possible.

*Example:*   *Yes, I do. I take after my mother. We're friendly and outgoing. I look*
        *like her, too.*   or

        *No, I don't. But I'd like to take after my father. He's really intelligent.*

1. _____

2. _____

3. _____

4. _____

5. _____

6. _____

7. _____

8. _____

9. _____

## 3 Complete the sentences with the correct words from the box.

| can't | may | ✓must |
|-------|-----|-------|

1. Cindy _____*must*_____ get along well with her family. She's at her parents' house every weekend.

2. I'm not sure, but I think I _____ know where the restaurant is.

3. Mark _____ be breaking up with me! He loves me!

| could | might not | must not |
|-------|-----------|----------|

4. Bev _____ come to work today. She felt sick yesterday.

5. Josh _____ be coming to the party. It started an hour ago, and he's not here.

6. You _____ run into Dan at the mall. I think he's shopping today.

## 4 Complete the conversation with *must, can't,* or *might*.

**Sandra:** Good morning, Paul. Do you know where Dan is? I didn't see his car outside.

**Paul:** I'm not sure. He _____*might*_____ be at a
                                        1
doctor's appointment.

**Sandra:** No, he _____ have a doctor's
                            2
appointment today. I have all his appointments
in my calendar.

**Paul:** You're right. He _____ be taking
                                  3
the bus today. The buses are often late.

**Sandra:** Well, he _____ have a good reason. He's never late.
                            4

**Paul:** Wait! My phone's ringing. It _____ be Dan. Let me see. . . .
                                            5
No. It _____ be Dan. It's not his number.
              6

**Sandra:** Well, you should answer it! Dan _____ be calling from a different
                                                      7
phone if there's a problem.

*A minute later . . .*

**Paul:** Yes. It was Dan. He _____ be feeling pretty stressed. He ran out
                                    8
of gas and had to ask a stranger to drive him to a gas station. But he left his cell
phone in his car, so he had to ask the stranger to use her phone.

**5** Answer the questions with your own ideas. Use words from the box to speculate and to say how sure you are.

| can't | could | may (not) | might (not) | must (not) |

*Example:* <u>I don't know. She might be looking for some money.</u>  or
<u>I see her car. She must be looking for her keys.</u>

1. What is the woman looking for?

_____

2. What animal is it?

_____

3. Why is the boy crying?

_____

4. Why are they arguing?

_____

5. Why is the woman late?

_____

6. Where are they going?

_____

# D Getting advice

**1** **Read the advice. Who is the speaker giving the advice to? Write the correct heading from the magazine article.**

1. "I'm sorry, but you need to get more organized. Your work is often late."     *To a co-worker*

2. "It must feel bad that James doesn't want to play with you. Could you ask Kahil?"     _____

3. "I don't think he's good for you. Do you ever think about breaking up?"     _____

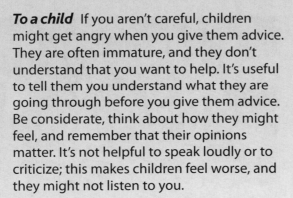

## How to Give Advice

Everyone has an opinion, but sometimes it's not easy to give advice. This is really true for important relationships. Here are some tips on how you can give advice in different relationships.

***To a child*** If you aren't careful, children might get angry when you give them advice. They are often immature, and they don't understand that you want to help. It's useful to tell them you understand what they are going through before you give them advice. Be considerate, think about how they might feel, and remember that their opinions matter. It's not helpful to speak loudly or to criticize; this makes children feel worse, and they might not listen to you.

***To a co-worker*** It can be difficult to give advice to people at work, so it's often good to apologize first. For example, say, "I'm sorry, but I think you could . . ." And remember that it's never a good idea to judge people. Give advice about what you think should change about the person's work, not about the person! Also remember that in work situations, you often have to compromise. You may give advice, but the person might not take it!

***To a friend*** Friends can be the hardest people to give advice to. It's important to be honest, but you should also be kind. When you give advice to a friend, don't argue. Try to communicate with your friend. Ask questions and really understand your friend's problem before you give advice.

These tips are useful in other types of relationships, too. The important thing to remember is to be patient with others, and give them a chance to respond to your advice. It's also helpful to give advice when the person is ready to listen. Don't give advice when the person is extremely upset or stressed. Try to find a time when he or she is more relaxed.

**2** **Read the article again. Check (✓) what the writer says about giving advice.**

1. Don't argue. ✓
2. You may need to compromise. ☐
3. You might need to get angry. ☐
4. Be honest. ☐
5. Don't give advice about work. ☐
6. Ask questions. ☐

# Living your life

## A *He taught himself.*

**1** Complete the puzzle with words for qualities for success. What's the mystery word?

1. a strong interest in something
2. the quality of showing no fear
3. the ability to change easily
4. a commitment to something
5. the belief that you can succeed
6. the ability to develop original ideas

|   | 1 | E | N | T | H | U | S | I | A | S | M |   |
|---|---|---|---|---|---|---|---|---|---|---|---|---|
|   | 2 |   |   |   |   |   |   |   |   |   |   |   |

(crossword puzzle grid with rows numbered 1–6, row 1 filled in as E N T H U S I A S M)

**2** Circle the correct words to complete the article.

## Man Saves Friend

Farmers Jim Rolland and Ryan Jensen were trying to take soybeans out of a large bin, but they wouldn't come out. Jim Rolland was (confident) / confidence that he could fix the problem, but his **confident / confidence** got him in trouble. He climbed some stairs and went into the bin. The beans moved and covered him completely!

Ryan Jensen told another worker to call for help. Then he had a **creative / creativity** idea. He wasn't sure it was **wise / wisdom**, but he also went into the bin. He got on his stomach on top of the beans. For four hours, he moved beans so Rolland could breathe. His **dedicated / dedication** and **brave / bravery** saved his friend's life.

Rescue workers finally came. They removed the beans and helped Rolland out of the bin. He was fine, and he was happy to have **talented / talent** people help him.

**3** **Put the words in the correct order to make sentences.**

1. a picture of / art class / myself / I / painted / in / .

   _I painted a picture of myself in art class._

2. by / The / isn't / itself / computer / going to work / .

   _____

3. brave / herself / doesn't / mother / My / consider / .

   _____

4. Japanese / themselves / taught / Kyle / and Mick / .

   _____

5. blame / Don't / for / my / yourselves / problems / !

   _____

6. did / Chris / When / hurt / himself / ?

   _____

7. yourself / by / draw / Did / you / that picture / ?

   _____

8. enjoyed / We / on / ourselves / trip to New York / our / .

   _____

**4** **Complete the sentences with the correct reflexive pronouns.**

What do people like to do by _____*themselves*_____ ? Here's what some
of our readers said:

- I like to travel by _____ . I always meet interesting people,
  and sometimes they teach me words of wisdom. (Tom P., Chicago)

- My brother and I love to play video games by _____ .
  We don't like our sisters to play with us. (Jake M., San Antonio)

- My husband likes to cook by _____ . And that's OK with
  me! (Lidia S., Boston)

- My daughter is very enthusiastic, and she likes to do extreme sports by
  _____ . It makes me nervous! (Na-young K., San Francisco)

What do you like to do by _____ ?

**5** Complete the conversations with the correct personal and reflexive pronouns.

A.  Rachel: _____I_____ like your scarf, Phoebe.
                      1

   Phoebe: Thanks. I made it by _____ .
                                          2

   Rachel: Wow. _____ have a lot of talent!
                         3

B.  Sheila: Look! My son painted this by _____ .
                                                  1

   Feng: _____ did a great job.
                2

C.  Joe: Did you hear what happened to Emily?

   Martin: No, _____ didn't.
                       1

   Joe: She hurt _____ skiing.
                         2

   Martin: Is _____ OK?
                    3

   Joe: Yes, she is.

D.  Laura: We really enjoyed _____ at your party, Pedro.
                                      1

   Pedro: I'm glad _____ had fun, but the food I made was terrible.
                          2

   Laura: Don't blame _____ . It was fine.
                              3

   Pedro: You're right. My friends enjoyed _____ . That's what counts!
                                                    4

**6** Answer the questions with your own information.

Example:  _Yes, I do. I'm very enthusiastic about good music._  or

          _No, I don't. I'm not enthusiastic about anything._

1. Do you consider yourself enthusiastic? What are you enthusiastic about? _____

_____

2. Do you consider yourself flexible, or do you like to do things your own way? _____

_____

3. What do you like to do by yourself? _____

_____

4. Have you ever painted yourself? What did the picture look like? _____

_____

5. Do you know someone who hurt himself or herself playing a sport? What happened? _____

_____

6. Do you think people should travel by themselves? Why or why not? _____

_____

## B   I'll give it some thought.

**1** Write the conversation in the correct order.

> Their prices are really high. You should go to Comp.com. It's an online store.
> ✓Hi, Tina. Where are you going?
> Hmm. . . . I'll give it some thought. Thanks.
> I don't think you should do that.
> I'm going to Tech-It to buy a new computer.
> Really? Why not?

Erin: _Hi, Tina. Where are you going?_

Tina: _____

Erin: _____

Tina: _____

Erin: _____

Tina: _____

**2** Complete the conversations. Use information from the pictures and sentences from the box. Use Exercise 1 as a model. Sometimes more than one answer is possible.

> I wouldn't recommend that.      I'll think about it.
> I'll see.                        I'm not sure that's the best idea.

1. **Ed:** Hi, Ali. Where are you going?

   **Ali:** I'm going to _____ to

   buy a new _____ .

   **Ed:** _____ .

   **Ali:** Really? _____ ?

   **Ed:** Their prices are really high. You should go

   to _____ . It's an

   _____ store.

   **Ali:** Hmm. . . . _____ .
   Thanks.

2. **Sasha:** Hi, Marc. _____ ?

   **Marc:** I'm going to _____

   _____ .

   **Sasha:** _____ .

   **Marc:** Really? _____ ?

   **Sasha:** Their prices are really high.

   _____ .

   _____ .

   **Marc:** Hmm. . . . _____ .
   Thanks.

1 Rewrite the sentences. Change the underlined words. Use the phrasal verb in parentheses and the correct pronoun.

1. Can you <u>show me where Linda is</u>? (point out)

   *Can you point her out?*

2. You need to <u>do your homework again</u>. It has a lot of mistakes. (do over)

   _____

3. I <u>didn't accept that job</u>. (turn down)

   _____

4. I'm going to <u>donate these shirts</u>. (give away)

   _____

5. Please don't <u>mention his daughter</u>. (bring up)

   _____

6. When are you going to <u>return the money I lent you</u>? (pay back)

   _____

7. We really should <u>discuss our problem</u>. (talk over)

   _____

8. Can I <u>use this computer</u> before I buy it? (try out)

   _____

9. I'll <u>return your camera</u> tomorrow, if that's OK. (give back)

   _____

10. Let's <u>do the conference call later</u>. (put off)

    _____

**2** Complete Bianca's email with the correct forms of the verbs in parentheses.
Use the second conditional.

To:       RobbieJ@cup.org
From:     Bianca54@cup.com
Subject:  What would you do?

Hi Rob,

I have some interesting news. My aunt might give me some money! I _would do_ _____
                                                                              1
(do) so many things if I _____ (have) a lot of money. If I
                              2
_____ (be) rich, I _____ (not work) anymore! That
        3                                    4
would be great. If I _____ (not have) a job, I _____
                            5                                          6
(travel) around the world. I _____ (feel) very lucky if I
                                      7
_____ (get) a lot of money. What would you do?
        8
Your friend,

Bianca

**3** Now complete Rob's email with the correct forms of the verbs in parentheses.
Use the second conditional.

To:       Bianca54@cup.com
From:     RobbieJ@cup.org
Subject:  RE: What would you do?

Hey Bianca!

Wow! It _would be_ _____ (be) great if your aunt _____ (give)
                1                                                2
you money. Is it a lot of money? If I _____ (have) a lot of money, I
                                              3
_____ (make) a big, beautiful garden. But I can't have a garden at my
        4
apartment, so I _____ (need) a house with a big yard. I
                        5
_____ (use) a lot of my money to buy a house, and there
        6
_____ (be) a lot of room for two big gardens: a vegetable garden and a
        7
flower garden. I _____ (give) some money to my brother, too, if I
                          8
_____ (be) rich. He _____ (not have to pay) me back.
        9                                    10
Take care,

Rob

**4** Write questions with the words in parentheses. Use the second conditional.

1. (What / you / do / if / you / be / braver)

   _What would you do if you were braver?_

2. (What / you / buy / for your friends / if / you / have / a lot of money)

   _____

3. (Where / you / go / if / you / have / a free ticket)

   _____

4. (What / you / do / if / you / have / 200 vacation days)

   _____

5. (What instrument / you / play / if / you and your friends / have / a band)

   _____

6. (What sport / you / try / if / you / try / an extreme sport)

   _____

7. (What / you / give away / if / you / move)

   _____

**5** Answer the questions in Exercise 4 with your own information.

Example:  _If I were braver, I would take a trip around the world by myself._

1. _____
2. _____
3. _____
4. _____
5. _____
6. _____
7. _____

# D What an accomplishment!

**1** Read the letter. Then circle the correct answers.

1. How old is Thomas?    99              100              101

2. Who is Peter?          his brother    his son    his grandson

Dear Peter,

Can you believe I'll be 100 years old next week? If I had a dollar for every great thing I did, I would be rich! I decided to write to you about a few important things that happened in each decade of my life.

1920s – These are the first years I really remember. Jazz music was extremely popular, and I was in a jazz band. We were very dedicated to our music!

1930s – Many people didn't have a lot of money in the 1930s, but I worked very hard. In 1937, I bought myself a car! If I had that car today, it would be worth a lot of money!

1940s – This was a sad decade because of World War II, but the 1940s were also happy for me in many ways. I met your grandmother in 1941 when I was a soldier. A friend pointed her out to me at the supermarket. We got married two years later. That was a wise decision! Your mother was born in 1944.

1950s – We bought our first TV. I remember trying it out in the store first. It was amazing! And with the Civil Rights Movement starting, it was a good time to have a TV.

1960s – This was a very creative time in my life. Your grandmother was painting, and I started taking pictures. In 1969, a man walked on the moon!

1970s – I was offered a promotion in 1972, but I turned it down. I retired six years later.

1980s – I started a volunteer program at a hospital in 1982 and was busy with that for several years.

1990s – In 1995, a park in our town was dedicated to me for the volunteer work I did at the hospital. Do you remember when you bought me a computer in 1997? I never taught myself how to use it!

2000s – The 2000s were a quiet decade, but I've had a lot of time to spend with family. I bought a cell phone this year, but I took it back. I didn't think I really needed it. I guess I'm a little old-fashioned!

See you next week for my birthday!

Your grandfather,

Thomas O'Malley

**2** Read the letter again. Then number the events in the correct order.

_____ He turned down a promotion.          _____ He got a cell phone.

_____ He got married.          _____ He bought a car.

_____ He started a volunteer program.          _____ He started taking pictures.

___1___ He was in a jazz band.          _____ He got a computer.

# Music

## A  *Music trivia*

**1** Put the words in the correct order to make phrases about music. Add hyphens, if necessary.

1. best / artist / selling        *best-selling artist* _____

2. video / winning / award        _____

3. performer / often / downloaded   _____

4. priced / high / ticket         _____

5. group / named / oddly          _____

6. singers / well / known         _____

7. breaking / hit / record        _____

8. nice / voice / sounding        _____

**2** Complete the webpage with the phrases from Exercise 1.

## Jake and Jill's Music Awards

Hello fans! Here's today's music news from your favorite music fans!

- Sting, a _*best-selling artist*_ from the 1980s, and his wife started the
  1
  Rainforest Concert in 1991. They have the concert every two years. This year,
  _____ , like Elton John and Bruce Springsteen,
  2
  performed. Tickets were $2,500 or more! That's a _____ ,
  3
  but all of the money helps save rain forests around the world.

- Listen to *Yellow Fever!* It's a great album by Señor Coconut and His Orchestra. Yes, this
  is a very _____ (*señor* is a Spanish word, but Señor
  4
  Coconut is actually German), but we think each singer has a very
  _____ !
  5

- Who is the most _____ on our website? Taylor Swift!
  6
  Her song "Love Story" has been downloaded over 4 million times, and the video won the
  Country Music Association Award for Best Music Video in 2009. To listen to her
  _____ , *click here*. To watch her
  7
  _____ , *click here*.
  8

**3** Complete the sentences with the correct forms of the words in parentheses. Use the past passive.

## We Are the World

*Kenny Rogers and Lionel Richie*

"We Are the World" _was recorded_ (record) in 1985.
                        1
The money it made _____ (give) to groups
                        2
that help hungry people in Africa. The song

_____ (write) by Michael Jackson and Lionel
        3
Richie. Many famous singers, like Kenny Rogers, Bob Dylan, and

Stevie Wonder, _____ (ask) to sing it.
                        4

A video _____ (make) while the singers were recording the song. The song
                5

and video _____ (play) on TV in the spring of 1985.
                6

In 2010, "We Are the World" _____ (record) again with new singers to help
                                    7

the people of Haiti. The song _____ (sing) by over 80 well-known musicians,
                                    8

like Justin Bieber and Jennifer Hudson. It _____ (see) on TV by many people
                                                9

on February 12.

**4** Rewrite each sentence in the past passive. If there is information about who did the action, use a *by* phrase.

1. Four men planned the Woodstock Festival in 1969.

   _The Woodstock Festival was planned by four men in 1969._

2. Someone asked many well-known singers to sing at Woodstock.

   _____

3. Someone gave information about the festival on the radio.

   _____

4. Someone allowed about 400,000 to 500,000 music fans into the festival.

   _____

5. People made a documentary about Woodstock in 1970.

   _____

6. *Rolling Stone* magazine listed Woodstock as one of "50 Moments that Changed the History of Rock and Roll."

   _____

**5** Look at the chart of some record-breaking hits. Then answer the questions. Use the past passive.

| Song | Singer(s) | Year of release | Millions of recordings sold |
|---|---|---|---|
| Candle in the Wind | Elton John | 1997 | 37 |
| White Christmas | Bing Crosby | 1942 | 30 |
| We Are the World | Many musicians | 1985 | 20 |
| Rock Around the Clock | Bill Haley and his Comets | 1954 | 17 |
| I Want to Hold Your Hand | The Beatles | 1963 | 12 |
| Hey Jude | The Beatles | 1968 | 10 |
| It's Now or Never | Elvis Presley | 1960 | 10 |
| I Will Always Love You | Whitney Houston | 1992 | 10 |

1. Who was "It's Now or Never" sung by?    *It was sung by Elvis Presley.*

2. When was "White Christmas" released?    _____

3. Who were "I Want to Hold Your Hand" and "Hey Jude" sung by?    _____

4. How many recordings of "We Are the World" were sold?    _____

5. What song was released in 1954?    _____

6. What song was sung by Elton John?    _____

7. How many recordings of "I Will Always Love You" were sold?    _____

8. When was "Hey Jude" released?    _____

**6** Answer the questions with your own information. Write complete sentences.

*Example:*   *My favorite song was "Candle in the Wind."*

1. What was your favorite song when you were 12?    _____

2. Who was it sung by?    _____

3. What kind of music was it?    _____

4. Was a video made of the song? What was it like?    _____

5. Was the singer or group well known?    _____

6. Is the singer or group well known today?    _____

7. Did you ever go to a concert of the singer or group? Where was it?    _____

8. Was a documentary ever made about the singer or group? What was it called?    _____

## B The first thing you do is . . .

Rewrite the instructions. Use the words in the box.

**A.**

> ### How to Buy a Song
> 1. Find the song you want, and click on it.
> 2. Enter your credit card number.
> 3. Read the information, and click "Yes."

> After that   ✓First   To finish

**How to Buy a Song**

*First, find the song you want, and click on it.*

_____

_____

**B.**

> ### How to Listen to Music on Your Phone
> 1. Open your music program.
> 2. Choose the song you want to listen to.
> 3. Click "Play."

> The last thing you do is   Then   To start

**How to Listen to Music on Your Phone**

_____

_____

_____

**C.**

> ### How to Record Your Voice
> 1. Put the recorder near you.
> 2. Hit the "Record" button.
> 3. Sing a song or speak into the recorder.

> Finally   Next   The first thing you do is

**How to Record Your Voice**

_____

_____

_____

# C  *Music and me*

**1** Complete the sentences and the puzzle with the correct verbs.

**Across**

1. My favorite band will _____ a new album next week.

5. Justin Bieber sang the song "My World," but he didn't _____ it.
   Usher was one of the producers.

7. Coldplay will _____ their tour dates on their website.

8. Beethoven couldn't hear anything, but he was able to _____ great music.
   Many people listen to his music today, almost 200 years after he died.

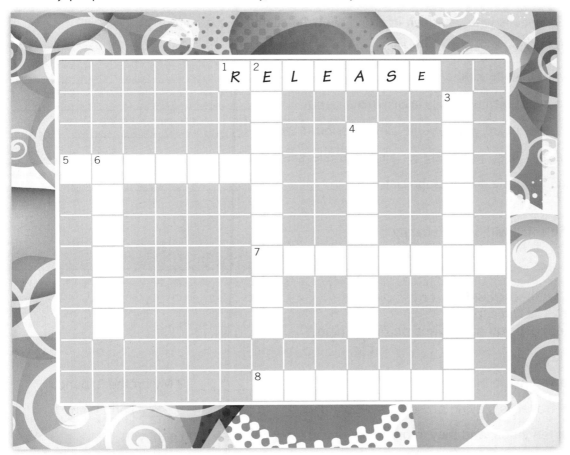

**Down**

2. Lady Gaga likes to _____ her audience in her concerts.

3. I can't sing very well, but I really _____ music. I listen to it all the time.

4. Do you know when your brother's band is going to _____ their new song?
   I really would like to go see his band.

6. We're going to _____ our new song in the studio next week.
   They have new computers we can use.

**2** Circle the correct word to complete each sentence.

1. Beethoven's Fifth Symphony is my favorite musical **compose** / **composition**.

2. My favorite band **released** / **a release** a new album yesterday.

3. My uncle **produces** / **production** songs, but he can't sing or play an instrument.

4. Jonathan found one of his father's old **record** / **recordings**.

5. Wendy loves to go to **perform** / **performances** at music festivals.

6. My sister likes to **entertain** / **entertainment** our family.

7. The band made an **announce** / **announcement** about their tour yesterday.

8. What time does the **produce** / **production** of *Hamlet* start?

**3** Answer the questions with your own information. Write complete sentences.

*Example:*  <u>My favorite kind of entertainment is the movies.</u>

1. What's your favorite kind of entertainment? _____

2. Have you ever taken a music class? When? _____

3. Have you ever heard your favorite singer perform? Where? _____

4. Have you ever been to a party for an album release? Where? _____

5. What kind of music do you appreciate? _____

**4** Complete the email with *yet* or *already*.

To:       Lee1988@cup.org
From:    JJJ@cup.com
Subject: Do you have plans on Friday night?

Hey Lee!

Have you made plans for Friday night _____*yet*_____ ? My brother's band,

Time Travel, is playing at the Music Café. I've _____ seen them

about ten times, and they're great! Have you listened to the CD I sent you

_____ ? I've _____ bought tickets for my sister

and me, but I haven't gotten a ticket for you _____ . Let me know

if you want to go. Tickets aren't high-priced. They're only $10. Time Travel has

_____ started recording their next CD. It hasn't been released

_____ , but they might play a few songs from it on Friday. I hope

you can come!

Jay

**5** Look at Carla's To-Do list. Then write sentences about what she has and hasn't done. Use the present perfect with *yet* or *already*.

> *To Do*
>
> ○ *Send Jen and Sandra information about the Coldplay concert* ✓
>
> ○ *Call Sandra and Jen about tickets to see Coldplay* ✓
>
> *Buy the tickets* ✓
>
> ○ *Clean the house*
>
> *Go to the airport to pick up Jen and Sandra*

1. *Carla has already sent Jen and Sandra information about the Coldplay concert.*

2. *She* _____

3. _____

4. _____

5. _____

**6** Look at Jen and Sandra's To-Do list. Then write questions and answers about what they have and haven't done. Use the present perfect with *yet* or *already*.

> *To Do*
>
> ○ *Do the laundry* ✓
>
> ○ *Clean the apartment* ✓
>
> *Listen to Coldplay's new songs*
>
> ○ *Give our parents Carla's cell phone number* ✓
>
> *Pay Carla for the tickets*

1. Question: *Have Jen and Sandra done the laundry yet?*

   Answer: *Yes, they have already done the laundry.*

2. Q: *Have they* _____

   A: _____

3. Q: _____

   A: _____

4. Q: _____

   A: _____

5. Q: _____

   A: _____

**1** Read the article. Then write why musicians don't want people to give music to their friends.

_____

# Music Laws

**Today, many people get their music from the Internet.** But is it legal? It depends on how you get the music and what country you live in. It's sometimes OK, but it's often against the law.

It is usually legal to buy songs from websites on the Internet. If you buy a song, you can make a copy for yourself. However, in the United States and some other countries, it is illegal to make copies of the song for your friends. This is because laws protect people's ideas and work. If everyone copied and gave music to their friends, people would not buy the singers' albums, and musicians couldn't make money for their work.

Also, in many countries it's illegal to *bootleg* music. This is a word that describes when people go to a live performance, record the music, and then upload the music to the Internet to give to their friends or to sell. Sometimes at concerts musicians perform new songs before they are recorded in a studio. They don't want their music released on the Internet before their albums are sold.

Some people *sample* music when they compose songs. This means they use a part of someone else's song in their music. This is often done in hip-hop music. Sampling is usually legal if you have permission from the singer, but it is usually not OK to use someone else's music without permission.

### Interesting Music Trivia

- In 1990, part of a David Bowie song was sampled by Vanilla Ice without permission. After the song was released, Vanilla Ice had to pay David Bowie a lot of money for using his music.

- In 1999, Napster was created as a way to get music from friends without paying for it on the Internet. Napster had to stop doing this in the United States, and now people have to pay for the music.

**2** Read the article. Then write L (legal – OK) or I (illegal – not OK) for these actions according to the laws in the United States.

1. You can buy songs on the Internet from websites. ___L___

2. You can get a song for free from a friend. _____

3. You can bootleg music from a live performance. _____

4. You can sample music without permission. _____

# On vacation

## A Travel preferences

**1** Complete the travel ads with the correct phrases from the box.

| | | | |
|---|---|---|---|
| buy handicrafts | listen to live music | ✓speak a foreign language | visit landmarks |
| go to clubs | see wildlife | try local food | volunteer |

### European Vacation

Can you _speak a_
_foreign language_ $_1$?
If you speak French,
Spanish, or Portuguese, this
is the vacation for you! Visit
France, Spain, and Portugal.
_____ $_2$,
like the Eiffel Tower in France and famous
museums in Spain, or stay near the ocean
in Portugal.

### Miami Dream

The weather is wonderful in
Miami for most of the year.
Visit beaches during the day.
At night,

_____ $_5$
to dance! There are also
many places to

_____ $_6$.
You can go to a concert or listen to free music
in the parks or even on the beach.

### South American Working Vacation

Visit Peru and Ecuador in a different way.
_____ $_3$ your time to
help people and animals. First, teach English
in Peru, and then work in the Amazon rain
forest. You'll _____ $_4$,
like frogs, river dolphins, and monkeys.

### Seoul Markets

Do you like shopping? Tour Seoul's markets.
Namdaemun is the largest market in Seoul, and
it sells many different things. You can

_____ $_7$, like bags and
jewelry. You can even _____ $_8$
while you are shopping at the market or take
some home to cook.

**2** Put the words in the correct order to make sentences. Make one of the words a gerund. Use the simple present forms of the other verbs.

1. be / by boat / Travel / very slow

    _Traveling by boat is very slow._

2. enjoy / I / foreign languages / speak / when I travel

    _____

3. buy / handicrafts for my cousins / I / in local markets / like

    _____

4. be / to cook / I / interested in / learn / Thai food

    _____

5. be / to do on vacation / landmarks / my favorite thing / Visit

    _____

6. be / concerned about / help / I / wildlife in the ocean

    _____

**3** Complete the conversation with the gerund forms of the correct words from the box.

| go | ✓hike | travel | volunteer | volunteer |
| --- | --- | --- | --- | --- |

**Mark:** Hey, Jesse. Where are you going for vacation?

**Jesse:** I don't know. I enjoy _____*hiking*_____ in
the mountains. Any suggestions?
$_1$

**Mark:** How about the Rockies in Canada?

**Jesse:** I don't think so. I prefer _____
somewhere warm.
$_2$

**Mark:** Why don't you go to Costa Rica? There are
mountains there, and it's warm.

**Jesse:** That's a good idea. You know, I'm interested in _____ .
Maybe I could help animals there.
$_3$

**Mark:** _____ is a great idea. It should make the vacation cheaper,
too. Are you going by yourself?
$_4$

**Jesse:** No, I'm not. I dislike _____ alone. I'm going with friends.
$_5$

**4** **Look at the chart. Then complete the sentences.**

| Name | Travel activity | Opinion | Preference |
|------|-----------------|---------|------------|
| Cara | travel / by bus | slow | go / by train |
| Diego | drive / a car | dangerous | ride / a bike |
| Donna and Nicole | visit / landmarks | boring | see / wildlife |
| Tom | go / to clubs | not fun | go / to concerts |
| Ian and Meg | travel / by plane | expensive | stay / home |
| Libby | learn / Chinese | difficult | study / Spanish |

1. Cara thinks  _traveling by bus is slow_  . She prefers  _going by train_  .

2. Diego thinks _____ . He _____ .

3. Donna and Nicole think _____ . They _____ .

4. Tom thinks _____ . He _____ .

5. Ian and Meg _____ . They _____ .

6. Libby _____ . She _____ .

**5** **Answer the questions with your own information. Use gerunds when possible.**

*Example:*  _I'm interested in buying handicrafts and trying local food._

1. What vacation activities are you interested in? _____

2. What do you enjoy doing on vacation? _____

3. What do you dislike doing on vacation? _____

4. What do you think is the easiest way to travel? _____

5. What do you think is the cheapest way to travel? _____

6. What do you dislike about planning a vacation? _____

7. What are you concerned about when looking for a hotel? _____

_____

8. What do you worry about when you travel? _____

9. Do you like listening to live local music when you travel? What kind? _____

_____

10. Are you interested in writing about your vacations? Why or why not? _____

_____

Complete the conversations with sentences from the box.

> Don't forget to get to the station 20 minutes early.
> Let me remind you to get there before 8:00 p.m.
> Remember to look for plane tickets today.
> ✓ Would you like a bus ticket or a train ticket?
> Would you prefer one bed or two beds?
> Would you rather go to a warm place or a cold place?

**A. Mr. Harris:** Hello. Can I help you?

    **Richard:** Yes. I'd like a ticket for Chicago, please.

  **Mr. Harris:** OK. _Would you like a bus ticket_
               <sub>1</sub>
            _or a train ticket_ ?
               <sub>1</sub>

    **Richard:** Oh, well, which one is better?

  **Mr. Harris:** The bus takes longer, but it's cheaper.

    **Richard:** Hmm. . . . I'll take the bus. I'm going on Saturday morning.

  **Mr. Harris:** Good. A bus leaves at 9:15. _____ .
                            <sub>2</sub>

    **Richard:** OK. Thanks.

**B.**    **Blanca:** Hey, Erica. _____ .
                    <sub>1</sub>

      **Erica:** Oh, yeah. Thanks. I'll look for the best tickets online after work.

           _____ ?
                 <sub>2</sub>

   **Blanca:** Let's go somewhere hot, like the beach.

      **Erica:** OK. I'll look for some cheap tickets, and we can make plans tonight.

   **Blanca:** Great. Thanks.

**C.**   **Ms. Ito:** Can I help you?

      **Shan:** Yes, I need a room for three nights.

   **Ms. Ito:** No problem. _____ ?
                   <sub>1</sub>

      **Shan:** One bed, please. Oh, and is there a restaurant in this hotel?

   **Ms. Ito:** Yes, there is. It's right over there. _____ .
                            <sub>2</sub>
           It closes at 8:30.

# *Rules and recommendations*

**1** Complete the words for the extreme sports.

1. p*aragliding*_____

2. r_____
   c_____

3. b_____
   j_____

4. w_____ -
   w_____
   r_____

5. k_____
   s_____

6. w_____

7. s_____

8. s_____

**2** Circle the correct expression to complete each sentence.

1. **Necessity:** _____ fill out this form before you go paragliding.

   a. You don't have to    (b.) You must    c. You'd better

2. **Recommendation:** Sandra _____ plan her vacation before she goes.

   a. doesn't have to    b. must    c. ought to

3. **Lack of necessity:** You _____ wear warm clothes when rock climbing in the summer.

   a. don't have to    b. have to    c. shouldn't

4. **Necessity:** Nancy and Carol _____ wear heavy boots when they go snowboarding.

   a. should    b. shouldn't    c. have to

5. **Recommendation:** _____ take sunglasses when you go white-water rafting.

   a. You must    b. You've got to    c. You'd better

6. **Lack of necessity:** Jorge _____ go skydiving if he doesn't want to.

   a. has to    b. doesn't have to    c. shouldn't

7. **Necessity:** _____ pay for my kite surfing lessons before I can take the first lesson.

   a. I've got to    b. I don't have to    c. I'd better

8. **Recommendation:** Sue and Teddy _____ go bungee jumping. It's very dangerous.

   a. don't have to    b. have got to    c. shouldn't

**3** Complete the article with *must* or *should*.

# ✈ *How to Get to Your Flight Faster*

Airports have a lot of rules. Here are some tips to help you get through the airport faster.

Airport Security

- You _____*should*_____ print your boarding pass at home,
  <sub>1</sub>
  if possible.

- You _____ get to the airport early. It's a good
  <sub>2</sub>
  idea to arrive an hour before your flight.

- You _____ have your passport or other ID.
  <sub>3</sub>
  You can't get on the plane without one of them.

- You _____ take off your shoes at security.
  <sub>4</sub>
  They won't let you go through with them on.

- You _____ wear shoes that are easy to take off.
  <sub>5</sub>
  You'll move faster.

**4** Circle the correct words to complete the instructions.

Welcome to the Riverside Park white-water rafting trip. We want you to
have a safe trip, so there are a few things that you (have to) / don't have to do.
1
First of all, **you'd better / you shouldn't** listen to your guide. That's me, so please
2
listen to me carefully. Now for the safety rules: **You must not / You must** sit on the
3
raft at all times. Stand only when you are getting on or off the raft. And while we are
riding, you **don't have to / ought to** hold on to the raft.
4

It's going to be warm today, so you **don't have to / must** wear a coat, but you
5
**should / shouldn't** wear a hat. It will protect your skin and eyes from the sun. Later
6
we'll stop at a beach and have lunch there. **You shouldn't / You'd better** eat on the raft.
7
Finally, don't forget that rafting can be dangerous. **You don't have to / You've got to**
8
be careful all day. If you follow my instructions, you'll be safe and have fun!

**5** Write your own rules and recommendations for each place. Use modals for necessity,
lack of necessity, and recommendations.

*Example:* **In a restaurant:** 1. *You must pay for your food.*

2. *You don't have to eat something you don't like.*

3. *You should leave a little extra money for the waiter or waitress.*

In a restaurant:

1. _____

2. _____

3. _____

At the movies:

4. _____

5. _____

6. _____

In your classroom:

7. _____

8. _____

9. _____

## D Seeing the sights

**1** Read the catalogue page. Then number the pictures to match the descriptions.

☐  ☐  ☐  ☐  ☐

### World Tour — The Catalogue for Travelers

Every year, World Tour chooses the top five items every traveler must have. Read about what you should buy this year.

**1. Digi-2300 Camera   $129.99**

Every traveler ought to have a good, reliable digital camera. We recommend the Digi-2300. It's small, so you can easily take it anywhere. It's great for taking pictures of landmarks or just for taking pictures of your friends. It's a reasonable price, and it takes great pictures.

**2. XP Binoculars   $52.99**

Look through these fantastic binoculars to see wildlife on your next safari. Using them is a great way to see animals safely and up close. They make the animals look ten times larger. You can also use these binoculars underwater, so they're great for looking at fish, too. They will fit easily in your bag because they're very small. Put them in your bag next to your new camera!

To order, call (800) 555-3400 or visit our website at www.worldtour.com/cup

**3. Simple Sarong   $18.50**

Sarongs are very useful, and there's one size for everyone. Women can use sarongs as a skirt or a dress, but men can use them, too. They work well as towels for the beach or to use after swimming, waterskiing, and kite surfing. Dry your body off, and then the towel dries in minutes! Get it in blue, black, red, orange, or green.

**4. Earplugs   2 for $3.50**

Earplugs are a cheap and practical gift for a friend or for yourself. Traveling on airplanes, buses, and trains can be noisy, but you won't hear any noise with these earplugs. Put them in your ears and fall asleep!

**5. The "It Bag"   $75.00**

Our best bag is called the "It Bag" because you have to have it! It can be small or large because it's expandable. It's perfect for a day trip or for a weekend vacation. Get it in black, brown, or red.

**2** Read the catalogue page again. Then write T (true), F (false), or NI (no information).

1. The binoculars are cheaper than the camera.  _T_

2. The camera only comes in one color.  _____

3. You have to wear the sarong.  _____

4. The earplugs aren't expensive.  _____

5. Expanding the bag is easy.  _____

# Credits

## Illustration credits

Kveta Jelinek: 1, 9, 47, 62, 73; Andrew Joyner: 12, 20, 45, 50; Greg Paprocki: 4, 10, 21, 36, 46, 55, 70, 77; Garry Parsons: 5, 14, 22, 25, 49, 71; Maria Rabinky: 33, 93; Rob Schuster: 76; Richard Williams: 23, 29, 68, 75

## Photography credits

6 ©Gulf Images/Alamy; 8 ©Media Bakery; 11 ©Juice Images/Alamy; 16 ©Michele Falzone/Alamy; 17 *(clockwise from top left)* ©Eva Mueller/Getty Images; ©Dorling Kindersley/Getty Images; ©Zee/Alamy; ©RT Images/Alamy; ©Shutterstock; ©Shutterstock; ©Siri Stafford/Getty Images; ©Ghislain & Marie David de Lossy/Getty Images; 18 ©Hulton Archive/Getty Images; 20 *(top to bottom)* ©Shutterstock; ©Kirsty McLaren/Alamy; 23 ©Media Bakery; 24 *(top to bottom)* ©Hulton Archive/Getty Images; ©Archive Photos/Getty Images; ©Ryan Miller/Getty Images; 26 ©Media Bakery; 28 ©Dreamstime; 30 *(top to bottom)* ©Media Bakery; ©Image Broker/Alamy; 32 ©Tyler Stableford/Aurora/Getty Images; 34 ©Asia Images/Getty Images; 35 *(left to right)* ©Hisham Ibrahim/Getty Images; ©Laura Ciapponi/Getty Images; 37 *(clockwise from top left)* ©Media Bakery; ©Paul Souders/Getty Images; ©Altrendo Travel/Getty Images; ©Media Bakery; ©Shutterstock; ©Oliver Strewe/Getty Images; 38 ©Media Bakery; 39 ©Image Makers/Getty Images; 40 *(left to right)* ©Doug Armand/Getty Images; ©Steve Bloom Images/Alamy; ©Philip & Karen Smith/Getty Images; 41 ©Ty Milford/Getty Images; 48 *(top to bottom)* ©Shutterstock; ©Tony Cordoza/Getty Images; ©Jack Hollingsworth/Getty Images; ©Jeffrey Coolidge/Getty Images; 51 ©Mike Powell/Getty Images; 52 *(top to bottom)* ©Iain Masterton/Alamy; ©Rene Magritte/Bridgeman Art Library/Superstock; ©Charles Stirling/Alamy; ©Oleksiy Maksymenko/Alamy; 57 *(clockwise from top left)* ©Media Bakery; ©Marlene Ford/Alamy; ©Franz Aberham/Getty Images; 60 ©Alamy; 61 *(clockwise from top left)* ©Justin Prenton/Alamy; ©Photo Library; ©Media Bakery; ©Media Bakery; ©Photo Library; ©Media Bakery; 63 *(top to bottom)* ©Fuse/Getty Images; ©Media Bakery; ©Fancy/Alamy; ©Media Bakery; ©Media Bakery; ©Media Bakery; 64 ©Media Bakery; 69 ©Media Bakery; 74 ©Tomás del Amo/Alamy; 79 *(left to right)* ©Ian Miles – Flashpoint Pictures/Alamy; ©Magdalena Rehova/Alamy; ©Media Bakery; *(bottom)* ©Tyler Stableford/Getty Images; 82 ©Redferns/Getty Images; 84 ©Frederick Bass/Getty Images; 87 ©Jason LaVeris/Getty Images; 89 *(clockwise from top left)* ©Jay Reilly/Getty Images; ©Media Bakery; ©Wendy Connett/Alamy; ©Alamy; 90 ©Nicolas Russell/Getty Images; 92 ©Photo Edit; 94 ©Alamy; 96 *(left to right)* ©Shutterstock; ©Shutterstock; ©Theo Fitzhugh/Alamy; ©Creative Crop/Getty Images; ©Creative Crop/Getty Images